Unveiled Love

10 Secrets to Working with God When Your Spouse Isn't!

Kim Moore

ISBN 978-1-68570-693-7 (paperback)
ISBN 978-1-68570-694-4 (digital)

Copyright © 2024 by Kim Moore

All rights reserved. No part of this publication may be reproduced, distributed, or transmitted in any form or by any means, including photocopying, recording, or other electronic or mechanical methods without the prior written permission of the publisher. For permission requests, solicit the publisher via the address below.

Christian Faith Publishing
832 Park Avenue
Meadville, PA 16335
www.christianfaithpublishing.com

Printed in the United States of America

Contents

Preface v

Acknowledgments xi

Part I: Take Your Mark!

    Secret 1:   Turn Your Weapons into Tools 1
    Secret 2:   Face Your Fear, Fulfill Your Desire 27
    Secret 3:   Build on Commonalities 49

Part II: Get Set!

    Secret 4:   Reclaim Your Freedom 81
    Secret 5:   Receive Love 113
    Secret 6:   Rely on God to Meet Your Needs 143

Part III: Go!

    Secret 7:   Live in Christ 191
    Secret 8:   Let God Do the Correcting 231
    Secret 9:   Endure the Contradiction 269
    Secret 10: Celebrate Victory! 297

Preface

Another book on marriage? Seriously? Already so much has been written, published, and preached on marriage. What possibly could anyone add, right? But then, there is God—always new, always relevant, always now. It reminds me of the prophet's words in Isaiah 43:19 (TPT).

> I am doing something brand new, something unheard of. Even now it sprouts and grows and matures. Don't you perceive it? I will make a way in the wilderness and open up flowing streams in the desert.

However, Solomon the wisest man that ever lived says that there is nothing new under the sun. In fact, he speaks this quite emphatically in Ecclesiastes 1:9 (MSG).

> There's nothing new on this earth. Year after year it's the same old thing. Does someone call out, "Hey, this is new"? Don't get excited—it's the same old story.

I believe the prophet and Solomon are both right because they are speaking about two different things. Solomon spoke of the unchangeable nature of man and God's laws. He is right in saying there is nothing new under the sun. There are no new laws, and at that time, no new nature of which mankind could avail himself.

But Jesus did not come from under the sun. He came from above. Jesus came from heaven to earth. Jesus represents a new nature.

This Divine Nature was in Christ, reconciling mankind to God. In Isaiah 43:19, the prophet is speaking of the coming of Jesus Christ. And Isaiah is right. Jesus came with a new nature, a new covenant, a new way, and new hope for mankind. God's will throughout the Old and New Testaments was and is to call, redeem, sanctify, direct, and instruct men and women in His ways. This hasn't changed. But the way God goes about this today is different than in the Old Testament. That's why it is called the New Testament.

Old vs. New

God's will for marriage is not new nor has it changed. The Bible states that marriage is between one biological male and one biological female. Genesis 2:21–24 (CSB) leaves no room for interpretation.

> So the Lord God caused a deep sleep to come over the man, and he slept. God took one of his ribs and closed the flesh at that place. Then the Lord God made the rib he had taken from the man into a woman and brought her to the man. And the man said: This one, at last, is bone of my bone and flesh of my flesh; this one will be called "woman," for she was taken from man. This is why a man leaves his father and mother and bonds with his wife, and they become one flesh. Both the man and his wife were naked, yet felt no shame.

God's will for marriage is that together, man and woman would rule the earth as He ruled the heavens. Genesis 1:28 (CSB) informs us:

> God blessed them (man and woman), and God said to them, "Be fruitful, multiply, fill the earth, and subdue it. Rule the fish of the sea, the birds of the sky, and every creature that crawls on the earth."

The will of God is the same, yesterday, today, and tomorrow, and forever this will be. God's will is implemented and upheld by inflexible laws. His will and His laws are consistent throughout the Bible. However, the methods God used to achieve His will in the Old Testament and the New Testament are different. One strong example is that in the Old Testament, God redeemed His people through animal sacrifice. Whereas in the New Testament, the method of redemption was Jesus Christ, a human sacrifice. God's will to redeem mankind was the same in both Old and New Testament. The law of the sacrifice upholds God's intention to redeem mankind. This, too, is consistent in both testaments. What is different is the method—human sacrifice replaced the animal sacrifice. God's will did not change. His law did not change. But His approach changed. It was new!

Then and Now

Few would argue that today's married couple looks very different than in the '50s and '60s. Back then, husbands were the primary source of income. Financial assets were purchased and owned by the husband who distributed as he chose. Wives were financially dependent on their husbands. Gender roles were clear. Husbands bore financial responsibility by working outside of their home. Wives maintained their home. She was solely responsible for raising the children, shopping, cooking, and housekeeping. The disparity in education between them contributed to wives' dependency on their husbands. Sex produced children. But also sex was thought to be the pleasure of husbands answered by their wives. Hence, male on top, female on the bottom. Going to church was common. Husbands and wives were locked into predetermined roles that governed every aspect of their relationship. Gender positions, gender roles and responsibilities were regarded as fixed, transcending every circumstance in marriage. Some have gone as far to treat these as doctrinal truths. To a recognizable degree, the church reinforced these ideas, without consideration for the individuality of each husband and wife, freedom of choice, personal responsibility, and God's unique assignment for each couple. Without freedom and personal responsibility, husbands and wives become clones. Feminism, the sexual revolution, and educated women challenged these ideas.

A 1975 (remade in 2004) satirical movie dramatizes this approach to marriage. It's called the *Stepford Wives*. The story is set in a small fictitious town in Connecticut called Stepford. The plot revolves around the role-restricted lives of financially successful husbands given to all kinds of sport. They are married to gorgeous women, impeccably dressed, with stunning homes and unconditionally agreeable. It seemed like a perfect town, with perfect men and perfect women, with perfect marriages. Joanna and her family are newcomers to the town. Initially, everyone seemed happy and agreeable. But as the story evolves, Joanna becomes disenchanted by all the perfection. She is increasingly disturbed by the lack of free will and the passivity of the wives, including her once independent friends. Joanna decides to research the town of Stepford and discovered that many of the wives were once feminist activists and very successful professionals. And that the husbands were engineers capable of making human-like robots. Your imagination need not run wild to figure out what took place and possibly how it ended.

As excessive as satire is, the thread of reality can still be seen today in traditional marriage approaches. The model for marriage is almost entirely gender driven. The word "hierarchy" characterizes this model.

I had been married for twenty-seven years when my husband followed through on his decision to divorce. Our marriage was based on hierarchy rather than relationship. We navigated life based on predetermined positions, roles, and responsibilities even though our skills and abilities did not match gender assignments. We tried. We gave up, then tried again. It just didn't work. It was frustrating for both of us. Whenever I exercised my free will, skills, and abilities and it did not agree with what was expected of me as a wife, I was met with disapproval. Not only from my ex-husband but also from the church.

Counseling reinforced the notion that my role and responsibility was to support my husband. On one occasion, I was advised not to speak to my then husband about my desires, as it related to ministry (we were in full-time ministry together). Rather, I should find ways to adapt and support him in his work. Another time, I was among wives whose husbands were also in ministry. We were admonished that it was our responsibility for setting the climate and conditions in our home. It was said that we were uniquely suited to support our husbands in this manner. Therefore, if something went wrong in our relationship, it was up to us to fix it. On countless occasions, I heard that I was not supportive. I became discouraged. My marriage seemed to revolve around me adapting to my husband's needs and wants. I often wondered how low I could go before I didn't exist. For me and many other wives, "supportive" was another word for "submission." And "unconditional" submission resulted in unchecked authority and accountability for husbands. Whether it is a system or a person, when questions are disallowed, freedom is denied. I felt trapped in a system I could not question.

In all fairness, we were both participants in a system that robbed each of us the freedom and right to think and decide what was best for our relationship. Repeatedly, we were told what made for a godly husband and wife—the positions we were to occupy, the roles we were to play, and what needs we had as a man and a woman. Supposedly, observing these things made for a happy marriage. But instead of a happy and harmonious relationship, we experienced turmoil. This was before my husband decided to think for himself and courageously chose divorce. I do not praise his decision. It was accompanied by more pain and anguish. What I praise is that my husband thought and acted for himself. His decision confronted an ungodly system in which we had been imprisoned for years! That this ungodly system of relating to each other was constructed and maintained by godly men and women made the hurt worse. You see, for years, I thought something was wrong with me. Why couldn't I just conform? If my husband hadn't initiated divorce, it is likely I would still be married today. And I would have suffered in ways God did not intend.

My husband's decision set both of us free. I am writing this book to offer frustrated husbands and wives hope and a new paradigm for marriage. I am writing to offer pastors, marriage ministry leaders, and Christian counselors a new strategy when working with pre—and post-marital couples. I am writing for my children and my children's children that they will know and experience the freedom Christ won for them in their relationships. I am writing to trumpet the sound of freedom, power, and love for those who may never hear my voice. I am writing for you. I am writing for me.

This is neither a theological nor philosophical study. That said, various translations of Scripture are used, noted, and repeated throughout the book. My aim is to promote the practicality of God's Word and to improve the readers' ability to engage with the material. I realize that some readers will straight away reject this paradigm. Others will find hope for their marriage. Still, others will be liberated by working together with God in new, exciting, and life-giving ways. To these I pray you discover more freedom, power, and love inside of marriage, overcoming the temptation to step outside. May the blessings of God's *Unveiled Love* be yours now and forever!

Acknowledgments

Truthfully, no great book is ever written alone. Whether it was praying, an encouraging word, just listening to my ideas, helping me clarify them, giving me a place of solitude to write, or contributing in many other ways, I owe a debt of love and gratitude to so many. Here are a few of the many that stand out.

Pam Ashby, Amy Bernal, and Patricia Shannon who prayed this book into being and that it would find its way to your eyes.

Clarence and Trish Wallace who gifted me the use of the solitude of their beach home to write.

The entire 2022 Unveiled Love Class who gave me the opportunity to teach and prove the applicability of the content to the newly married, as well as those married for over forty years. A special thank you to Phillip and Mandy Cate for hosting the class in their home.

Norman Dale is one of the smartest, and most tender-hearted, men I know. Norman verified every reference source and challenged me to write with greater clarity, thereby improving the overall readability of the book.

John Alberta, formerly with Microsoft, after reviewing the manuscript, came alongside to lend his business acumen to the project. John is also one of the voices on the audiobook, *Unveiled Love.*

My clients who contributed real-life scenarios to *Unveiled Love.* In most cases, the names were changed to ensure their privacy.

Relationship Game Changers who, for the past four years, have faithfully showed up every Wednesday evening for a conference call to hear and engage many of the truths espoused in this book.

All who texted or called to let me know they were praying for me during this three-year writing journey. Your thoughts, prayers, cards, and kind words were well placed in moments of opposition.

A special thank you to Amy Bernal. Getting this book into your hands has been no small feat. It has been a difficult journey lasting four-and-a-half years. It began as a workbook under a different title. Midway through, I turned it into a chapter book with questions at the end of each chapter. Then, we decided to change its title to convey its message better. Afterward, Amy recorded part of the audiobook. I owe a debt of gratitude to my business partner and friend. Thank you!

Last, and first is God, My Father and my Savior and Lord Jesus Christ. Although I have written several books before, this book compelled me to dig deeper in His word, curating truths that apply to all men and women and husbands and wives—*and especially to those that proclaim Christ.* Becoming the first partaker of the truths in *Unveiled Love* was grueling at times and gratifying at other times. I can honestly say that *Unveiled Love* has changed my life and relationships for the better, and hopefully, it will do the same for you!

Part I—Take Your Mark!

Like a swimmer hearing a whistle and the starter's command during pre-race preparation, in Part I, we will learn how to ready ourselves, confront and overcome our challenges, and build relationships with others.

> I will climb up to my watchtower and stand at my guard post. There I will wait to see what the Lord says and how he will answer my complaint (Habakkuk 2:1 NLT).

Secret 1

Turn Your Weapons into Tools

> He'll settle things fairly between nations. He'll make things right between many peoples. They'll turn their swords into shovels, their spears into hoes. No more will nation fight nation; they won't play war anymore. Come, family of Jacob, let's live in the light of God. (Isaiah 2:4 MSG)

Let's face it, by the time we become adults, we are skillful at surviving in relationships. We have exercised thoughts, feelings, and behaviors so often and for so long they are native to us. This means they are automatic responses when presented with certain stimuli or triggers. Each of us has a sophisticated array of weapons, defensive and offensive. It's an arsenal designed to protect us mentally, emotionally, physically, and even sexually. These weapons are powerful, effective, and sometimes destructive in marriage.

Anything can become a weapon. They come in many different types, forms, sizes, and strengths. That's what can make them so hard to detect. But also we have relied on them so heavily, they instinctively become a part of us. We may even *think* that our weapons are us and we are them. But we are not these things; they are separate from us. It's just that we use them to survive.

A weapon can be a learned skill. It could be mental, behavioral, or emotional. Here are some examples of weapons you may recognize. The performance weapon can be used to get love and acceptance and avoid rejection. The compliance weapon may be used to get connected and avoid abandonment. The academic knowledge of anything, even the Bible, can be a weapon that calls for respect and puts off feelings of insecurity. The "ability to win friends" weapon succeeds in gaining friends and influence and keeps loneliness at bay.

Consider "helicopter parents" who pay exceptional attention to their children's academics, activities, and friends to ensure their success and well-being. This can also be a weapon. By living vicariously through their children, helicopter parents may be addressing the disappointment and emotional absence they felt from their parents. Or a spouse that uses anger to gain control when feeling insecure or incompetent. Maybe it's the nice, overly forgiving spouse that is unable to draw boundaries for fear of abandonment. And how about the one with an inflated sense of responsibility for people for fear of being out of control. All are further examples of how different people may use varied weapons for an array of reasons. This is but a short list of weapons and the kinds of people that may use them. Whether it is performance, compliance, knowledge, material success, vicarious emotional living through children, anger, misuse of forgiveness, or hyper-responsibility, all are examples of weapons designed to eliminate threats to our mental, emotional, and physical well-being. Whether it is a spouse, a parent, someone else, you, or me, we all have learned that our weapons are reliable, and they are effective, keeping others out and us in. They just work for us. So we use them—*extensively*.

Weapons to Tools

In marriage, these weapons *must* be turned into tools that husbands and wives can use to build something amazing together. Every marriage is supposed to look different, feel different, and do different. Yet it must be the same God working all and in all. While the weapons that must become tools are different for every husband and wife, the way God turns them into tools is the same. An illustration will help. Think of the different weapons of war used by warriors in the Bible as an example. There are the belt, the breastplate, the shoes, the helmet, the spear, the bow and arrow, and of course, the sword and shield. The helmet, breastplate, and shield are for defense. They are designed to protect the wearer from bows and arrows and spears. The latter enable the bearer to advance. For this reason, they are offensive weapons. All weapons, both offensive and defensive, are learned. They are the result of training. And until placed on God's altar, all weapons have one goal—that is, to keep you alive physically and emotionally. No matter how beautiful or grotesque, no matter how godly or ungodly, until God has opportunity to cleanse our intention, the weapon is self-serving. The sword is unique in that it is both an offensive and defensive weapon. What must happen before these weapons can be turned into tools? First, they must be taken off or laid down so that craftsmen can turn them into tools. But something happens to the warrior that removes his weapons, he becomes *vulnerable, undefended*.

In like manner, before the learned weapons and the defense mechanisms of husbands and wives can be turned into tools, they must be cast off and laid down. Each spouse, husband and wife, each soul must become vulnerable and undefended. Or better stated, *they must* become vulnerable and undefended again. When we were children, we were vulnerable and undefended. We were as sponges, absorbing and responding to everything without insight or intent. We had all the faculties of an adult and control over none of them— *not our arms, hands, legs, or feet, not even our bladder or bowels.* As we grew, we gained control over these and other faculties like thinking, reasoning, and choosing. Over time, we learned, exercised, and controlled our responses without giving much thought to them.

In the process, we gained weapons, and we lost our vulnerability. That is, we forfeited so many of the skills and abilities not necessary or helpful to remaining connected to the parents and people important to us. These skills were set aside, and therefore, undeveloped. Since we didn't need them, we didn't use them. We didn't even think they were a thing. And when we did recognize these things are as important as forgiveness or rest, we ignored, devalued, and even condemned them as unnecessary. But they aren't. While we may not have been raised to need and appreciate them, God made us to need them. God-given needs do not go away because we reject them. They become our elevator music in a crowd of people. God uses this music to summon us by introducing us to people that represent answers to our need. A quick survey of the type of people to whom we are drawn and those drawn to us often reveals something about the needs and answers present.

Raised vs. Made

Turning weapons into tools means learning to accept and behave how God made us, instead of how we were raised. The one keen on performing for love must learn that God loves us because He made us, and there is nothing we can do to earn love. We are lovable because He loves us. Period. And the one bent on being compliant must learn that God made us to take dominion—to initiate, to activate, and to motivate. It is in relationship with others that both learn. Oftentimes, these two individuals will marry each other! Although what they need is different, the requirement of vulnerability is the same. We will continue to unpack these ideas throughout the book.

God's Precision

Unveiled Love is like a homing pigeon. Homing pigeons are noted for their ability to find their way home from very long distances. The Bible credits the dove with finding its way back to the ark after released by Noah. Genesis 8:8–11 (CSB) reads:

> Then he sent out a dove to see whether the water on the earth's surface had gone down, but the dove found no resting place for its foot. It returned to him in the ark because water covered the surface of the whole earth. He reached out and brought it into the ark to himself. So, Noah waited seven more days and sent out the dove from the ark again. When the dove came to him at evening, there was a plucked olive leaf in its beak. So, Noah knew that the water on the earth's surface had gone down.

Doves symbolize the Holy Spirit in scripture (Matthew 3:16–17; Mark 1:10) and are also symbolic of love. Speaking of her beloved, the bride in Song of Solomon 5:12 (AMPC) says,

> His eyes are like doves beside the water brooks,
> bathed in milk and fitly set.

Male doves also *coo*. This low-tone distinctive sound woos a potential mate.

Like the undeterred devotion of Noah's dove, *Unveiled Love* searches for us and finds us. Like the lover of the bride in Song of Solomon, *Unveiled Love* woos the undefended parts of our soul. That is, the deepest, most vulnerable, undefended, and unloved parts of ourselves. Then it romances us and captures our affections. It fans even the embers of our innermost desires into flames. It shows us life and even allows us to taste the possibility of a forever experience. We feel whole and complete. So we keep on accepting its invitations to spend time together. We lose track of time. When *Unveiled Love* is present, hours can pass without notice. That's because we are on the soul's time. The soul is both present and eternal. It exists *inside and outside of the time God created to hold our physical bodies.* In eternity with Christ, souls are defenseless and time ceases.

Timelessness

Timelessness is when the hours pass by without notice. That timeless experience is real, like conversations that last into the wee hours of the morning—when words cease and turn into breathing. The preoccupation with another soul in a state of euphoria evades time. In this place of timelessness, the glory aspects each one possesses are exaggerated. Time is prevented from filling in the less than glorious details. Some call this timeless experience of two lovers (the law of) attraction. Whether you call it attraction, infatuation, limerence, or lust, it is the feeling of being alive and perfect that is so irresistibly compelling. All our guards are down. Our souls are free and defenseless.

Could it be that the timeless experience that some call falling in love is the personal best of each soul, combined with a tasting of a more exquisite Soul, that is, Christ? What I mean is this. God creates every man and woman to express an aspect of His glory to the world. Each aspect is magnificent, despite being marred by sin and impure motives. When *Unveiled Love* finds and connects the souls of a man and a woman, each one experiences the other's God-given glory. In marriage, it is the very thing each one, each soul needs to become the person God intends. In the light and warmth of this God-given glory, each experiences the other as an answer.

In heaven and in the new earth, weapons are obsolete. Souls are borne, naked if you will, that is, until God clothes us, our souls with incorruptible bodies. As it were the bodies of the souls in the Garden of Eden before sin, so will it be again. Pure love. Pure acceptance—a celebration of openness, bareness, or nakedness minus the guilt and shame. What's so fantastic is that with *Unveiled Love*, husbands and wives can preview this now!

When *Unveiled Love* gets a hold of two souls, it is as though they are caught up in a divine eternal affair—*and they are*. It is an atmosphere unique to them. For this reason, a man and woman may find each other irresistible. Everything: the looks, the feel, and the essence of each one, is present. So fiery is this aspect of God's glory! He created each one to affirm and supply answers to the deepest needs of the other's soul. And the soul in need knows this, if only subconsciously. *Unveiled Love* gently awakens the hidden longings deep within our souls. Like a favorite love song, *Unveiled Love* goes where fingers cannot, touching and whispering, "Awaken, my love." *Unveiled Love* calls for who you are and have yet to become.

Healing Wholeness and the Defended Soul

When two souls are removed from the influence of caregivers who may have been harsh and controlling or permissive and unrestrained, there is a fresh opportunity for *Unveiled Love* to offer healing and wholeness. That's because *Unveiled Love* addresses fear. It offers a safe place for the soul to undress and discard defense mechanisms. Defenses are our unhealthy ways of responding to threats to our safety and well-being. Defended souls use all types of coping skills. They are the thoughts and behaviors we engage to protect our emotional or physical well-being. Sometimes, they can be healthy, unhealthy, or cease to serve us the way they once did. For instance, the child who feels unimportant to parents and siblings learns to feel important by excelling in school or sports. Importance feels good, so this child develops into a well-disciplined overachiever, acquiring all the bells and whistles that go along with success. This person brings a high regard for discipline and performance into marriage and family. Not only so but insists a spouse and children live up to his or her discipline and performance expectations. When they don't, they are condemned as if something is wrong with them. What were excellent and necessary life skills learned in response to feeling unimportant as a child have become weapons used to injure others as an adult. Others are injured by unrealistic expectations, anger, criticism, et.al. The very skills that kept the child in relationship with biological or custodial parents and siblings now undermine the relationship with spouse and children. That's because this person's performance expectations were and are about self-esteem. It's about an adult using childish ways to manage an adult relationship. This is a soul defending itself against feelings of insignificance. And since God gives us the desire and need to feel important and that we matter, we will not outgrow it. Rather God's *Unveiled Love* shows us how God can meet it in a way that benefits others.

When we defend our souls, we deny ourselves the freedom to create the relationships we desire. That's why in 1 Corinthians 13:11 (AMPC), Paul writes:

> When I was a child, I talked like a child, I thought like a child, I reasoned like a child; now that I have become a man, I am done with childish ways and have put them aside.

In verses 1–3 of 1 Corinthians 13, Paul describes defended souls. He says that defended souls can speak well, possess above average understanding and knowledge of spiritual matters, as well as enjoy great faith to move mountains, perform signs and wonders. He concludes by stating that defended souls can be generous givers and display sacrificial love. Then He says without love (God's *Unveiled Love*), defended souls are noisy, useless bodies who, in the end, gain nothing. Wow!

Beginning in 1 Corinthians 13:4–8 (AMPC), Paul tells us what this love and undefended soul looks like. That means God intends for *Unveiled Love* to be seen, felt, and heard. God's plan is that we reproduce, illustrate, and sanctify each other through this love. And there is no better relationship to start with than marriage!

> Love endures long and is patient and kind; love never is envious nor boils over with jealousy, is not boastful or vainglorious, does not display itself haughtily. It is not conceited (arrogant and inflated with pride); it is not rude (unmannerly) and does not act unbecomingly. Love (God's love in us) does not insist on its own rights or its own way, for it is not self-seeking; it is not touchy or fretful or resentful; it takes no account of the evil done to it [it pays no attention to a suffered wrong]. It does not rejoice at injustice and unrighteousness but rejoices when right and truth prevail. Love bears up under anything and everything that comes, is ever ready to believe the best of every person, its hopes are fadeless under all circumstances, and it endures everything [without weakening]. Love never fails [never fades out or becomes obsolete or comes to an end]. As for prophecy the gift of interpreting the divine will and purpose), it will be fulfilled and pass away; as for tongues, they will be destroyed and cease; as for knowledge, it will pass away [it will lose its value and be superseded by truth].

Verses 9–10 Paul speaks about our current condition. He says what we know and teach is incomplete and imperfect. That means to one degree or another, each of us have based our lives on partial and faulty information. Proof lies in the unattractive, unrewarding state of many marriages. Paul's answer, I repeat.

> When I was a child, I talked like a child, I thought like a child, I reasoned like a child; now that I have become a man, I am done with childish ways and have put them aside.

In other words, whatever costume you wore to adulthood no longer serves you. Recurring relationship breakdowns are proof. There is a saying that goes, "What got you here isn't sufficient to keep you here." It's true of marriage. Whatever brought you into marriage alone isn't enough to keep you there. Falling in love is easy, it's staying there that's hard! That's because true love, God's *Unveiled Love*, requires naked, undefended souls. This is its one and only unrelenting pursuit. The core and visible indicators of a defended or weaponized soul are summarized below:

A Defended Soul is . . .	How Defended Souls Behave?	
Closed	Angry (Passive and Active)	Need to be right/best/heard
Fixed	Humor to Avoid Serious Dialogue	Overly Responsible for Others
Subjective	Intellectualizes	Irresponsible
Withholding	People Pleasing	Addictions
Lives in the past or future	Difficulty Admitting Wrong	Abusive
	Difficulty Owning Need	Overly Opinionated
	Unable to Ask for Help	Lacks follow through
	Unable to Ask Forgiveness	Critical/Demanding/Impatient
	Over-achievers/Work-Alcoholics	Unforgiving
	Blames Others	Maximizes or Minimizes
	Co-dependency	Lies

Undressing the Soul

Unveiled Love does this by gathering, holding, transforming, and then releasing each one again and again until all conforms to Christ. God is gracious like this. *Unveiled Love* inspires a soul to want to undress and be fully seen. But also it can provoke some souls to reject such nudity altogether. Our souls were not made to hide. We were taught to hide in rigid, graceless, and permissive parented homes. The result has been that many of us contend with fear, guilt, and shame. The answer is God's *Unveiled Love*!

Fear, guilt, and shame and the lying and pretending that follow are the works of the devil. God's *Unveiled Love* personified in Jesus came to overthrow these things.

> "The Son of God was revealed for this purpose: to destroy the devil's works." (1 John 3:8 CSB)

It is for this reason that *Unveiled Love* can also be violent. It seeks to root out, pull up, and destroy every thought, idea, attitude, manner, and way that opposes the Lordship of Jesus Christ.

There are no exemptions. *Unveiled Love* will turn over every stone, remove every roadblock, interrupt every evil plan, disrupt every relationship, break down every wall, and confront virtually anything that stands in the way of its unrelenting fury for pure, undefended souls of men and women. *Unveiled Love* is a threat to pride and every false notion we have of ourselves.

It is unmoved by forms and pretenses of godliness. It demands substance—godly substance. That's because God desires for the souls of husbands and wives to experience deep intimate fellowship with each other and with God's Divine Nature. There is absolutely no way for this to occur other than reducing each one to their lowest common denominator that is Christ—*the Christ life!* This process of reducing can feel mean. When it feels this way, it's only because we are either refusing love by clinging to something condemned or we are grieving and recovering from what we chose to give to *Unveiled Love*.

Christ is the best example of the beauty and inspiration to take part in *Unveiled Love*. He opened and offered His soul to us. He withheld nothing. *Unveiled Love* did not hurt Jesus. What Jesus chose to do for God's *Unveiled Love* hurt deeply and fatally.

Paul describes his experience with this *Unveiled Love*. After sharing the horrible physical, mental, and emotional experiences he encountered, Paul writes these words to his friends in Corinth:

> My friends at Corinth, our hearts are wide open to you, and we speak freely, holding nothing back from you. If there is a block in our relationship, it is not with us, for we carry you in our hearts with great love, yet you still withhold your affections from us. So, I speak to you as our children. Make room in your hearts for us as we have done for you.[1]

Paul wasn't talking only about his spirit being open and vulnerable to his friends, but his soul too. His thoughts and affections were toward his friends. Paul longed for his friends to experience *Unveiled Love* that sets them free to think, decide, and act for themselves. He hoped they would choose to engage in an unfathomable fellowship together with him. Like Jesus, Paul presented his soul defenseless, offering it to God for the benefit of others. He says so in Colossians 1:24 (AMPC).

> [Even] now I rejoice in the midst of my sufferings on your behalf. And in my own person I am making up whatever is still lacking and remains to be completed [on our part] of Christ's afflictions, for the sake of His body, which is the church.

The Message Translation conveys the goal of *Unveiled Love* in marriage. That is, that the souls of husbands and wives would open

---

[1] 2 Corinthians 6:11–13 (TPT)

with nothing to hide, nothing to lose, nothing to prove—everything to gain! This is the freedom to which we are called!

> I'm speaking as plainly as I can and with great affection. Open up your lives. Live openly and expansively!

The core and some visible indicators of an undefended soul, that is, a soul whose weapons have been transformed into tools are summarized in the chart below.

An Undefended Soul is . . .	How Undefended Souls Behave?	
Open	Owns His/Her Thoughts, Feelings, Actions	Gives freely
Fluid	Respects Others Freedom	Admits Wrong
Objective	Doesn't Try to Control Outcomes	Asks for Forgiveness
Liberating	Loves freely	Loyal/Faithful
Lives in the Present	Helps Others	Acknowledges Limitations
	Displays Patience	Open to Constructive Feedback
	Displays Kindness	Doesn't Retaliate
	Forgives	Empathetic
	Honest to His/Her Own Hurt	Peaceful
	Safe Mentally, Emotionally, Physically, Sexually	Celebrates/Cries with Others
	Vulnerable	Willing to Learn from Others
	Asks for help	Grateful

Undefended—Not Only Possible but Also Practical

Live open, in the light. Present your soul defenseless. This certainly is possible! It is also practical. If it were not, Jesus would not have told us to follow Him. He would not have taught the disciples to become fishers of men. The truth is, we can live as human beings, who are vulnerable males and females by the power of the Holy Spirit. We can experience the intimacy that comes from the undressing of our souls.

We can only experience the intensity of love and intimacy to the degree we are honest with ourselves and others. This requires each one's willingness and ability to reflect on his or her thoughts, feelings, actions, motives, and outcomes. It requires the willingness to consider the impact of our actions on others. It requires empathy. While willingness is a decision, the ability to meet these requirements is learned. The only alternative is to hide and deny. All have been taught the art of unhealthy hiding. Everyone hides. None are immune. *Unveiled Love* is designed to assist those who desire to come out of hiding, experience freedom and new levels of authority, and influence in relationships.

Defended souls becoming undefended is about turning weapons into tools to build deeper connections and intimacy in marriage. God takes what we offer Him and transforms it into something new! He has both history and a track record of doing this very thing! The skills we developed to stay alive in our families of origin, whether biological or custodial, become our defense mechanisms. These became obsolete the day you entered marriage and all other significant relationships God uses to transform your soul. The recurring breakdowns are oftentimes the result of relying on skills that have not been cleansed from the selfish motive to remain alive.

José was raised in a machismo culture. He had a strong sense of family and community. He learned to be protective. José worked construction, but also was a jack of all trades. Give him space and time and he could repair anything. He spent weekends with his wife and kids. José liked a clean home and disciplined children. Maria loved José. They married young. She appreciated his regard and provision for their family. And she enjoyed maintaining the house and children. They enjoyed a traditional marriage, and it seemed to work for them. However, several years into their marriage, Maria confided in me that she experienced José as possessive and controlling. When going out, he wanted to choose the outfit she should wear. He instructed her as to how to discipline the kids and how he wanted the house. José was a micromanager. He wanted to influence every detail of their lives together. Initially, Maria was responsive to José, but as the years went by, she felt suffocated and irrelevant. Maria's attempts to voice her frustration were met with reassurances of his love for her and all that he does is for her and their family.

José had a wonderful array of skills. He learned and developed them growing up in his family. José's dad worked hard. He had a lawn care and home repair business. Through these, he was able to provide his family many things that others could not. His dad was very disciplined and disciplined his sons accordingly. His mother was a silent, supportive, and submissive woman. José learned how to take care of people and things. When José married, he began taking care of people, the same way he was taking care of things—*like a business with employees*. The problem is Maria is not a business, and in their case, not an employee. She grew resentful of José's possessive and controlling behavior. But it's what José knew. And what he knew, he did. José learned to hide his real feelings growing up as his dad made no space for them. He was afraid of not measuring up to his dad. So he worked and worked and worked. Maria wanted his vulnerability.

José represents a defended soul. His skills were weapons he used to defend against feelings of inadequacy while growing up. Marriage asks for those weapons that they may be turned into tools to build something greater than he or Maria could alone, without sacrificing their relationship. That meant José must decide to become vulnerable with Maria.

So let's take another look at the distinctions between defended vs. undefended souls.

Defended vs. Undefended Soul

Soul = Mind, Will and Emotions

Defended Soul	Undefended Soul
Closed	Open
Fixed	Fluid
Subjective	Objective
Holds On to Others	Releases Others
Lives in the Past/Future	Lives in the Present

Becoming an undefended soul is a process, not an event. It takes many new experiences over time. Working with God's *Unveiled Love* to turn our weapons into tools requires significant relationships. We must have stock in the relationship. God intends for marriage to be one of the main relationships for this work to occur. But there are other important relationships God uses to invite us to take part in *Unveiled Love*. Parenting, employment, church, friendships, and teams are all relationships God uses. For the one bent on learning and taking part with *Unveiled Love*, God can use any relationship. That's because nothing is wasted on the one learning how to hear, respond, and work with God's *Unveiled Love*!

Unveiled Love and Abuse

In any conversation on marriage, it is important that we recognize abuse is real. Scripture has been used disgracefully to perpetuate abuse. If you are in an abusive situation: verbally, emotionally, physically, or sexually—whether married, cohabitating, or boyfriend and girlfriend, I strongly recommend addressing the abuse first, then using the principles in God's *Unveiled Love* to establish and maintain proper boundaries. The presence of abuse is unsafe, and safety in a relationship is of primary concern. Taking steps to ensure your safety is the first course of action. This may mean involving a trusted friend, pastor, professional, and when appropriate, law enforcement. It may also mean separating from the abuser so that you have the freedom to think clearly and make informed decisions about how to go forward. Establishing and/or maintaining a relationship with a local church provides community that can support you in navigating these kinds of circumstances.

God does not support victimization for the sake of spreading the gospel or discipling another. Victimization robs us of the very thing Christ died for: our freedom. Anyone and anything that attempts to steal or destroy your freedom is not of God and should be regarded as a threat. We love others best when we love God first! Let us all return to our first love.

A Contrasting Look at the Undefended Soul

Hopefully, you are beginning to see and feel the passion in God's *Unveiled Love*! There is just no other way to explain the fiery, invincible nature of God's *Unveiled Love*. Song of Solomon 8:6–7 (MEV) tries to explain.

> Set me as a seal upon your heart, as a seal upon your arm; for love is strong as death, passion fierce as the grave. Its fires of desire are as ardent flames, a most intense flame. Many waters cannot quench love, neither can floods drown it. If a man offered for love all the wealth of his house, it would be utterly condemned.

Unveiled Love reveals itself and works most powerfully through undefended souls. Jesus lived the human life as an undefended soul by the indestructible power of the Holy Spirit. Jesus abandoned His soul to God's *Unveiled Love* for Him and humanity. Everything Jesus said and did, He received from His Father. Jesus even acknowledged that His capture and crucifixion were from the Father. Pilate was so frightened and frustrated by Jesus's confidence and silence that he tried to convince Jesus to speak. The Scripture records what happened next.

Pilate contentiously pulls Jesus aside and asks,

> "Why don't you talk to me?" Pilate demanded. "Don't you realize that I have the power to release you or crucify you?" (John 19:10 NLT)

Jesus responds in verse 11:

> You would have no power over me at all unless it were given to you from above. So, the one who handed me over to you has the greater sin.

Jesus understood that whatever power we possess has been given to us. Correcting his brothers and sisters, Paul writes in 1 Corinthians 4:7 (CSB).

> For who makes you so superior? What do you have that you didn't receive? If, in fact, you did receive it, why do you boast as if you hadn't received it?

Jesus saw beyond the power granted Pilate from the Sanhedrin to the ultimate power of God. In his book *Crucified by Christians,* Gene Edwards describes it this way: "Behold how he reacted to betrayal, to lies to false witnesses. Jesus Christ absorbed these pains, even as they added to the shamefulness of being crucified in public. Humiliated, degraded, defamed, tortured, and then murdered. That day he raised acceptance of the cross to an art form. He learned to accept all things from His Father."

Jesus made no effort to defend Himself against what He recognized as His Father's will. Defending His soul from that which He came to do would be to abort God's plan. Jesus took authority over demons, casting them out and commanding them to leave. Jesus did not argue with people, be they His accusers, skeptics, other friends, followers, or even His disciples. However, there may have been times He was disappointed, dissatisfied, or even exasperated with them. Especially with His disciples when He overheard them arguing, but He didn't argue or join their arguments. Jesus did not blame. He did not blame Judas nor did he condemn the Roman soldiers who escorted Him. He offered no rebuttal. He understood His Father's will and timing and consented. Jesus showed up, presenting His undefended body and soul to the moment. He cared more for His Father than His own life. It reminds me of John speaking about the brethren in Revelation 12:11:

> They conquered him completely through the blood of the Lamb and the powerful word of his

testimony. They triumphed because they did not love and cling to their own lives, even when faced with death.

A Gruesome Display of *Unveiled Love*

Some may be thinking what a severe illustration of an undefended soul. Why on earth would a man or woman or husband or wife sign up for something like this? And what if anything does this rendering of an undefended soul have to do with marriage? Everything. At the deepest part of our humanity, that is our soul, we have a profound, irresistible desire to receive and give love. This desire is so compelling and at times overwhelming that we do almost anything to experience it. As forceful as the desire for sex is to the body, the emotional desire for love to the soul is even greater. The fellowship between sex and body and love and soul can be breathtaking. Still, it pales in comparison to the fellowship we will one day experience with Christ when the corrupted veil of our flesh is removed.

Adam and Eve knew the wonder and awe of another undefended human soul. Although they were clothed in flesh, it was unspoiled before sin. Genesis 2:23–25 (MSG) writes of the married couple.

> The Man said, "Finally! Bone of my bone, flesh of my flesh! Name her Woman for she was made from Man." Therefore, a man leaves his father and mother and embraces his wife. They become one flesh. The two of them, the Man and his Wife, were naked, but they felt no shame.

An undefended soul is naked and not ashamed. And while nakedness of body and soul makes us vulnerable, *Unveiled Love* doesn't mind. That's because *Unveiled Love* has no fear. Adam and Eve's decision to pursue information to guide their lives from a source other than God, led to their demise. When confronted, Adam gave this response in Genesis 3:10 (MSG):

> He said, "I heard you in the garden and I was afraid because I was naked. And I hid."

Fear and blame caused conflict and eroded the relationship between Adam and Eve. Adam blamed Eve, and in turn, Eve blamed the serpent. Betrayal and distrust replaced love. Adam and Eve suffered for it. What God intended to be held together through an inner bond of love would now be held together through external rules. This was not a blessing; instead, it was a curse.

It is interesting to consider that a man and woman spend lots of time and money to dress up for the wedding day. From that night on, they begin disrobing, the outmost garments first! Few imagined that this undressing wouldn't stop with the body. But God doesn't excuse us from the disrobing of our soul, which is wonderful at times and painful work at other times. Perhaps we ought to counsel couples to plan a life that includes a wedding day instead of the wedding day alone.

Unveiled Love Is Inescapable

Wherever we are, *Unveiled Love* is there. The degree to which this love is present is explained in Psalm 139 (HCSB). In twenty-two verses, David describes an all-knowing and always present God. And in verse 23 and 24, he gives us this wise response.

> Lord, you have searched me and known me. You know when I sit down and when I stand up; you understand my thoughts from far away. You observe my travels and my rest; you are aware of all my ways. Before a word is on my tongue, you know all about it, Lord. You have encircled me; you have placed your hand on me. This wondrous knowledge is beyond me. It is lofty; I am

unable to reach it. Where can I go to escape your Spirit? Where can I flee from your presence? If I go up to heaven, you are there; if I make my bed in Sheol, you are there. If I fly on the wings of the dawn and settle down on the western horizon, even there your hand will lead me; your right hand will hold on to me. If I say, "Surely the darkness will hide me, and the light around me will be night"—even the darkness is not dark to you. The night shines like the day; darkness and light are alike to you. For it was you who created my inward parts; you knit me together in my mother's womb. I will praise you because I have been remarkably and wondrously made. Your works are wondrous, and I know this very well. My bones were not hidden from you when I was made in secret, when I was formed in the depths of the earth. Your eyes saw me when I was formless; all my days were written in your book and planned before a single one of them began. God, how precious your thoughts are to me; how vast their sum is! If I counted them, they would outnumber the grains of sand; when I wake up, I am still with you. God, if only you would kill the wicked—you bloodthirsty men, stay away from me who invoke you deceitfully. Your enemies swear by you falsely. Lord, don't I hate those who hate you, and detest those who rebel against you? I hate them with extreme hatred; I consider them my enemies. Search me, God, and know my heart; test me and know my concerns. See if there is any offensive way in me; lead me in the everlasting way.

Hide and pretend as we often do, nothing is hidden from God. He sees everything—*everything we think, feel, say, and do.* Paul agrees. Hebrews 4:13 (HCSB) reads,

> No creature is hidden from him, but all things are naked and exposed to the eyes of him to whom we must give an account.

Everything hidden will be exposed. Luke 8:17 (AMPC) agrees.

> For there is nothing hidden that shall not be disclosed, nor anything secret that shall not be known and come out into the open.

And in chapter 12, verse 3 (AMPC), Luke adds.

> Whatever you have spoken in the darkness shall be heard and listened to in the light, and what you have whispered in [people's] ears and behind closed doors will be proclaimed upon the housetops.

David offers us a humble response to the God who knows everything, about anything there is to know something about. In Psalm 139:23–24 (MSG), David requests God to:

> Investigate my life, O God, find out everything about me; Cross-examine and test me, get a clear picture of what I'm about; See for yourself whether I've done anything wrong—then guide me on the road to eternal life.

David was an undefended soul. He knew God's *Unveiled Love.* Upon the ark returning to his city, David danced unrestrained, with all his might before God and in front of the people (2 Samuel 6:14). David didn't care what others thought of him. He was motivated by

Unveiled Love! David's wife, Micah, had a problem with his over-the-top behavior. Her response is captured in 2 Samuel 6:16 (KJV).

> And as the ark of the Lord came into the city of David, Michal Saul's daughter looked through a window, and saw king David leaping and dancing before the Lord; and she despised him in her heart.

When confronted by the prophet Nathan for arranging to have Bathsheba's husband, Uriah, killed, David did not defend his actions. But not at first. You recall, David slept with Bathsheba, and she became pregnant. David then plotted to kill Uriah to hide his sin. Hiding is a form of defending one's soul and behavior. When found out, David simply said to Nathan these words in 2 Samuel 12:13 (CSB):

> I have sinned against the Lord.

David's behavior had consequences. Verses 10–12 and 13–14 explain.

> Now therefore, the sword will never leave your house because you despised me and took the wife of Uriah the Hittite to be your own wife. This is what the Lord says, "I am going to bring disaster on you from your own family: I will take your wives and give them to another before your very eyes, and he will sleep with them in broad daylight. You acted in secret, but I will do this before all Israel and in broad daylight." Then Nathan replied to David, "And the Lord has taken away your sin; you will not die. However, because you treated the Lord with such contempt in this matter, the son born to you will die."

Psalm 51 reveals the depth of *Unveiled Love* working in David's defenseless soul. Verse 17 (CSB) sums it up nicely.

> The sacrifice pleasing to God is a broken spirit.
> You will not despise a broken and humbled heart,
> God.

And the Message translations drives the point home even more emphatically.

> Going through the motions doesn't please you, a flawless performance is nothing to you. I learned God-worship when my pride was shattered. Heart-shattered lives ready for love don't for a moment escape God's notice.

And Psalm 34:18 (CSB) assures us that God remained close by.

> The Lord is near the brokenhearted; he saves those crushed in spirit.

David was vulnerable to *Unveiled Love*. On one occasion he danced wildly before the Lord. And on another occasion, he was broken and contrite. *Unveiled Love* is both magnificent and humbling. We know that God was not finished with David nor is He finished with us. *Unveiled Love* seeks a soul that offers itself to the light whether on its own or when confronted with truth. One of the disciples captures the essence of this idea in John 3:19–21 (MSG).

> This is the crisis we're in: God-light streamed into the world, but men and women everywhere ran for the darkness. They went for the darkness because they were not really interested in pleasing God. Everyone who makes a practice of doing evil, addicted to denial and illusion, hates God-light and won't come near it, fearing a pain-

ful exposure. But anyone working and living in truth and reality welcomes God-light so the work can be seen for the God-work it is.

People who routinely defend themselves do so to preserve their life. It could be their reputation, a title or position, things, relationships, or whatever ideas about themselves or others that reinforce their significance. All defend. All possess self-preservation techniques. And we are good at it! So natural and universal is this need to survive, Jesus speaks to it in Matthew 16:25–26:

> For whoever is bent on saving his [temporal] life [his comfort and security here] shall lose it [eternal life]; and whoever loses his life [his comfort and security here] for My sake shall find it [life everlasting].
>
> For what will it profit a man if he gains the whole world and forfeits his life [his blessed life in the kingdom of God]? Or what would a man give as an exchange for his [blessed] life [in the kingdom of God]?

Unveiled Love Gets in Our Way

Unveiled Love disrupts and dismantles our defenses. And what better relationship than the permanency of marriage to pursue us? By the time we reach adulthood, our defense mechanisms are automated. They are involuntary. Consider the husband or wife whose first response to most things is "no," then goes away and has a change of heart. Or the husband or wife who grew up heavily criticized. When confronted, the automatic assumption is he or she must have done something wrong. Our initial responses to situations often reveal a well-oiled, well-timed, well-primed machine hidden in the recesses of our souls. It is natural to want to preserve our life. It's what we learned to do early on to stay alive—*emotionally and sometimes even physically.* We've succeeded!

Here's the thing God's *Unveiled Love* addresses. When we insist on preserving our lives, we engage a variety of tactics. We may dismiss constructive feedback, fail to consider the impact of our words and actions upon others, we may blame others for our behavior, say one thing and do another, criticize others, lie, cheat, steal—*whatever it takes!* Still, there are less obvious ways we defend our souls. They are almost undetectable to those lacking discernment. For instance, the person that uses humor to hide offense and pain. We all laugh. But on the inside, that person may be crying invisible tears. Then there are behaviors that appear virtuous and Christian. Yet behind these admirable behaviors, there lives a proud, unbroken soul simply insisting on his or her own life, emotional security, and way of doing things.

Unveiled Love begins turning weapons into tools by drawing a man and a woman together, connecting their innermost beings, building them up, breaking them down, and sharing the spoils among them again and again. Job 33:29 (MSG) says:

> This is the way God works. Over and over again
> He pulls our souls back from certain destruction,
> so we'll see the light—and live in the light!

Questions to Learn By

1. What experience brought you into *Unveiled Love*? Did you experience the timelessness of *Unveiled Love*? If so, describe what it was like (i.e., constant thoughts, rearranging your priorities, loss of appetite, increased sexual desire, et.al.)
2. What attracted you to your spouse? Did you feel a sense of completeness?
3. Based on what you have read, what does it mean to be an "undefended soul"?

Questions to Grow By

1. Read Psalms 139 in the Passion Translation.
   How do these verses support God's desire for an undefended soul?
   What one to three verses resonate with you? Why? (The verses do not have to be consecutive.)
2. Proverbs 4:23 (TPT) reads, "So above all, guard the affections of your heart, for they affect all that you are. Pay attention to the welfare of your innermost being, for from there flows the wellspring of life." According to this verse, what does the Bible say "guarding your soul" looks like? How might this differ from defending your soul?
3. What are some things you learned to do to emotionally protect yourself?

Questions to Change By

1. In Matthew 15:11, Jesus states, "What truly contaminates a person is not what he puts into his mouth but what comes out of his mouth. That's what makes people defiled." This means that although your spouse may provoke you (and he or she certainly will), God ultimately holds you responsible for your own responsive words and/or actions. What has been your recurring response when your spouse provokes you? Does it meet God's criteria for defilement in Matthew 15:11?
2. What might your recurring response be hiding? (i.e., What fear, shame, or guilt?)

Secret 2

Face Your Fear, Fulfill Your Desire

> There is no fear in love; instead, perfect love drives out fear, because fear involves punishment. So, the one who fears is not complete in love. (1 John 4:18 CSB)

All desire love and intimacy. All desperately fear it. To refute this reveals an ignorance about God, human beings in general, and us. We were created by love to receive and give love. Love is an innate desire. We were born with it. Thereafter, we learned to fear love. Ever since then, there has been a gut-wrenching tension between love and fear. It contributes to anxiety and stress. It's like trying to drive a car in forward and reverse at the same time! It's absurd! It's unreasonable because what we want most, we also fear.

If husbands and wives hope to experience the beauty and grace of two undefended souls coming together in a feast of love, then they first must recognize that God creates all things for His pleasure. God created us to be open, fluid, objective, and to live in the present with Him and each other. This naked, surrendered soul is for God to enjoy and commune. John says as much in Revelation 4:9–11:

> And whenever the living creatures gave glory, honor, and thanks to the One who is enthroned and who lives forever and ever, the twenty-four

> elders fell facedown before the one seated on the throne and they worshiped the one who lives forever and ever. And they surrendered their crowns before the throne, singing: You are worthy, our Lord and God, to receive glory, honor, and power, for you created all things, and for your pleasure they were created and exist.

It's worth repeating. God creates each one for His pleasure. We exist for Him. We do not have life in ourselves. Speaking to the Jews in John 6:53 (CSB), Jesus said:

> Truly I tell you, unless you eat the flesh of the Son of Man and drink his blood, you do not have life in yourselves.

Therefore, we are alive because God made us alive. And He did so for His pleasure. And what is His pleasure, except that we bear His image and likeness. And why? So that our souls—*mind, will, and emotions* can engage in the fellowship of the Spirit. This fellowship is unique to healthy intimacy and intercourse. God intends this communion of spirit, soul, and body to produce and reproduce families, communities, and nations of people that also share the joy of this fellowship. Moreover, that these rule the earth as He rules the heavens.

More than anything in the whole wide world, God desires friendship and intimacy with the souls of men and women. He longs to relate to us and us with Him. He loves us. This truth alone makes each one of us lovable and deserving of love. Paul states it this way in Romans 13:8 (CSB).

> Do not owe anyone anything, except to love one another, for the one who loves another has fulfilled the law.

A Personal Relationship vs. Intimacy

I am suggesting that even more important than ruling the earth, God longs for us to be with Him, to know Him, and for us to desire to be with Him and be known by Him. Above anything we can ever do for God is His desire for us to be an intimate partner. For many Christians, this desire has morphed into the worn-out phrase, "God wants a personal relationship with—*you, me, us.*" But the phrase "personal relationship" does not even begin to scratch the surface for what God seeks. In fact, these two words have contributed to more erroneous teaching than one can shake a stick at! A personal relationship with God has become synonymous with working for God—through intercessory prayer, winning souls, reading our Bibles, attending church, working in ministry or the marketplace, just to name a few.

These activities have come to characterize a personal relationship with God. The more we engage in these activities, the more confident we feel about our personal relationship with God. The less we engage, the worse we feel. Our personal relationship with God rises and falls on the quantity and/or quality of our work. To ask another whether he or she has personal relationship with God is easier, less pushy, and less interfering than saying, "Are you intimate with God?"

Telling another that you have a personal relationship with someone can mean many things. But to say you are intimate with another implies so much more. To say you are dating is one thing. To say you are engaged is another. And being married is yet another. That we have a personal relationship with God or anyone else does not necessarily imply that we are intimate. It could mean that you relate to each other at work or church. Or that you volunteer together at your children's school. I have a personal relationship with my gardener, but we are not intimate. I have a personal relationship with my hairstylist, but we are not intimate. I have a personal relationship with my clients, but we are not intimate. By contrast, intimacy always indicates a personal relationship with another.

Many will lean into the work of having a personal relationship with God and their spouse. They are serious. They work hard and long. When they declare exhaustion, you can feel it. They will say things like, "I'm tired," "I really tried," "I don't know what he or she wants," "I can't do this anymore." It's like being on a treadmill, and the only thing running somewhere is the sweat running down the face. Sadly, the repetitiveness of doing the same thing and expecting different outcomes produces dutiful, at-risk husbands and wives.

The struggle is real, complete with the temptation to step outside of marriage and in any number of ways. The sincere, albeit futile efforts of husbands and wives reminds me of Jesus's description of a generation in Matthew 11:16–19 (AMPC).

> But to what shall I liken this generation? It is like little children sitting in the marketplaces who call to their playmates, We piped to you [playing wedding], and you did not dance; we wailed dirges [playing funeral], and you did not mourn and beat your breasts and weep aloud. For John came neither eating nor drinking [with others], and they say, He has a demon! The Son of Man came eating and drinking [with others], and they say, Behold, a glutton and a wine drinker, a friend of tax collectors and [especially wicked] sinners! Yet wisdom is justified and vindicated by what she does (her deeds) and by her children.

In verse 20, Jesus's conclusion is this. Despite all the good and mighty works He had done, their hearts were unchanged. This is Jesus, the Son of God, saying that even His work alone was insufficient to change the hearts of the people. Jesus makes this explicitly clear in John 5:19 (NKJV).

> Then Jesus answered and said to them, "Most assuredly, I say to you, the Son can do nothing of Himself, but what He sees the Father do; for whatever He does, the Son also does in like manner."

If you feel like you've hit the wall, having tried everything you knew to do to improve the quality of your relationship with your spouse or others, I strongly encourage you to stop. It hasn't worked. It isn't working nor will it work! Just stop it. As noble and godly as your best efforts might be, they aren't working. Give up to Him who knows all things. Give up to Him who loves you best and knows your spouse completely. Reread Psalm 139 inserting your spouse's name and then leave him or her on this altar of Solomon's God-given wisdom.

Polluted Works

Here's the thing. There is God's work and there is our work. Oftentimes, they are not the same. Certainly, from time to time we can and do engage God's work. It is the genuine and unselfish acts of love and kindness. Of this, we are capable. However, our work often is polluted by self-preservation. Couples know this to be true. What attracted you to one another eventually becomes an irritation. Does it not? With many experiences over time, our spouse sees us for what we are—*self-serving and preserving.* It is initially about survival. Both husband and wife are skilled at surviving the challenges faced growing up.

Consider the wife attracted to her husband's charm and hospitality. He's a great listener, very laid-back, and really likes to be with his wife. She enjoys his attentiveness and readiness to help. Sometime after their honeymoon, laid-back becomes lazy. Great listening turns into seldom talking. And just wanting to be with her morphs into him doing little and leaving chores incomplete. A once warm admiration turns to irritation, for the wife who equates being still with doing nothing.

Or the husband who is drawn to his wife's structured, tasked approach to life. He finds comfort in knowing she will take care of things. Sometime after the honeymoon, he realizes taking care of things doesn't mean taking care of him. Structure becomes imposing. The list of tasks becomes rigid and inflexible. He feels controlled. For the husband who feels his performance won't measure up, his initial attraction to his wife becomes a real irritation with his wife.

The irritation can become threatening for reasons we will discuss later. For now, consider this. Your frustrations, irritations, and lack of marital fulfillment prove that your best work will continue to fail to produce the relationship God intends and you desire. That's because God's ways are different than our ways. Our ways are polluted with pride, selfishness, and elaborate survival techniques.

God's ways promote life, hope, and opportunity. Our ways result in death, despair, and loss of relationship. Isaiah 55:8–9 (CSB):

> "For My thoughts are not your thoughts, nor are your ways My ways," says the Lord. For as the heavens are higher than the earth, so are My ways higher than your ways, And My thoughts than your thoughts.

For many, work is about survival—whether to secure physical or emotional food, clothing, and shelter. For Adam, survival depended on outside work—*tilling the ground, forcing it to give him what he wanted and needed.* It was a consequence of doing things his way rather than God's way.

Adam's Story Is Our Story

When we work for what God promises to provide, work becomes a brutal taskmaster. The punishment of working to survive came because Adam disobeyed God. Genesis 3:17–20 (MSG):

> He told the Man: "Because you listened to your wife and ate from the tree that I commanded you not to eat from, 'Don't eat from this tree,' The very ground is cursed because of you; getting food from the ground will be as painful as having babies is for your wife; you'll be working in pain all your life long. The ground will sprout thorns and weeds, you'll get your food the hard way, planting and tilling and harvesting, sweat-

ing in the fields from dawn to dusk, until you return to that ground yourself, dead and buried; you started out as dirt, you'll end up dirt."

Respected forefathers in the faith, including Martin Luther, John Calvin, and John Wesley, have used the words, *"Because you listened to your wife and ate…"* to condemn women and wives to objects of scorn.[2] These men believed and taught that a woman caused Adam to sin. I challenge this notion as you will see in the pages to follow. For now, let's be clear. Adam was not punished because he listened to his wife. If his wife truly was the problem, it would have been a simple fix. Swap out the wife. Adam was punished because he disobeyed God. He chose to eat from the tree of the knowledge of good and evil. Adam was not forced to eat. He chose to eat. Genesis 3:17 (CJB):

> To Adam he said, "Because you listened to what your wife said and ate from the tree about which I gave you the order, 'You are not to eat from it,' the ground is cursed on your account; you will work hard to eat from it as long as you live."

Measuring out punishment begins with God addressing Adam's confession in verse 12 (NKJV):

> The woman whom You gave to be with me, she gave me of the tree, and I ate.

But Adam's confession fell short of the truth. It did not address the heart of the matter. Blame never will. God reveals the truth and heart of the matter by posing a question to Adam in verse 11.

> Who told you that you were naked? Have you eaten from the tree of which I commanded you that you should not eat?

---

[2] https://valerietarico.com/2013/07/01/mysogynistquoteschurchfathers/

The first punishment occurred when God removed His Spirit and covering from Adam, which resulted in death, fear, and an awareness of his nakedness. "Who told you that you were naked?" For the second punishment, God cursed the ground for Adam's sake.

The third punishment was work. God removed the ground's eternal fertility. The ground was afflicted and would no longer readily offer its strength or sweetness to Adam. Adam would sweat from dawn to dusk to force the ground to surrender to his needs. What God intended the ground to produce effortlessly, now required Adam to work for hard and long. This sentence of hard labor would occur, *"until you return to that ground yourself, dead and buried."* Thankfully, Jesus returned to the ground for us! By so doing, the nature of our work has changed.

It is interesting to consider how husbands and wives challenge each other to surrender to one another's needs. We have an entire theology wrapped around a barter system. I call it "need theology." It goes like this: "You meet my needs, and I will meet your needs." And we know what these needs are, because well-meaning pastors and teachers repeatedly tell us. A few well-placed scriptures aid in persuasion. But more about needs later. Sufficient here is that need theology robs husbands and wives of the very things they desire. That's because much of it proceeds from fear of not believing they can get what they want. And this leads to a fourth punishment—distrust between Adam and Eve. Distrust can result from many things. Here, blame is the culprit. Adam held the woman responsible for his behavior.

So why was Adam punished? The second half of verse 11 is explicit. Again, God poses the answer in a question to Adam. The right questions have an uncanny way of getting to the heart of the matter. Adam disobeyed God's command. The punishments were the consequences.

> Have you eaten from the tree of which I commanded you that you should not eat?

For her part, the woman would suffer in childbearing, and she would be subject to her husband. Adam would suffer in the soil. But the woman would suffer in her body. The woman suffered internally, while Adam suffered externally. And since Adam held the woman accountable for his actions by blaming her, God punished Adam by making him accountable for the woman.

Adam's first act of accountability was to name Woman. Adam called her Eve, designating her the mother of all living. Through one man disobeying God, death, fear, and work came into humanity. But through one man, that is Jesus Christ, grace, mercy, and freedom from these punishments became available to men and women. Those that receive the life of God through Christ can enjoy new life, spiritual, mental, emotional, and physical reconnection as well as freedom from fear and punishment. Today, husbands and wives are accountable to God. Each one is responsible for what he or she thinks, feels, says, and does.

Jesus satisfied Adam's need, and by extension, our need to return to the ground, die, and be buried. As we died in Christ, we are raised from the dead by Him. Romans 6:3–4 (MEV) explains:

> Do you not know that we who were baptized into Jesus Christ were baptized into His death? Therefore, we were buried with Him by baptism into death, that just as Christ was raised up from the dead by the glory of the Father, even so we also should walk in newness of life.

Paul speaking to the believers in the church at Ephesus clarifies the meaning of all this in Ephesians 2:8–9 (TPT).

> For by grace you have been saved by faith. Nothing you did could ever earn this salvation, for it was the love gift from God that brought us to Christ! So, no one will ever be able to boast, for salvation is never a reward for good works or human striving.

Jesus Christ not only restored us, but also He went into the ground and restored its fertility. For us who believe in Jesus Christ, the ground has been restored to its original condition. It means that the ground is ripe and ready to release its sweetness. It is alive and rich with all that is necessary to produce and not by the sweat of our brows. This is the good news of the kingdom: God has given us ground to develop to His pleasure and our benefit. He wants us to be fruitful, multiply, replenish the ground, and subdue it. Moreover, Christ restored our ability to engage God intimately. This was His original intent.

> God blessed them and said to them, "Be fruitful and multiply, and replenish the earth and subdue it. Rule over the fish of the sea and over the birds of the air and over every living thing that moves on the earth." (Genesis 1:28 CSB)

God did not intend our rule over the earth to supersede an intimate fellowship with Him. No matter how well we manage the earth and its resources, it will never replace God's desire for us to have an intimate relationship with Him and each other. External successes will never satisfy the internal need for intimacy—to know and be known by another. Jesus makes this abundantly clear when condemning the Pharisees and Scribes in Matthew 23; Jesus made some very scathing statements calling these deceived, blind guides, frauds, and pretenders. In verse 23 (TPT), Jesus summed up the heart of the matter.

> Great sorrow awaits you religious scholars and Pharisees—frauds and pretenders! For you are obsessed with peripheral issues, like insisting on paying meticulous tithes on the smallest herbs that grow in your gardens. These matters are fine, yet you ignore the most important duties of all: to walk in the love of God, to display mercy to others, and to live with integrity. Readjust your values and place first things first.

This about sums up what Jesus thinks about a personal relationship with God based on works. Here's the bottom line according to Jesus in Matthew 15:8 (TPT):

> These people honor me only with their words,
> for their hearts are so very distant from me.

Intimacy with God and Your Spouse

Still today, many otherwise godly men and women offer God words and works instead of communion with their naked souls. As fascinated as husbands and wives are with each other's naked body, so God is fascinated by our naked soul. Yet many souls remain fully clothed and heavily guarded by poor, ineffective coping skills. Men and women arrive to adulthood disguised and fully armored. Fear, guilt, and shame are cleverly concealed. We baffle some and fool others. But not God nor our spouse. The deep God-given desire for intimacy causes hunger pangs. We become "hangry." We find all kinds of ways to feed and satisfy our hunger for intimate love. Still, we suffer. Marriage, like no other relationship, offers the greatest opportunity to experience such intimacy because it includes sex.

Intimacy is about connecting with another deeply at a spiritual, mental, emotional, and physical level. It's seeing and hearing another, all to the awareness of the person. It's like watching another person see you. In this place, there are no covers, no pretense, no excuses—just an undefended soul. It is here in this place that the weakness of one and the strength of another collide for the better. When *Unveiled Love* is present, it makes for a beautiful healing, and unforgettable experience. Those that know the empathy and freedom that comes from intimacy want it again and again. That's because intimacy rekindles and restarts us mentally and emotionally. It feels clean and innocent because it distinguishes who we are from the unlovely things that have happened to us or that we may have done. Intimacy is our best hope to become courageous men and women. It's the only option to become what God intends individually and relationally. *Unveiled Love* is a gift to those that receive it and to those that offer it. That's because *Unveiled Love* destroys fear and replaces it with hope.

Fear of Vulnerability

Fear is a lock that prevents us from entering the door of intimacy. The key that opens the lock is vulnerability. Vulnerability is about showing up mentally, emotionally, and physically. It's about all of us—our thoughts, feelings, memories, and all our willing and choosing parts being in the same room, at the same time with another. In this condition, we render our souls defenseless. Unarmed and in full view of another, we are susceptible to harm. Vulnerability is like standing completely naked in front of a full-length mirror that happens to be a live human being. Did you feel that? Chances are you just experienced what it means to be vulnerable.

Our hunger, thirst, and appetite for intimacy is built into the Divine Nature which we received upon creation, lost through sin, and regained upon taking Christ as Savior and Lord. It's an inescapable aching for connectedness that God shares with us as He did with Jesus. But for many couples, the desire for intimacy and reality are often worlds apart. This is true for our relationship with God and the relationship between husbands and wives. Herein lies the paradox. Above all things, the innate desire for intimate love is the very thing we fear. It's a paradox that causes internal conflict. That which we want and need most is also what we desperately fear. For all, this is a challenge of epic proportions! Solving the riddle is the chief aim of *Unveiled Love*.

No other book in the Bible makes this plainer than the Song of Solomon. It is the most complete and concise account of intimacy and sex between a man and a woman. In fact, the entire book is only about intimacy and sex and the fear of it. The book showcases the challenge and the solution in an unending circle of emotional connection, fear of exposure and vulnerability, sexual fulfillment, and freedom. It's the repeated invitation to bear one's soul and the consequence of refusing and the freedom that accompanies accepting.

To fully appreciate the erotic, albeit difficult language used by the man and the woman in this book, it helps to know that the climatic end of intimacy is sex. And the climatic end of sex is orgasm.

Weaved throughout all is the dismantling of the soul's elaborate defense system. Understandably, the disarming of the soul does not provide the same immediate gratification of sex and orgasm. It's easy to see why many husbands and wives prefer sex over intimacy. Comparatively, sex is quick. It's satisfying, although not for some. A couple can have great sex without intimacy! Unlike sex, intimacy involves the disclosure of the soul. In marriage, the presentation of the body, without the presentation of the soul is a sham—and an unsustainable one at that. Worse still, sex without the soul is an insult to the soul. That's because Genesis 2:25 says that both the man and woman were naked. They had no shame. Guilt and fear had not entered humanity. They were naked body, soul, and spirit.

Unfortunately, intimacy effectively has been reduced to sex, which causes many relationships to suffer from what only intimacy can provide. Intimacy provides for deep emotional connection between two souls. It is part of what makes up the glue in marriage. Sex can undress the body without undressing the soul. Undressing the soul is the work of intimacy. Throughout its eight chapters, the book of Song of Solomon intertwines the themes of intimacy and sex. Each one aiding and strengthening the other. *Unveiled Love* enables intimacy. As intimacy increases, so does the healing and transformation of the soul. No wonder fear seeks to restrain the soul. Only *Unveiled Love* is powerful enough to break this restraint of fear and strong enough to move the souls and men and women to voluntary disclosure.

Song of Solomon helps explain the paradox of *Unveiled Love*, as a fierce competition between love and fear of intimacy. It's about desiring, hiding, and unrelenting invitations to come out of hiding, pretending, and being found out by *Unveiled Love*. Song of Solomon is about the messiness of love. It's about overcoming fear and quenching the thirst for intimacy. God creates all human beings with intimate fellowship in mind. The desire is built in. We cannot remove it. However, we can deny it, ignore it, or satisfy it with substitutes—*like work, ministry, hobbies, children, social media, drugs, pornography, and adultery to name a few.*

Intimacy is about the private details of our life on display before another. Worse than the details just being on display before another is that those details are also in their hands. It's scary. We cannot control how others will respond. Most of us have not had genuine experiences with love. God's *Unveiled Love* draws people close to one another so that what is wounded and broken in one, can receive life and healing from the other. This can happen in relationships other than marriage. But marriage stands above all other relationships. It is the only relationship God has given for men and women to experience the fullness of love—spirit, soul, and body intercourse. This fact alone makes marriage the most powerful human relationship on earth.

Rejecting Intimacy

The world and religion socialize us to reject such intimacy. When we sense and feel another approaching those wounded broken places, we rebel. We fear moral judgment, rejection, or abandonment. Consequently, the dirty facts of our lives become the secrets we vow never to tell. When asked, we lie. We hide. We deny. Yet and still, it's these traumatic, embarrassing, humiliating experiences that have contributed to the persons we have become. It's our (own) unloveliness, lack of admission, and acceptance of love that causes many of the challenges with which we contend. These jaw-dropping, life-sucking details tempt us to preserve our lives. And we do. In doing so, we reject intimacy. We refuse to be seen as we truly are, and therefore, forfeit hope and healing.

But it's *Unveiled Love's* demand for intimacy that keeps reducing us to vulnerability. For after Christ, this is the lowest common denominator between souls. Jesus is the great equalizer between men and women. He leverages the playing field so that all have opportunity to play and win! For many, vulnerability means more pain and suffering. Understandably, we desperately want to avoid such pain. So we avoid allowing ourselves to be known—*our goodness, badness, and the ugliness.* But it's mostly the bad and ugly we shun others from seeing. In marriage, dodging invitations to be open, honest, and vulnerable breeds a resistant strain of pride. Paul writing to the church at Corinth has this to say in 2 Corinthians 6:11–13 (AMPC):

> Our mouth is open to you, Corinthians [we are hiding nothing, keeping nothing back], and our heart is expanded wide [for you]! There is no lack of room for you in [our hearts], but you lack room in your own affections [for us]. By way of return then, do this for me—I speak as to children—open wide your hearts also [to us].

Unveiled Love desires us to open, show up, and receive healing. Healing requires the exposure of hurts, habits, and hang-ups that undermine love. What better place than marriage. What better people than safe husbands and wives. Perhaps, the same vulnerability we fear could lead us to re-injury could also fling wide open the doors of love, acceptance, and healing. This is the nature of *Unveiled Love*. It is committed to resolving the discrepancies between who we pretend to be, who we are, and who we hope to be. And most importantly, who God created us to be.

Habits and Idols

It's the information about our unloveliness—what has happened to us along life's way, who we really are, and what we have done—that we hide. These are the skeletons in our closet: it's the stuff we don't want anyone else to know. These things become our sacred cows—the stuff no one is allowed to touch, ask, or talk about with us. We set them apart from our lives or so we think. They are our hurts. We have dressed them in what become self-defeating habits. By isolating our hurts and adopting poor coping skills that later become habits, we enshrine the pain that feeds our fears. They become the idols for which we build beautiful and sometimes ugly temples. Unknowingly, in the process, we become idol worshippers. Both Old and New Testament scripture make clear that we cannot experience intimacy with God or each other and worship idols. Jeremiah 1:16 (AMPC):

> And I will utter My judgments against them for all the wickedness of those who have forsaken Me, burned incense to other gods, and worshiped the works of their own hands [idols].

Psalm 115:4–8 (AMPC):

> The idols of the nations are silver and gold, the work of men's hands. They have mouths, but they speak not; eyes have they, but they see not; They have ears, but they hear not; noses have they, but they smell not; They have hands, but they handle not; feet have they, but they walk not; neither can they make a sound with their throats. They who make idols are like them; so are all who trust in and lean on them.

First Corinthians 10:7, 14 (AMPC):

> Do not be worshipers of false gods as some of them were, as it is written, "The people sat down to eat and drink [the sacrifices offered to the golden calf at Horeb] and rose to sport (to dance and give way to jesting and hilarity)." Therefore, my dearly beloved, shun (keep clear away from, avoid by flight if need be) any sort of idolatry (of loving or venerating anything more than God).

God's *Unveiled Love* is zealous to be intimate with us. *Unveiled Love* detests idols. It unleashes its fury against anything that seeks to steal, kill, or destroy our ability to be intimate with God and each other. It is the archenemy of pride. *Unveiled Love* picks, prods, and provokes until pride rears its ugly head. Oftentimes, these come in the form of offenses. In Matthew 18:7, Jesus said that offenses are inescapable. Therefore, they are necessary. Offenses expose what is in us whether fear or love or pride or humility. Such exposure injures pride, weakens fear, and gives expression to real hurts and pains. First John 4:18 (TPT) explains it this way:

> Love never brings fear, for fear is always related to punishment. But love's perfection drives the fear of punishment far from our hearts. Whoever walks constantly afraid of punishment has not reached love's perfection.

Consider this scripture, in the Amplified Classic version:

> There is no fear in love [dread does not exist], but full-grown (complete, perfect) love turns fear out of doors and expels every trace of terror! For fear brings with it the thought of punishment, and [so] he who is afraid has not reached the full maturity of love [is not yet grown into love's complete perfection].

Unveiled Love desires to reduce us to pure, naked, undefended souls in which husbands and wives can experience intimacy and sex. And that both become natural and spontaneous. Perhaps this is what is meant by Genesis 2:25 (NIV).

> Adam and his wife were both naked, and they felt no shame.

This means delivering us from every hurt, pain, and fear for which we have built a temple, around which we placed armed guards. *Unveiled Love* seeks to destroy idol and altar. In no other relationship is *Unveiled Love's* determination to facilitate emotional intimacy more apparent than in marriage. In no other relationship is there such a full front on, unrelenting assault on weaponized, proud souls than in marriage.

Unveiled Love resolves the conflict between a man and a woman's innate desire for emotional intimacy with each other and their enormous fear of it. The menacing nature of this paradox is captured by British writer, Iris Murdoch.

> I hate solitude, but I'm afraid of intimacy. The substance of my life is a private conversation with myself which to turn into a dialogue would be equivalent to self-destruction. The company which I need is the company which a pub or a cafe will provide. I have never wanted a communion of souls. It's already hard enough to tell the truth to oneself.[3]

Holding the Tension

Many are unaware of the magnitude of tension that exists between love and fear. All have felt it. Few can express it. Ignored, the tension fuels our already anxious, defensive souls. *Unveiled Love* can ease the tension through its gentleness. When we recognize this anxiety in another, we can respond calmly. Proverbs 15:1 (GNT) reads:

> A gentle answer quiets anger, but a harsh one stirs it up.

While this doesn't always guarantee a peaceful outcome, it removes any fuel we contribute to the fire. *Unveiled Love* is gentle, but also honest. Proverbs 27:6 (TPT) explains:

> You can trust a friend who wounds you with his honesty, but your enemy's pretended flattery comes from insincerity.

---

[3] Iris Murdoch, "Under the Net," Penguin Books, Ltd, 27 Wrights Lane, London, W8 5TZ England

Honesty is not intended to harm, rather to help. But let's face it, honesty can hurt!

Marriage is not for fearful, fragile souls that must be carefully kept and properly esteemed. And yet, marriage is comprised of these very souls. Consequently, we need *Unveiled Love*. Moreover, we need souls willing to work with God's *Unveiled Love*. *Unveiled Love* makes us strong and able to endure the fragileness of others. *Unveiled Love* offers wisdom unique to each marriage. First Peter 3:20 (AMPC) reminds us of God's patience with the souls of men, while Noah built the ark.

> [The souls of those] who long before in the days of Noah had been disobedient, when God's patience waited during the building of the ark in which a few [people], actually eight in number, were saved through water.

Concerning Jesus, it is written in 2 Peter 3:15 (AMPC):

> And consider that the long-suffering of our Lord [His slowness in avenging wrongs and judging the world] is salvation (that which is conducive to the soul's safety), even as our beloved brother Paul also wrote to you according to the spiritual insight given him.

Christians have developed an affinity for praying, declaring God's word, and expecting things to change immediately. Certainly, this approach is far cleaner and neater than having to gut out the sometimes slow, painful, bloody, messy grinding wheels of change. To many Christians, the idea that we might suffer at the hands of those we love, is both unthinkable and unbelievable—until it happens! In Psalm 55:12–14 (AMPC), David speaks:

> For it is not an enemy who reproaches and taunts me—then I might bear it; nor is it one who has hated me who insolently vaunts himself against

me—then I might hide from him. But it was you, a man my equal, my companion and my familiar friend. We had sweet fellowship together and used to walk to the house of God in company.

Peter writes:

> Therefore, since Christ suffered in the flesh, arm yourselves also with the same understanding—because the one who suffers in the flesh is finished with sin—in order to live the remaining time in the flesh no longer for human desires, but for God's will.[4]

Eleven verses later in First Peter 4:12–13 (CSB), Peter encourages his friends.

> Dear friends, don't be surprised when the fiery ordeal comes among you to test you, as if something unusual were happening to you. Instead, rejoice as you share in the sufferings of Christ, so that you may also rejoice with great joy when his glory is revealed.

Unveiled Love is committed to transforming the souls of men and women. It does this by resolving the inner conflict between our desire for intimacy that produces healing and strengthens the connection between husbands and wives and our fear of it. That's why *Unveiled Love* is so stubborn and always advancing. It wants pure, undefended souls fully engaged with God and manifesting His Kingdom on earth. Philippians 2:13 (AMPC) reveals God's determination.

---

[4] 1 Peter 4:1–2 CSB

> For it is (not your strength, but it is) God who is effectively at work in you, both to will and to work (that is strengthening, energizing, and creating in you the longing and the ability to fulfill your purpose) for His good pleasure.

And Paul assures us in Philippians 1:6 that we can be confident in this.

> That He who began a good work in you will carry it on to completion until the day of Christ Jesus.

Like no other relationship, marriage is uniquely suited to bring us to spiritual, mental, and emotional maturity. Marriage is a divine invitation for both husband and wife to come out of hiding and be seen.

The deep-seated hostility between the love and fear; the innate desire for intimacy and the fear of it make *Unveiled Love* a riddle to be solved. It's a mystery revealed to those who embrace and take part in God's *Unveiled Love*. These become pure, naked, undefended souls through which God can perform miracles. Today, more than ever, we need miracles in marriage. That husbands and wives desire love and intimacy and that *Unveiled Love* makes a way for them to experience it is miraculous! It is nothing short of a divine invitation!

Questions to Learn By

1. The author makes the statements, "All desire intimacy. All desperately fear it." What do you think this means?
2. What is the difference between a personal relationship and an intimate relationship?

Questions to Grow By

1. Recall a time when you succeeded at something. Did you encounter fear along the way? If so, describe your experience.

2. What are some things that might make an intimate relationship invasive and uncomfortable at times?
3. What does the author say is the problem with work?

Questions to Change By

1. Do you feel like you can be completely yourself with your spouse? Why or why not?
2. What behaviors do you display that make your spouse feel safe or unsafe emotionally?
3. What behaviors does your spouse display that make him or her safe or unsafe to you?
4. What is your biggest fear about intimacy?

Secret 3

Build on Commonalities

> If we walk in the light as he himself is in the light, we have fellowship with one another, and the blood of Jesus his Son cleanses us from all sin. (1 John 1:7 CSB)

We can face fear when we recognize that God created marriage to be a safe place. One thing that helps make marriage a safe place is starting with and continuously reinforcing what you and your spouse have in common. Sadly, this principle of connection flies out the window when your relationship repeatedly breaks down. That's because conflict reveals differences. Finding sameness in the differences is an intentional matter made harder by conflict. But also the church places a great deal of focus on the differences between men and women, husbands and wives. Emphasizing differences as the primary means through which husbands and wives relate to each other contributes to power and control struggles. Since so much focus in marriage has been placed on gender distinctions, I want to take a few minutes to address this further. That's because starting with commonalities in marriage represents a major paradigm shift.

Not only does the church promote differences as the way for husbands and wives to connect and build intimacy, but books also reinforce this notion. Books like *Love and Respect* (2004) and *His Needs, Her Needs* (1986) differentiate men and women. These books describe characteristics and behaviors of husbands and wives that are rooted in their different needs. The writers go further to prescribe behavior based on these differences. No doubt, there are differences between men and women. However, these books and others like them lead husbands and wives into one-directional thinking they can build and sustain a satisfying intimate relationship by working within the confines of their respective gender differences. If this were true, then we would see less carnage among Christians in marriage. We would see less abuse, less pornography, less abandonment, less separation, and less divorce. But our own stories prove that we are more than male or female. We are more than our differences. We are human beings who happen to be male and female. More importantly, we are spirit. As Christians, we have been reborn of the Spirit and thereby recreated in the image of God. This goes beyond what we commonly teach, that is, as Christians, we should identify with Christ. That we are recreated in God's image means that we come from Him and therefore belong to Him and Christ. We do not merely identify with Christ as someone looking from the outside in, rather we look from the inside out. We do not live in response to an external Christ or its accomplice, which is religion. We live in response to the indwelling Christ. This transcends our differences as men and women. Galatians 2:20 (CSB) says it neatly.

> I have been crucified with Christ, and I no longer live, but Christ lives in me. The life I now live in the body, I live by faith in the Son of God, who loved me and gave himself for me.

In this matter, husbands and wives are no different. Trying to develop emotional connection and intimacy by giving undue attention to what divides us is ineffective. Worse still, it is almost impossible. It's like trying to swim upstream in a rapidly moving river, or trying to walk up the down escalator. It's a recipe for failure.

Overemphasizing Differences Leads to Dysfunction and Demise

While differences may draw us to one another, alone they cannot keep us together. Other words for difference(s) include, but aren't limited to: contrast, deviation, disparity, divide(d), distinction, diversity, opposition, and separation. All these words support the improbability of building and maintaining emotional connection, intimacy, and togetherness. Jesus settles it when He speaks concerning a house which is divided in Mark 3:25 (CSB).

> If a house is divided against itself, that house cannot stand.

In fact, Jesus repeats this truth in Matthew 12:25 and Luke 11:17. These scriptures apply to marriage as well as other entities as seen in Matthew. This includes a divided city coming to peril. In all three gospels, Matthew, Mark, and Luke, Jesus states that a divided kingdom will collapse. It should be clear that the principle that Jesus was teaching is the truth that any relationship built solely on disparities will breakdown. This is true of the smallest community that is husband and wife to the largest community that being a nation and a kingdom and every type of community in between!

Differences

The beautiful upside of differences is that they allow husbands and wives to see an aspect of God's glory in each other. Differences also enable couples to accomplish more together than either can alone. But before couples experience such a breakthrough, there will certainly be breakdowns. That's because it's nearly impossible to see differences and not attach values. We have a human tendency to label things good or bad, best or worse, right or wrong, first or second, et.al. We can't help it. It's natural.

For instance, I have a client who I'll call Jasmine. Jasmine loves everyone. The worse off a person, the more she loves them. Jasmine has an uncanny ability to see beyond a person's presenting behavior to what they really need—*love*. Jasmine is known for going the extra mile whether it's spending time or money. What a blessing Jasmine is to her local church. She is always the first to give and the last to leave a situation. Jasmine's upbringing placed great value on serving others in this manner.

But Jasmine's husband, whom I'll call Mike, had concerns with Jasmine's tendency to give so much time and resources to others because it often came at his expense. And not only at Mike's expense but Jasmine's as well. Mike felt that Jasmine seldom had time for him. He preferred being with Jasmine, more than being with Jasmine and others. He felt that they did not have enough alone time.

In addition, Jasmine's generosity often meant Mike constantly juggled money to meet their financial obligations. To manage their money, Mike often disagreed with Jasmine's generosity. Mike desired greater financial stability. Mike and Jasmine might affectionately be called the saver and the spender. Both saving and spending are important aspects of negotiating life on earth. Both have value. But they comprise different behaviors. Mike values personal financial security. He believes being prepared for rainy days and retirement are worth whatever tightening of the wallet *and purse* may be necessary. Jasmine values people. She believes serving others is her responsibility as a Christian. Whatever sacrifices she *and Mike* may incur are worth it. Neither are wrong. Jesus values generosity. He also values time with loved ones and financial stewardship. Who's right? Who's first? Who should lead? Who should follow? How would religion answer these questions?

In marriage, it is seldom either/or, as disparities seem to imply. With *Unveiled Love*, there is space to hold and act on competing values. Mike and Jasmine's differing values reflect an aspect of God's glory or presence! God's presence is secure. God promises to never leave us nor forsake us.⁵ He will provide for His people. Psalm 37:25 (CSB) confirms this.

> I have been young and now am old, yet have I not seen the [uncompromisingly] righteous forsaken or their seed begging bread.

God provides resources. We can take it to the bank. We can count on it. Mike knows this innately and practically. He patterns his financial life accordingly.

God's glory is also generous. That is, when God is present so is generosity. He is always seeking to do good. Jeremiah 29:11 (CSB) declares this:

> For I know the plans I have for you—this is the Lord's declaration—plans for your well-being, not for disaster, to give you a future and a hope.

Mike and Jasmine offer each other different aspects of God's presence. It is up to each one to recognize them, move beyond personal fear to trust and embrace them. Both must grow. Both must establish new comfort zones, leaving the past behind. Their differences are wonderful and needful to God's assignment for them individually and collectively. But first, we must unearth these differences. When we do, we discover that fear drives Mike and Jasmine. Mike fears poverty. Jasmine fears not being a generous, giving, good Christian. A worse fear is the threat of being abandoned by her faith. Facing fear leads to freedom and wealth (spiritually, mentally, emotionally, and in some case financially).

More Alike than Different

The church in the book of Acts was radical. They grew and thrived. They began building on the foundation of the apostles and

---

⁵ Deuteronomy 31:6, 8; Isaiah 41:17; Hebrews 13:5

prophets, with Christ Jesus himself as the chief cornerstone.[6] Acts 2:42, 44–47 (CSB) tells us how they did it.

> They devoted themselves to the apostles' teaching, to the fellowship, to the breaking of bread, and to prayer. Now all the believers were together and held all things in common. They sold their possessions and property and distributed the proceeds to all, as any had need. Every day they devoted themselves to meeting together in the temple, and broke bread from house to house. They ate their food with joyful and sincere hearts, praising God and enjoying the favor of all the people. Every day the Lord added to their number those who were being saved.

The first church built on what they had in common. No one lacked what he or she needed. The people were filled with awe; signs and wonders were evident, they praised God and enjoyed the favor of one another. And daily, God added to their numbers. Husbands and wives would benefit from learning this method of growth, multiplication, and favor with God and each other. They built on commonalities, then multiplied and diversified through their differences. When we build on commonalities, it is sustainable.

Unlike building exclusively on differences, building on what husbands and wives have in common endures. Moreover, it leads to long-term satisfaction and success. Amos 3:3 (KJV) asks:

> Can two walk together, unless they be agreed?

In other words, a husband and wife cannot walk together unless they first come together. Though they try, unless they have a common starting point and clear destination, they will suffer unnecessarily. Sadly, many couples today, are trying to walk their differences,

---

[6] Ephesian 2:20

rather than harnessing the strength of their commonalities. The truth is men and women, husbands and wives have more in common than different. So if we are going to build on commonalities, let's consider some of them. We have physical and biological things in common. For biological parents, children are the most obvious and irrefutable commonality. We have mental and emotional things in common. And we have spiritual things in common.

While the size and shape of our bodies are quite different, men and women are designed with the following systems in common: circulatory, digestive, exocrine, skin and nails, skeletal, muscular, respiratory, renal, immune, and nervous (brain, spinal cord, and peripheral nerves). Parts of the endocrine system (hormonal glands), the genitourinary and reproductive systems are uniquely different in men and women. But the design and function of the main human body systems are the same. In summary, while physical and hormonal differences contribute to the attraction men and women have toward each other, marriage does not negate these similarities. But there are not only physical, biological, and functional commonalities, but there are other tangible ones as well.

Mental and Emotional Commonalities

God created all human beings, that is male and female with the ability to think, feel, and decide for self. This is clear to any parent who has or is raising a two-year-old. Possessiveness, big feelings, temper tantrums highlight this phase of development. Whether male or female, "It's all about me—mine." They think and act accordingly. It is most obvious during play. My two-year-old grandson believes all things belong to him. When he is ready to use something, he promptly tries to take it from his older brother or sister. When he fails, it is accompanied by a temper tantrum. It also happened with my granddaughter. As they grow, so do the ways they think to control their environment and the people within it!

In addition to our bodies, the ability to think and feel is also part of what makes us human. God created every human being, male and female, husband and wife, with the capacity to feel. Unless tampered with, all can experience happiness, sadness, love, fear, anger, surprise, shame, and guilt, as well as many more variations of these emotions. Feelings influence how we respond and interact with life, circumstances, and people. A husband and wife may feel the same emotion for different reasons. For instance, the wife who commits adultery may be hurt and angry at herself for betraying her marriage vow. She may feel guilt for what she has done and shame for what it has made of her. Her husband could be hurt and angry because he perceives she chose herself over him. He could be angry at the other person, whether male or female. He may feel guilty for not protecting her. And perhaps he feels shame for failing to satisfy her need. They share the same feelings, but for different reasons. Our feelings do more to connect us than what we think or how we think.

Feelings are extremely powerful in this way. Feelings are not independent. They follow thoughts, and in turn, influence action. Like our physical similarities, emotions facilitate connection. Husbands and wives that can own and share their feelings with each other, especially the more vulnerable ones, have the best opportunity to connect deeply and meaningfully.

Spiritual Commonalities

We are not only more alike than different physically and emotionally but also spiritually. There is one God and Father of all. Jesus Christ is the only name given whereby men and women must be saved from eternal separation from God. Whether male or female, Jesus is the only mediator between human beings and the Creator of the universe. There is not a separate gospel for men and another for women. All men and women have sinned and routinely fall short of God's desire. John 1:12–13 (MEV) advises:

> Yet to all who received Him, He gave the power to become sons of God, to those who believed in His name, who were born not of blood, nor of the will of the flesh, nor of the will of man, but of God.

Here's how the Amplified Bible Classic Edition records it.

> But to as many as did receive and welcome Him, He gave the authority (power, privilege, right) to become the children of God, that is, to those who believe in (adhere to, trust in, and rely on) His name—Who owe their birth neither to bloods nor to the will of the flesh [that of physical impulse] nor to the will of man [that of a natural father], but to God. [They are born of God!]

Notice there is no distinction or order among men and women. Each one must choose Christ as an independent act of his or her will. When they do, they become sons of God. God gives full authority to men and women who receive Him to become His sons. Today, most agree with the truth that women and wives are not inferior to men or husbands. However, when most of the emphasis is placed on differences and hierarchy in marriage, we contradict that truth. Of the sons of God, Paul writes that we are joint heirs and co-laborers with Christ. He does not distinguish male and female believers in Romans 8:16–17 (CSB):

> The Spirit himself testifies together with our spirit that we are God's children, and if children, also heirs—heirs of God and coheirs with Christ—if indeed we suffer with him so that we may also be glorified with him.

And in 1 Corinthians 12:13 (CSB), Paul makes no distinction between Jews and Greeks in Spirit.

> For we were all baptized by one Spirit into one body—whether Jews or Greeks, whether slaves or free—and we were all given one Spirit to drink.

While this verse removes the distinction between Jews and Greeks, its fundamental truth applies to both men and women also without distinction. Paul elaborates in Ephesians 2:13–18 (TPT):

> Yet look at you now! Everything is new! Although you were once distant and far away from God, now you have been brought delightfully close to him through the sacred blood of Jesus—you have actually been united to Christ! Our reconciling "Peace" is Jesus! He has made Jew and non-Jew one in Christ. By dying as our sacrifice, he has broken down every wall of prejudice that separated us and has now made us equal through our union with Christ. Ethnic hatred has been dissolved by the crucifixion of his precious body on the cross. The legal code that stood condemning every one of us has now been repealed by his command. His triune essence has made peace between us by starting over—forming one new race of humanity, Jews and non-Jews fused together in himself! Two have now become one, and we live restored to God and reconciled in the body of Christ. Through his crucifixion, hatred died. For the Messiah has come to preach this sweet message of peace to you, the ones who were distant, and to those who are near. And now, because we are united to Christ, we both have equal and direct access in the realm of the Holy Spirit to come before the Father!

Through Jesus Christ, God's *Unveiled Love* tears down the dividing wall of hostility between men and women. By fulfilling the law comprised of commands designed to regulate human beings' behavior toward God and each other, Jesus is free to create in Himself one new man out of two. Paul explains it as a promise, the result is peace. He gives us Jesus's reason in verse 16 (CSB):

> He did this so that he might reconcile both to God in one body through the cross by which he put the hostility to death.

But some will read and say that Paul is speaking with respect to the Jews and Greeks. Genesis 2:24–25 (CSB) suggests that God not only had racial and ethnic unity in mind but also humanity—*all men and all women.*

> This is why a man leaves his father and mother and bonds with his wife, and they become one flesh. Both the man and his wife were naked yet felt no shame.

If this is not convincing enough, then consider Galatians 3:28 (CSB).

> There is no Jew or Greek, slave or free, male and female; since you are all one in Christ Jesus.

Paul makes a big deal about our sameness in Christ. Marriage does not remove our differences, but rather desires to use them to produce something much more spectacular than husband or wife can alone. That husbands and wives can become one makes reproducing a child possible. The truth that they can become one in Christ also makes reproducing in their God-given assignment possible. But Genesis 1:28 informs us that reproducing is not enough. Husbands and wives must also multiply. Early farmers and armies, as well as loggers today, understand the power of multiplication. It is well documented that by harnessing draft horses together, they can move heavier loads than either could alone. One Belgian draft horse can pull eight thousand pounds. Two can pull almost three times the weight of one. Their combined ability is more than a coupling or doubling, rather a multiplying. Today, draft horses are used in logging. Two can haul up to eight tons of logs per day.[7] What God finds good is the inherent ability of all created things to multiply. Husbands and wives together are supposed to reproduce and multiply. When they don't, dysfunction and demise of the relationship is likely. The process of reproduction and multiplication begins with two becoming one.

That's because when God begins building, He starts with one and those that enter oneness. That's why praying together, reading scripture together, and sitting quietly together in full awareness of God's presence matters. He uses these activities to bring husbands and wives into unity. It's not about who prays or reads first, the best, or even the loudest. It's about being real and honest, turning our weapons into building tools. God also uses adverse circumstances and challenges to escort husbands and wives to oneness. This is so that we might better reflect Him and that He may relaunch us for His glory and our benefit.

The Bride—the Wife of the Lamb

Just as believing men and women are the sons of God, they both will make up the woman, the Bride of the Lamb that is Christ. The Old Testament develops the idea that Israel, collectively, is God's wife. Speaking to Israel in Isaiah 54:5 (MEV), God declares Himself her husband.

> Indeed, your husband is your Maker—his name is the Lord of Armies—and the Holy One of Israel is your Redeemer; he is called the God of the whole earth.

Jeremiah 3:14 (CSB) affirms Israel as God's wife.

> "Return, O backsliding children," says the Lord, "for I am married to you. I will take you, one

---

[7] https://www.besthorserider.com/how-much-weight-can-a-draft-horse-pull/

from a city and two from a family, and I will bring you to Zion."

And Deuteronomy 7:7–9 (CSB) tells us that God's covenant is with Israel.

> The Lord had his heart set on you and chose you, not because you were more numerous than all peoples, for you were the fewest of all peoples. But because the Lord loved you and kept the oath he swore to your ancestors, he brought you out with a strong hand and redeemed you from the place of slavery, from the power of Pharaoh king of Egypt. Know that the Lord your God is God, the faithful God who keeps his gracious covenant loyalty for a thousand generations with those who love him and keep his commands.

Preparation of the Bride

The pattern of the Old Testament is to show us outwardly with Israel, what the New Testament says will take place inwardly with Jew and Gentile, male and female. In the Old Testament, the wife of God is Israel—*the Jewish people.* In the New Testament, the wife of the lamb is inside the church. She is preparing herself for the marriage ceremony. Revelation 19:7–8 (CSB):

> Let us be glad, rejoice, and give him glory, because the marriage of the Lamb has come, and his bride has prepared herself. She was given fine linen to wear, bright and pure.

Together, men and women who receive the fine linen and wear it are bright and pure. Linen is harvested from the flax plant. It is organic. It is naturally resistant to pests, therefore requires no pesticides, little fertilizer, or water. In the Bible, flax or linen symbolizes purity. It requires that we receive truth and establish right alignment in relationship with God, self, and others. I believe Revelation 19:7–8 is referring to men and women that receive truth and live uprightly as fine linen. These are being made one in Christ. The ideal relationship for men and women to experience this oneness is in marriage.

Through Jesus Christ, the Gentiles are grafted into the vine such that there is no distinction between Jews and Gentiles. Romans 11:17 (TPT) speaks about the splicing that occurred.

> However, some of the branches have been pruned away. And you, who were once nothing more than a wild olive branch, God has grafted in—inserting you among the remaining branches as a joint partner to share in the wonderful richness of the cultivated olive stem.

Jesus Christ made it possible for us that believe to become a part of His bride. We do so by receiving and conforming to truth. He is the truth.[8] He is also the way the bride must follow and the life she must live. All of this expressed in our relationships, beginning with marriage. Paul writes in 2 Corinthians 11:2 (CSB):

> For I am jealous for you with a godly jealousy, because I have promised you in marriage to one husband—to present a pure virgin to Christ.

There are not many brides. There is only one. The bride is made up of men and women who are making themselves ready. Song of Solomon 6:8–10 (MEV) makes this clear.

> There are sixty queens and eighty concubines, and virgins without number. My dove, my perfect one, is the only one, the only one of her mother, choice to her who bore her. The maid-

---

[8] John 14:6

ens saw her and called her blessed; the queens and concubines also, and they praised her. Who is this who looks forth like the dawn, fair as the moon, radiant as the sun, awesome as an army with banners?

Marriage is for the overarching purpose of preparing men and women to wed Christ. Every other purpose of marriage is an aspect of this one thing. All those preparing *and some who are not* have residence in the church.

Residence of the Bride

The bride currently resides in the Body of Christ, which is the church. Ephesians 5:23 (GW) explains:

> The husband is the head of his wife as Christ is the head of the church. It is his body, and he is its Savior.

To appreciate this further consider the Old Testament example of Adam and Woman. Genesis 2:21–22 (GW):

> So the Lord God caused him to fall into a deep sleep. While the man was sleeping, the Lord God took out one of the man's ribs and closed up the flesh at that place. Then the Lord God formed a woman from the rib that he had taken from the man. He brought her to the man.

Woman resided inside of Adam until God removed her and presented her to him. Adam's body had to be broken to remove the woman. Following God's example, it is easy to see that the wife of the Lamb is presently in His Body, that is in the church. That means the church is not the bride of Christ, nor the wife of the Lamb of God. Like the woman hidden inside Adam's body, so the wife of Christ is hidden and residing in Him. While the bride is residing in Him, she is preparing herself.

A rib was broken from Adam's body. And with that rib, God made Woman. Jesus often broke bread, releasing the life that was in the bread. In John 6:48 and 51, Jesus tells us He is the living bread. Jesus's death, the ultimate brokenness, resulted in the release of the Holy Spirit. This release of the Holy Spirit is so that we might have a more abundant life. Now are you ready for this? Like Adam's body, like Jesus's own body, His current body, that is the church must be broken, if not destroyed so the bride of Christ can fully emerge. And this will happen at God's appointed time!

In Ephesians 5:31–32 (CSB), Paul writes once more.

> For this reason, a man will leave his father and mother and be joined to his wife, and the two will become one flesh. This mystery is profound, but I am talking about Christ and the church.

That there will be no marrying in the resurrection makes this mystery even more profound. In Matthew 22:30 (CSB), Jesus states it this way:

> For in the resurrection they neither marry nor are given in marriage but are like the angels of God in heaven.

I must admit I do not comprehend the depth of all that I write. What is clear to me is this: in Christ, there is no male and female. We are one, though we are not all equal in knowledge, skill, or position. Still, it is the equality of who we are as sons and bride that is the strength of the union. The depth and power of marriage lies in husbands and wives' willingness to embrace their oneness. This is a big deal when navigating challenges whether externally or internally. You can start by acknowledging, accepting, and continuously reinforcing what you have in common. When husbands and wives hug, hold on to, and talk about their physical, biological, mental, emotional, and spiritual similarities they improve their relatability. They also strengthen their emotional connection. For instance, all human beings have felt guilt and shame. All have the capacity to feel joy, pain, love, and anger. Moreover, when perceived the same—*equally in need of the Savior and Lord, equally in need of love and respect, equally in need of forgiveness*—a certain humility is present. God is drawn to humility and so are we. James 4:6 (CSB) emphasizes:

> But he gives greater grace. Therefore he says: God resists the proud but gives grace to the humble.

Adam said it best in Genesis 2:23:

> And the man said: "This one, at last, is bone of my bone and flesh of my flesh; this one will be called woman, for she was taken from man."

For the first time, Adam saw himself and he was spectacular. Likewise, if man saw himself, then woman also saw herself in Adam! Paul writes of the experience this way in Ephesians 5:28–29 (MEV):

> In this way men ought to love their wives as their own bodies. He who loves his wife loves himself. For no one ever hated his own flesh, but nourishes and cherishes it, just as the Lord cares for the church.

Wives, too, ought to love their husbands for this is the will of God that we love one another as Christ loves us.[9] Commonalities enable a husband and wife to build sustainably. Building on their commonalities provides the support required to expand, diversify, reproduce, and multiply. This results in long-term success, and in

---

[9] John 13:34–35

turn, leaves a legacy. Shared physical, mental, emotional, and spiritual attributes are as important as having common ground.

Common Kingdom Ground

The Kingdom of God represents solid common ground for husbands and wives. It is not subject to the changeability of either husband or wife. It is no respecter of persons, whether male or female. The Kingdom of God is not regulated by the will of men and women. It does not rise and fall on our faithfulness or unfaithfulness. Paul summed it up in Romans 11:18 (TPT) when cautioning the Gentiles being grafted into the vine not to be arrogant.

> There's no reason to boast, for the new branches don't support the root, but you owe your life to the root that supports you!

The Kingdom of God authorizes and supports all that enter and adhere. All kingdoms and many nations have a king, still others have a president or leader by some other name. The Kingdom of God has a king. His name is Jesus Christ. Kingdoms also have cultures, laws, norms, and practices. Together, they comprise a network, a system that rewards and punishes behavior. To illustrate, let me borrow an analogy from technology.

Mobile phones, smart home automation (i.e., Alexa), Cash App, Venmo, Apple Pay, debit cards, Facebook, YouTube, and 5G operate on a network. A network is a centralized system of rules, routers, switches, and access points. Whoever is connected to the network and observes the rules can communicate effectively with other users. Whoever is not connected to the network has limited ability to communicate with those on the network and sometimes not at all. This is because each network has rules that determine access and usability. If we follow the rules, then we enjoy the benefit of communicating and connecting with others. Some activities are only available to those on the same network. For instance, two iPhones can FaceTime. But an android phone and an iPhone cannot without different software that links two networks. In addition to rules, every network has an owner, operator, and users.

The Kingdom of God is a network. God is its Owner and the Holy Spirit its operator. Jesus is the blueprint—*the firstborn among many sons.*

Once connected to the network, God and Holy Spirit have access to users' profile, personal information, likes, dislikes, contacts, and other sensitive details. They have access to everything there is to know about us, even those things we may neither know nor understand about ourselves. This can be both comforting and unsettling to the defended soul. Unlike the self-serving, power-hungry ploys of big tech, God's Kingdom is for you, not against you. Romans 8:31 (AMPC) reassures us.

> What then shall we say to [all] this? If God is for us, who [can be] against us? [Who can be our foe, if God is on our side?]

Network Systems

Networks are comprised of systems. A computer has a hardware system, an operating system, and a security system among others. The Kingdom of God has systems also. *Unveiled Love* is a system for living in relationship with God, self, our spouse, and others. Although we are focusing on the *Unveiled Love* system as it applies to marriage, it is applicable to all relationships. We have already discussed two aspects of the system. The desire to become an undefended soul before God and our spouse is the first prerequisite to take part in *Unveiled Love*. This leads to the second aspect of engaging *Unveiled Love*, that is, the willingness to face fear to fulfill your desire and destiny. The third aspect of the *Unveiled Love* system requires husbands and/or wives to begin building on commonalities. This is our best hope of using differences to scale adversities, multiply, and diversify.

To use the *Unveiled Love* system effectively, each of these three components (secrets) must be engaged, as well as the remaining seven. All components align with the values and rules of conduct for the Kingdom of God. All citizens of the Kingdom and participants in *Unveiled Love* are required to adopt and adhere to these values and rules or suffer the consequences. The values and rules serve as common ground as they apply to husbands and wives equally.

Shared Values

Examples of shared values include honesty, integrity, compassion, and growth. As it relates to handling money with honesty and integrity, Paul writes this to the church in 2 Corinthians 8:18–22 (TPT):

> So we're sending with him the brother who is greatly honored and respected in all the churches for his work of evangelism. Not only that, he has been appointed by the churches to be our traveling companion as we carry and dispense this generous gift that glorifies the Lord and shows how eager we are to help. We are sending a team in order to avoid any criticism over how we handle this wonderfully generous gift, for we intend to do what is right and we are totally open both to the Lord's inspection and to man's. So we're sending with them another brother who is faithful and proven to be a man of integrity. He is passionate to help you now more than ever, for he believes in you.

Concerning compassion, Paul writes to the church in Colossians 3:12–13 (TPT):

> You are always and dearly loved by God! So robe yourself with virtues of God, since you have been divinely chosen to be holy. Be merciful as you endeavor to understand others, and be compassionate, showing kindness toward all. Be gentle and humble, unoffendable in your patience with

others. Tolerate the weaknesses of those in the family of faith, forgiving one another in the same way you have been graciously forgiven by Jesus Christ. If you find fault with someone, release this same gift of forgiveness to them.

And about our need to grow up, Paul, writing to the church in Ephesians 4:14 (TPT), has this to say:

And then our immaturity will end! And we will not be easily shaken by trouble, nor led astray by novel teachings or by the false doctrines of deceivers who teach clever lies.

Speaking concerning himself in 1 Corinthians 13:11 (TPT), Paul writes these familiar words:

When I was a child, I spoke about childish matters, for I saw things like a child and reasoned like a child. But the day came when I matured, and I set aside my childish ways.

Marriage is one of our last chances to grow up emotionally, mentally, and spiritually. It's required. When we refuse, we suffer—*individually and relationally.* Growing up involves honesty, integrity, and compassion. These are some of the values of God's Kingdom and *Unveiled Love.* They apply to all and thus represent common ground for husbands and wives.

Impartial Rules

The rules of engagement in the Kingdom of God and *Unveiled Love* are impartial. They contain no gender bias nor positional bias. Husbands and wives are well-advised to obey the rules. When a husband or wife violates the rules, penalties result. That's the inherent nature of a rule or law. They punish disobedience. Some of the problems husbands and wives experience in marriage are a direct result of violating God's rules. When one violates a rule, all suffer. God joins husbands and wives in part, so there will be no lack or division in His body. First Corinthians 12:26 (TPT) summarizes God's intention.

> In that way, whatever happens to one member happens to all. If one suffers, everyone suffers. If one is honored, everyone rejoices.

It's important to know and practice the rules. They represent common ground and carry authority to bless and punish behavior. Some of these rules include the law of freedom, the law of love, and the law of submission.

The Law of Freedom

God created us to be free. That is to be free to choose Him or not. Hence there are two trees in the Garden of Eden. One tree represents a life of perpetual friendship and fellowship between God and mankind. The other tree represents death or detachment between God and mankind. Today, thank God through Jesus Christ, each of us has the freedom and opportunity to choose life or not. Even after we accept Christ as our Savior from the wrath of God, we retain the freedom to choose God's way of life or not. We may not like others' choices, but we can respect their freedom to choose.

For freedom, Christ set us free. In Galatians 5:1 (NLT), Paul encourages us that when taking this freedom, we must be diligent to remain free. But also it means honoring the freedom of others to think and decide for themselves. When we do not, we violate the law of freedom.

> So Christ has truly set us free. Now make sure that you stay free, and don't get tied up again in slavery to the law.

James 2:12 (CSB) informs us that each of us will be judged by what we do with our freedom:

> Speak and act as those who are to be judged by the law of freedom.

Finally, James 1:25 (AMPC) assures us of the benefits of using our freedom to honor God and His word:

> But he who looks carefully into the faultless law, the [law] of liberty, and is faithful to it and perseveres in looking into it, being not a heedless listener who forgets but an active doer [who obeys], he shall be blessed in his doing (his life of obedience).

The entire premise of *Unveiled Love* recognizes and honors the freedom of each one of us to think and decide for ourselves, and the personal responsibility that accompanies our decisions.

The Law of Love

When asked by a Pharisee which is the greatest commandment, Jesus had this to say in Matthew 22:37–40 (TPT):

> Love the Lord your God with every passion of your heart, with all the energy of your being, and with every thought that is within you. This is the great and supreme commandment. And the second is like it in importance: You must love your friend in the same way you love yourself. Contained within these commandments to love you will find all the meaning of the Law and the Prophets.

These two commandments fulfill all the laws of the Old Testament prophets! The law of love provides no exception to husbands or wives. Whether we experience joy or pain depends on our response to love. Whether our spouse experiences joy or pain in part depends on our response to the law of love. The law is simple: love or suffer. Though harsh, this is the nature of God's rules.

The Law of Submission

This one is a big deal. One reason is because traditional marriage teaching emphasizes wives' submission to husbands as the cornerstone of a good relationship. As a member of a church since 1982, a pastor on staff at two local churches for a combined fifteen years and having counseled hundreds of married couples over the past twenty-five years, I confidently say that submission has been chiefly taught as the wives' responsibility. Emphasis on hierarchy as a model for relating in marriage reinforces this notion.

Submission is a law of the Kingdom of God. This means it applies equally to husbands and wives. We need look no further than our Savior and Lord, Jesus Christ to verify this truth. Jesus obeyed His Father to His demise. He chose His Father's will over His own. Jesus says so Himself in Matthew 26:39 (CSB).

> Going a little farther, he fell facedown and prayed, "My Father, if it is possible, let this cup pass from me. Yet not as I will, but as you will."

In John 17:4 (CSB), Jesus speaking to the Father says this:

> I have glorified you on the earth by completing the work you gave me to do.

In verse 10, He adds:

> Everything I have is yours, and everything you have is mine, and I am glorified in them.

The law of submission concerns men and women, husbands and wives. Rebellion is a violation of the law. I have spoken to many husbands frustrated by their wives' lack of support. In some cases, wives are truly rebellious toward authority. In other cases, husbands may not discern their wives are supporting them—*just not in the manner desired*. In still other cases, it is the husband and not the wife who is rebellious, all the while demanding submission from his wife. In all cases, submission is required of both husband and wife. First and foremost, they must submit to God. Colossians 3:17 (AMPC) suggests that we do all things unto God.

> And whatever you do [no matter what it is] in word or deed, do everything in the name of the Lord Jesus and in [dependence upon] His Person, giving praise to God the Father through Him.

First Corinthians 10:31 (AMPC):

> So then, whether you eat or drink, or whatever you may do, do all for the honor and glory of God.

Husbands and wives are also advised to submit to each other. In Ephesians 5:21 (KJ21), Paul writes the following:

> Submitting yourselves one to another in the fear of God.

In God's Word Translation, this verse is more explicit.

> Place yourselves under each other's authority out of respect for Christ.

After submitting to Christ and practicing submission to one another, then Paul instructs wives to submit to their own husbands. Ephesians 5:22 (AMPC) records it this way:

> Wives, be subject (be submissive and adapt yourselves) to your own husbands as [a service] to the Lord.

There are many other laws as well. A few of them are the law of forgiveness, the law of gratitude, the law of kindness, the law of self-control, and the law of humility. The big idea here is this. The laws of the Kingdom of God and *Unveiled Love* pertain to husbands and wives, wives and husbands. There is no distinction between men and women or husbands and wives. The laws represent common ground for relating. That they are laws means that while applicable to all, they are enforced by One, who is God.

Husbands and wives must face fear to overcome near obsession with differences to avoid their demise. This begins with identifying, embracing, and creating conversations around their similarities. When God wanted to reconcile human beings' relationship with Him, He began with a human being—*like us*. Like Adam, God made this human being male. As Woman was hidden in Adam's body, so the bride is hidden in Jesus Christ's body. About this Jesus, it is written in John 1:14 (NASB, 1995):

> And the Word became flesh, and dwelt among us, and we saw His glory, glory as of the only begotten from the Father, full of grace and truth.

Philippians 2:7–8 (CSB) writes of this Man named Jesus.

> Instead he emptied himself by assuming the form of a servant, taking on the likeness of humanity. And when he had come as a man, he humbled himself by becoming obedient to the point of death—even on a cross.

And Hebrews 4:15 refers to Jesus as a High Priest saying:

> For we do not have a high priest who cannot sympathize with our weaknesses, but One who has been tempted in all things as we are, yet without sin.

Paul tells Timothy that for all humanity—*male and female*—there is one mediator. First Timothy 2:5 reads:

> For there is one God and one mediator between God and mankind, the man Christ Jesus.

If husbands and wives ever had opportunity to turn the tide of adultery, abuse, and divorce, it is now. It will require at least one to initiate a reset by building on commonalities. The following chart is a summary of the many things husbands and wives have in common. It does not include things like air, food, water, and shelter as these are obvious. Keep in mind, growth occurs on a continuum. It is not a destination. However, celebrating goals and milestones is important. Each one grows and changes (or not) at his or her own pace. We best help God by maturing in our ability to hold tension for each other. Holding the tension means being the space between who one's spouse is and who God desires him or her to be. To do this is good. To do this gracefully is God working with the sovereign act of your will!

Things Husbands and Wives Have in Common

Physical	Mental	Emotional	Spiritual	Kingdom
Body	Ability to think	Feel happiness/joy	Father	Law of Love
Major Organs*	Ability to reason	Feel sadness	Christ	Law of Submission
Circulatory System	Ability to decide	Feel anger	Holy Spirit	Law of Forgiveness
Skeletal System	Ability to act	Feel love	Authority	Law of Gratitude
Muscular System	Conscience	Feel pride	Power	Law of Kindness
Digestive System	Ability to self-reflect	Feel shame	Sonship	Law of Self-Control
Nervous System**	Ability to change mind	Feel guilt	Bride	Law of Sowing/Reaping
Immune System		Feel pain		Law of Humility
Endocrine System**				
Respiratory System				

Everyone has ability to grow and change with new experiences over time!

*Does not include reproductive organs
** Does not include sex specific sensory nerves or glands

By shifting your paradigm and starting with commonalities, you position yourself to multiply and diversify based on your differences. No longer will they contribute to divisiveness, rather they become tools to appreciate, applaud, and freely engage. It stems the tide of competition in marriage. That's because what you applaud removes the need for your spouse to have to prove. When you or your spouse no longer must prove yourselves, you are free and totally devoted to being yourselves. Isn't that what we want in marriage—to just be ourselves?

Beginning Alone

Building on commonalities does not always mean beginning together. When it does happen, it is beautiful and impressive! By all means, husbands and wives experiencing this synergy do well to enjoy it. That's because every earnest husband and wife will know what it feels like to carry an uncalled for, perhaps even unjust weight in marriage. It's inescapable. The ability to bear weight is how we grow strong. It's how our muscles get bigger. It's how muscles are transformed. This is true physically, mentally, emotionally, and spiritually. Jesus is quite familiar. Remember, Jesus did not carry His own sin to the cross. It was our sin—the weight of our sin. He wasn't forced to do so. He chose to do this as an independent act of His will by the power of the Holy Spirit. Paul writes of Jesus's decision this way in Romans 5:8 (CSB):

> But God proves his own love for us in that while we were still sinners, Christ died for us.

In other words, we were distant, incapable, and unhelpful to Jesus. We offered sin to the redemption process. Jesus working together with His Father and the Holy Spirit secured our freedom from eternal judgment. He also won our right to reclaim our sovereignty with the hope that we would fully surrender to God.

Questions to Learn By

1. When it comes to differences and similarities, in your experience, which one is emphasized the most?
2. The author provides five areas in which husbands and wives are alike. Which two areas would you like to learn more about?

Questions to Grow By

1. In your marriage, what is emphasized most—your differences or similarities? Give an example.
2. How many times a week (i.e., 0, 5, 10, 25, or more) do you talk about the things you have in common? In what area on the chart: "Things Husbands and Wives Have in Common" do these conversations land?
3. What reason does the author give for calling love, submission, forgiveness, et.al., rules or laws?

Questions to Change By

1. What do you have in common with your spouse that is easy to accept? What do you have in common with your spouse that is hard to accept?
2. Which of the laws do you struggle with the most? Why do you think this is the case?
3. What commonality with your spouse would interest you in starting a conversation with him or her? What are some things you could say to begin a conversation? What are some open-ended questions you might ask your spouse to validate this commonality? What are some things you could do to make it fun?
4. Are you in a season of building together or building alone? Describe your experience.

Part II—Get Set!

Like the swimmer, immediately after hearing the command "Take your marks" the athlete thinks "Okay I have to get set now". In Part II, we will learn how to reclaim our freedom, ready ourselves to receive love, and set our heart on trusting God to meet our needs.

    Adopt the same attitude as that of Christ Jesus,
    (Philippians 2:5 CSB)

Secret 4

Reclaim Your Freedom

> Now, the "Lord" I'm referring to is the Holy Spirit, and wherever he is Lord, there is freedom.
> (2 Corinthians 3:17 TPT)

Freedom matters. Your freedom matters. Your spouse's freedom matters. Freedom especially matters in marriage! If we hope to stem the tide of abuse, adultery, and divorce, each one must reclaim his or her freedom.

In the above verse, the only condition of freedom is that the Holy Spirit must be Lord. Wherever the Holy Spirit reigns, there is freedom. Wherever He does not, there is bondage. It's either that simple or we make God a liar. Contrary to the "old ball and chain" metaphor, God does not intend for your spouse to strangle your freedom. God offered man a rather dangerous proposal in the Garden of Eden. He gave mankind freedom to choose which tree He would use as a food source. God did this knowing full well Adam would not choose Him. And yet He left the choice with mankind anyway. Genesis 2:8–9 (CSB) explains:

> The Lord God planted a garden in Eden, in the east, and there he placed the man he had formed. The Lord God caused to grow out of the ground every tree pleasing in appearance and good for

food, including the tree of life in the middle of the garden, as well as the tree of the knowledge of good and evil.

In verses 15–17 (CSB), God instructs man concerning the trees. Here's what he says:

> The Lord God took the man and placed him in the garden of Eden to work it and watch over it. And the Lord God commanded the man, "You are free to eat from any tree of the garden, but you must not eat from the tree of the knowledge of good and evil, for on the day you eat from it, you will certainly die."

Freedom is choice. Without choice, we are not free. We can be committed and dutiful, but not free. Unless choice is at the core of our marriage commitment, we become slaves to whatever and whomever we serve—whether for good or evil. It's inevitable. Paul writes it this way in Romans 6:16 (AMPC):

> Do you not know that if you continually surrender yourselves to anyone to do his will, you are the slaves of him whom you obey, whether that be to sin, which leads to death, or to obedience which leads to righteousness (right doing and right standing with God)?

Freedom and responsibility are inseparable. It is only a matter of whether we are responsible or irresponsible with freedom. Writing to the Church at Galatia, Paul has this to say:

> Beloved ones, God has called us to live a life of freedom. But don't view this wonderful freedom as an excuse to set up a base of operations in the

natural realm. Constantly love each other and be committed to serve one another.[10]

First Peter 2:16 in God's Word Translation adds:

> Live as free people, but don't hide behind your freedom when you do evil. Instead, use your freedom to serve God.

Both Paul and Peter (in verse 17 below), link freedom to how we respond and relate to others.

> Honor all people. Love the brotherhood. Fear God. Honor the king.[11]

Religion teaches husbands and wives to serve one another by husbands loving their wives and wives respecting their husbands. Serving your spouse does not always mean you are serving God. But serving God always means you are serving your spouse. And this only can be when our ability to choose remains intact. Commitment is long term, but choosing is a daily decision. When there is a breach like adultery, commitment is questioned. And choices are revisited as each one contemplates what happened. The spouse who is the victim almost always contends with the question: "Why him or her over me?" In other words, why was this person chosen instead of me? What did the other person possess that I did not?

Side Note: Adultery

I know some reading this have been or maybe are wounded by adultery. So it's important enough to take a moment to address. That way, all will have the best chance of moving forward in freedom. Your spouse's "why" will never satisfy you. Here's why. Asking why your

---

[10] Galatians 5:13 (TPT)
[11] 1 Peter 2:17 (MEV)

spouse chose someone other than you is the wrong question. The question is wrong because it is false. It is false because it assumes that adultery is about the other person. Adultery occurs when a married person gratifies his or her sexual desires through someone other than his or her spouse. This question is like a carrot on a stick. The carrot—*the promise of truth*—and the stick—*the fear of punishment for not finding the truth*. It could be the fear of it happening again, or the fear of loss of relationship as in divorce, and a myriad of other things. Repeatedly asking why your spouse chose another rather than you will keep you on the hunt and your spouse hiding behind possible, albeit unhelpful reasons.

That's because the real question and its answer provide the best opportunity for husbands and wives to move beyond adultery and even strengthen their relationship. What Joseph said to his unfaithful brothers in Genesis 50:20 (CSB) offers us hope.

> You planned evil against me; God planned it for good to bring about the present result—the survival of many people.

We aid God's plan in prevailing when we ask the real question and offer the real answer. The real question is not for the victim to answer, but rather for the adulterer to answer. The real question is this: Why did he or she choose him or herself over you, the other person, and God? The real question and its answer offer the possibility for more honest conversation about wants, needs, and how God might have each one respond. This leads to intimacy. And keep in mind, husbands and wives have more things in common than different. Though one may not have committed adultery, most can relate to an underlying need and/or want.

Here's the idea. All have chosen self over others and to their hurt. Some of the most valuable things we learn often come at others' expense. It is part of the nature of the flesh. It's just one more thing husbands and wives have in common. How and to the degree we hurt each other may be different. That we hurt each other is the same. So the real question for the victim of adultery is this. How will you use your freedom afforded to you by this knowledge?

Our Choice—His Outcome

Freedom belongs to us. Therefore, choose we must. However, God determines the outcome of choice—*whether blessing or consequence*. Of every tree in the garden, man could eat freely and receive the blessing of God. But of the tree of the knowledge of good and evil, God forbade man from eating, saying as a result he would die. God gave Adam the power to choose but retained ultimate control over the outcome. God specified how Adam was to interact with the earth and all therein. In Genesis 1:26 (CSB), God provides the scope of this interaction.

> Then God said, "Let us make man in our image, according to our likeness. They will rule the fish of the sea, the birds of the sky, the livestock, the whole earth, and the creatures that crawl on the earth."

Man was given to rule the earth and every living thing, except for other human beings. Originally, man and woman were assigned to rule the earth and relate to each other. Instead, men and women try to rule each other and relate to the earth and its resources. And we wonder why so many marriage relationships fail.

Religion and Freedom

Sadly, religion is all too easily manipulated by the devil to control husbands and wives. Religion hijacks their freedom, replaces their will to choose with prescribed positions, roles, responsibilities, and assigns each one needs. Worse still, is when bad theology continues, despite it wreaking havoc upon the family. Let me be clear, I do not condemn positions or roles for husbands and wives. However, I find it problematic when partial truths are extolled and reinforced as if they are the whole truth. For instance, it may be often true that men are more suited for outside work and women inside work. But it is not true that all men or women are effective in their respective domains simply because they are men and women. Consider the generation of men that have been raised and praised in playing sports, video games, and women. And the generation of women that have be raised and rewarded for taking responsibility for people, places, and things. Marry the two. He wants her to play more. She wants him to be more responsible. Now insert these two into a hierarchical model of marriage based on gender positions, roles, and needs. Can you picture this? Perhaps some readers are experiencing this in their marriages right now. Maybe we should ask this: how is it working for you?

Without the freedom to create the marriage God has for you and your spouse, you become nothing more than what religion has taught you. And we wonder why cohabitation competes with marriage today. Freedom is everything. To lose it is to have lost all. Not only did Jesus die for our sins, but also He won back our freedom. When we receive Jesus, we are free. Paul underscores this in Galatians 5:1 (CSB):

> For freedom, Christ set us free. Stand firm, then,
> and don't submit again to a yoke of slavery.

Marriage does not change this nor does marriage modify it. You can still do everything you did as an unmarried person. That you do not is a matter of choice. Every day, every moment of the day, and in every adverse situation you face in relationship to your spouse, you are making a choice. To regard it any other way is bondage.

Freedom and Sovereignty

Freedom gives us both the right and the responsibility to govern our lives. Sovereignty is about governance. How we govern depends on to whom we belong, whatever is our source and what we believe. Freedom makes all things allowable, just as it was in the Garden of Eden. Likewise, all things were not profitable then or now. Paul explains it this way in 1 Corinthians 6:12 (CSB):

> Everything is permissible for me, but not everything is beneficial. Everything is permissible for me, but I will not be mastered by anything.

Paul repeats these words in 1 Corinthians 10:23–24, informing us that our freedom is not without responsibility that includes regard for others. Therefore, freedom is not a license to do whatever we want, whenever we want with whomever we want. Freedom is precious. To regard our own is to regard another's. Freedom is essential to working with God's *Unveiled Love*. That's because without freedom we cannot choose sovereignty.

When we receive Christ, we are free. We are free to think and act differently. This gives us the opportunity to exercise sovereignty. God is sovereign, and He recreated us in His image. Therefore, each one—*husband and wife*—is a sovereign being.

God is sovereign because He is the owner and maker of the heavens and earth.[12] God is sovereign because he holds ultimate authority over all created things.[13] He is sovereign because He lives in His words.[14] God does what He says and says what He does. Finally, God is sovereign because He thinks, decides, feels, and acts on His own will. God alone decides who He will be at any given time, in every situation, with whomever He interacts. Not even to those He loves does He give authority to define Him or decide who He will be. When Moses asked God His name, the name He should use when addressing the Israelite leaders, God explained it this way in Exodus 3:14 (AMPC):

> And God said to Moses, "I Am Who I Am and What I Am, and I Will Be What I Will Be; and

---

[12] Genesis 14:19; Psalm 24:1, 50:10–12; Haggai 2:8
[13] Deuteronomy 10:14
[14] John 1:14

He said, You shall say this to the Israelites: I Am has sent me to you!"[15]

God told Moses that He is who is and can become whatever He needs to be to fulfill His word. Despite Moses's sincere need to know who was sending Him, God refused such limitation. If God refused to concede to the sincere, then how much more unwilling might He become when questioned by the deceitful, disordered desires of human delight. Both husband and wife are free and sovereign human beings. The most obvious proof of this is our physical bodies. Our physical bodies represent borders that separate us, one from another. To disrespect the boundaries of your spouse is akin to abuse. As we guard our own freedom and sovereignty, so too must we become the guardians of the same for our spouse.

For His Name's Sake

A recurring observation in the Psalms and among the Old Testament Prophets is God doing things for His name's sake. Here are a few examples. Psalm 23:3 (MEV):

> He restores my soul; He leads me in paths of righteousness for His name's sake.

In Psalm 106:8 (CSB), we read:

> Yet he saved them for his name's sake, to make his power known.

Isaiah speaks:

> I will act for my own sake, indeed, my own, for how can I be defiled? I will not give my glory to another.[16]

---

[15] Exodus 3:14 (AMPC)
[16] Isaiah 48:11 (CSB)

Daniel appeals:

> Lord, hear! Lord, forgive! Lord, listen and act! My God, for your own sake, do not delay, because your city and your people bear your name.[17]

And then there is Ezekiel 20:9 (MEV):

> But I acted for My name's sake, that it should not be polluted before the nations among whom they were, in whose sight I made Myself known to them in bringing them out of the land of Egypt.

God intervenes on behalf of mankind because He chooses to intervene. Oftentimes, we neither deserve it nor appreciate it. God acts in honor of His name. He performs His word because He *is* His word. He intercedes for the sake of His reputation. God acts in His own interest for His own good to satisfy His eternal purposes. He can because He is free and maintains His freedom at all costs.

God is not only free but also freedom itself. That He is sovereign is apparent in Paul's writing. Hebrews 6:13–14 (MEV) reads:

> For when God made promise to Abraham, because He could swear by no greater, He swore by Himself, saying, "Surely in blessing I will bless thee, and in multiplying I will multiply thee."

God made a promise to Abraham based on His will, ability, and integrity. He required no one else to carry out His word. He did it by Himself. God kept His word to Abraham. Read this slowly: God kept His word. Hebrews 6:15 says that Abraham obtained the promise. This means God fulfilled His word. God proved He is self-governing by keeping His word. Freedom requires choice. Choice is the authority and power necessary to govern our lives according to God's plan.

---

[17] Daniel 9:19

God gives each of us a purpose and destiny. Marriage is never intended to derail destiny, rather to aid us in fulfilling it. Ephesians 1:11 (TPT) says this:

> Through our union with Christ we too have been claimed by God as his own inheritance. Before we were even born, he gave us our destiny; that we would fulfill the plan of God who always accomplishes every purpose and plan in his heart.

Destiny is more than what God creates us to do. Equally important is who God creates us to be.

Freedom to Be

To be who God desires requires that you are free to govern yourself. This means thinking, deciding, and acting for yourself. This is one reason we are made in God's image and likeness. Like God, we too can own and make things. We can exercise authority over that which we create. We, too, can live in our words and keep them at all costs. And like God, we can think, decide, and act for ourselves. Freedom grants us the opportunity to determine who we will be at any given time, in every situation, in whatever relationship we find ourselves. This unquestionably includes marriage. Here's what Paul tells the Corinthians:

> Only, let each one live the life which the Lord has assigned him, and to which God has called him [for each person is unique and is accountable for his choices and conduct, let him walk in this way]. This is the rule I make in all the churches.[18]

---

[18] 1 Corinthians 7:17 (AMPC)

Paul writing to the believers in 1 Thessalonians 4:10–12 (CSB) has this to say:

> But we encourage you, brothers and sisters, to do this even more, to seek to lead a quiet life, to mind your own business, and to work with your own hands, as we commanded you, so that you may behave properly in the presence of outsiders and not be dependent on anyone.

How many husbands and wives can honestly say that they feel free to be themselves with their spouse? Understandably, one must guard his or her heart and soul from a spouse that is mentally, emotionally, or physically unsafe. That is a calculated decision. However, I am speaking about the willingness and ability to show up when safety is present. But how would we know? Showing up is learned and practiced. The inability to speak up or be quiet when God prompts is one indicator that we are not free. Freedom is the awareness and ability to speak or be quiet, sit or stand, give or receive with equal determination. And this requires that we govern ourselves.

Unfortunately, sovereignty or self-government is seldom taught in churches. That Christ set us free so we can think, decide, and act independently is threatening to those that need us to behave a certain way. Religious marriages work when both husband and wife buy into the narrative. This narrative reduces husbands and wives to gender positions, roles, and needs. It is dismissive of all the other ways this couple is unique as individuals and as a pair. There is no other couple like you and your spouse. Sure, you may have similarities with other couples, but no other person is you and no other person is your spouse. Each one of you is an unrepeatable miracle. God designed it this way. Therefore, there is no other marriage like the one you create. Anyone that robs you of the creative energy to make something greater and more magnificent than either of you could alone is an enemy of God! You may be criticized, but let it be because the pair of you are creating something so fantastic that all see your jaw-dropping beauty! This is what will draw men, women, and children to Christ!

Therefore, create we must. Each couple has a unique expression. *Unveiled Love* removes the shackles of religion so that husbands and wives are free to create. Paul testifies of our freedom in Galatians 5:1 (CSB):

> For freedom, Christ set us free. Stand firm, then,
> and don't submit again to a yoke of slavery.

You are free. You are free to be. You are free to create. Your art as an individual and as a couple is exceptional. Though it is different from all others, it is the same Spirit that works through all and in all. When speaking about the uniqueness of gifts in 1 Corinthians 12, four times Paul concludes by saying it is the same Spirit.

Being and Ownership

Freedom is what Christ gives us. Who we are is what we give to Him. And we cannot give God what we do not own. The freedom to think, decide, and act for ourselves is our opportunity to own who we are and who we are not. Our ability to will and to do, apart from others, is an essential component of *Unveiled Love*. Therein is the authority to influence the destiny of others—without trying to control the outcomes.

Abigail was married to Nabal. The Bible describes Nabal as very rich, but harsh and evil in his dealings with others. One of Nabal's young men, when speaking to his wife, described Nabal as a worthless fool to whom nobody can talk. While there is no record of Abigail encouraging the young man by agreeing with him, she does disclose her thoughts to David. Abigail tells David that he should disregard her husband for he is a worthless fool. She goes on to say that Nabal is living up to his name which means "stupid," and stupidity is all he knows.

Abigail was beautiful, intelligent and discerning. She was a prophetess and an intercessor. Abigail was married to Nabal; however, they were individuals and God treated them so. Their character and actions provide evidence. Abigail was free, though married to a foolish tyrant. She did not cover her husband's foolishness as so many wives have been taught. Instead, Abigail exposed it to another human being and type of Christ, who is David. Speaking to the church at Ephesus in Ephesians 5:6–14 (CSB), Paul warns against deception and disobedience. Having been delivered from darkness, Paul admonishes them to live in truth and light. In verse 11, he plainly tells the believers this.

> Don't participate in the fruitless works of darkness, but instead expose them.

Paul makes no exception for the married. Abigail neither took part in her husband's foolishness nor did she try to cover it up. The freedom to think, decide, and act apart from her husband enabled Abigail to intercede on his behalf, but also act in her own best interest. After interceding for Nabal and prophesying David's future, here's what Abigail asked of David in 1 Samuel 25:30–31 (CSB):

> When the Lord does for my lord all the good he promised you and appoints you ruler over Israel, there will not be remorse or a troubled conscience for my lord because of needless bloodshed or my lord's revenge. And when the Lord does good things for my lord, may you remember me your servant.

The full story is told in 1 Samuel 25. No spoiler alert here because I think it's a worthwhile read to find out what happened to Nabal and Abigail. Especially so since this marriage seldom makes the headlines when delivering the yearly sermon series on marriage. Abigail was a different kind of wife—*a help, appropriate to Nabal's obvious need for wisdom.* Yet foolish pride and arrogance got the better of him, and he refused wisdom. Abigail was Nabal's wife. She owned her thoughts and decisions and acted upon them accordingly. It was then that she offered herself to David, *a type of Christ*, in Nabal's place. Abigail makes it clear that we can only offer to God that which we own. Abigail owned Nabal's sin, telling David the guilt is hers.

Abigail's authority to speak frankly to David concerning his fate is a result of living in freedom, owning her life and choices and trusting God, not man with the outcome.

How different is this than the advice given many wives whose husbands behave as Nabal? For the longest time, wives have been pastored to pray, fast, forgive, and cover their husbands' sinful behavior no matter the cost.

Unveiled Love honors the freedom of husbands and wives to think and act as each one chooses. Taking part in *Unveiled Love* means embracing your freedom, right, and responsibility to govern your life. It also means dignifying your spouse by allowing him or her to do the same. This is just one more thing husbands and wives have in common. Each one must use their freedom to take possession of his or her spirit, soul, and body. Practically, this includes our thoughts, feelings, decisions, actions, and motives. In 1 Thessalonians 4:3–5 (AMPC), concerning sexual immorality and by extension all immorality that flows from the lust of the flesh, lust of the eyes, and pride, Paul has this to say:

> For this is the will of God, that you should be consecrated (separated and set apart for pure and holy living): that you should abstain and shrink from all sexual vice, That each one of you should know how to possess (control, manage) his own body in consecration (purity, separated from things profane) and honor, Not [to be used] in the passion of lust like the heathen, who are ignorant of the true God and have no knowledge of His will.

When we refuse to use our freedom to take personal responsibility, inevitably, we will hold others accountable for our behavior. It's blame. It's unavoidable. Think of it like this. All need oxygen to breathe. It's not optional. Therefore, if I am not using my own oxygen, then I must take yours if I want to survive. You have heard it said that a certain individual is sucking all the oxygen out of the room. This means that a certain individual is dominating the conversation at the expense of anyone else joining in. In marriage, this can happen. A husband or wife's need for attention, power, praise, or you fill in the blank robs the other of the same. When we refuse to take responsibility to breathe for ourselves, we make others responsible to give us oxygen. The problem is no one can inhale and exhale enough oxygen for another. Nor can we eat enough food, drink enough water, or eliminate enough waste to sustain the life of another—*though we try.* Each one is responsible for his and her thoughts, feelings, decisions, and actions.

Sarai didn't think so. Sarai blamed Abraham for Hagar's attitude. After Hagar became pregnant, the Bible says she despised Sarai. Sarai was barren for years when Hagar became pregnant by the man Sarai loved. I can only imagine jealousy seeping into her soul. Sarai mistreated Hagar provoking her to run away.

Sarai blames her wrong on Abraham. Here's what she said to him in Genesis 16:5 (CSB):

> May [the responsibility for] my wrong and deprivation of rights be upon you! I gave my maid into your bosom, and when she saw that she was with child, I was contemptible and despised in her eyes. May the Lord be the judge between you and me.

Sarai was the perpetrator, yet she behaves as the victim. She behaves as though she had been wronged. This is what happens when we don't take ownership for our actions and dislike the outcomes. God blessed Sarai despite her impatience and criticism of Abraham and Hagar.

Jesus tells the disciples in Luke 21:19 that in patience, they are possessing their souls. Each one is responsible for him or herself. One day, each of us will give an account to God concerning the deeds done in our flesh. Every husband and wife will answer for his and her own behavior. Each one of us is called to freedom. Freedom grants us opportunity to take possession of our lives. For the Christian, freedom and ownership must lead to total surrender to the Lord Jesus Christ.

Jesus's Example

Without the component of surrender, Jesus's words in John 10:17–18 seem pompous and unbridled and given to rebellion. That whole idea that "I can do whatever I want because I am an adult" mentality. Or "I can do whatever I want because I am in charge" mentality. Or "I can do whatever I want because I own this" mentality. Or "I can do whatever I want because no one can stop me" mentality. Or "I can do whatever I want whatever the reason." One who thinks like this does not see him or herself as a custodian of all that belongs to God.

I recall a good friend who after many years of struggling, God turned his business into a huge success. His success led to the purchase of more and more things. It was fun watching God bless him and he, in turn, blessing God. However, somewhere during his success, each new purchase was accompanied by the following words, "Why? Because I can." I was so happy for him that I began repeating these words as well. As I am writing these words, I was reminded of the joy and laughter we shared. Then I realized that because we can do something doesn't always mean we should.

In John 10:17–18, Jesus speaks as one under authority. He speaks as one who has received human life and is managing that life in unerring response to the giver. Read what Jesus says in John 10:17–18 (CSB).

> This is why the Father loves me, because I lay down my life so that I may take it up again. No one takes it from me, but I lay it down on my own. I have the right to lay it down, and I have the right to take it up again. I have received this command from my Father.

Jesus is the personification of freedom. At no time did Jesus give up the freedom to govern His life. Freedom was given and lost in the Garden of Eden and won back in the Garden of Gethsemane. Jesus made it clear that human desire would have God find some other way to redeem mankind. Nevertheless, Jesus used His freedom to surrender His life to the Father. These are Jesus's words in Matthew 26:39 (CSB):

> Going a little farther, he fell facedown and prayed, "My Father, if it is possible, let this cup pass from me. Yet not as I will, but as you will.

On another occasion, Jesus makes known to the Roman soldiers His freedom and authority to choose His destiny. Upon turning Himself into the Roman soldiers, Peter cut off one of the soldier's ears. Matthew 26:52–54 (CSB) records what Jesus said to Peter and all those listening.

> Then Jesus told him, "Put your sword back in its place because all who take up the sword will perish by the sword. Or do you think that I cannot call on my Father, and he will provide me here and now with more than twelve legions of angels? How, then, would the Scriptures be fulfilled that say it must happen this way?"

At all times, Jesus retained full possession of His soul. At no time did Jesus give to another His authority to be who His Father desired. Let me say this again. In no circumstance, condition, or challenge faced did Jesus let go of His authority to be who God desired. Just so we are clear, this means that in no relationship did Jesus give up the right and responsibility to govern His life. Jesus is free. Maintaining authority is the symbol and seal of freedom. Jesus is our example. John testifies:

> By living in God, love has been brought to its full expression in us so that we may fearlessly face the

day of judgment, because all that Jesus now is, so are we in this world.[19]

Freedom and Authority in Marriage

Marriage neither alters nor diminishes our God-given freedom, right, and responsibility to govern our lives. James writes it this way:

> But he who looks carefully into the faultless law, the [law] of liberty, and is faithful to it and perseveres in looking into it, being not a heedless listener who forgets but an active doer [who obeys], he shall be blessed in his doing (his life of obedience).[20]

"He" here is inclusive of all humanity—*male and female*. It does not say he (or she) that looks carefully into the law of liberty for another. Nor does it say he (or she) who adheres and perseveres for another. It says to the one (male and female) who observes the law of freedom, sticks to it, actively engages, using freedom to obey God's word (general context), this one is blessed in his or her obedience. In James 1:26 (AMPC), we are advised that self-control is essential to the freedom Christ won for us.

> If anyone thinks himself to be religious (piously observant of the external duties of his faith) and does not bridle his tongue but deludes his own heart, this person's religious service is worthless (futile, barren).

Here James speaks of controlling the tongue. That's because like the rudder of a ship, though very small, the tongue steers the body. In 2 Timothy 3:1–5 (CSB), Paul lists eighteen things that would

---

[19] 1 John 4:17 (TPT)
[20] James 1:25 (AMPC)

characterize the last days. The lack of self-control appears. Men and women would lack restraint. In other words, although free, they would behave irresponsibly.

Jesus Christ sets us free. The Father calls each of us to a life of responsibility—*married or not*. If God asks a husband what he did with the wife given him, then He will also ask the wife what she did with the husband to whom she was given. External limitations like gender, bodies, positions, and roles, do not relieve us of internal accountability.

With God, there is no favoritism.[21] James 2:1–11 warns against the sin of favoritism. As an example, James uses distinguishing between the poor and the rich. The truth is favoritism is a sin. Whether we favor the rich over the poor, the educated over the uneducated, or men over women (and vice versa) it is sin and therefore wrong. Sadly, many have used honor as a cloak for preferential treatment of leaders in the church and husbands in marriage. When this occurs, hurt is the certain outcome. Reclaiming authority in marriage begins with understanding that before you are a husband or wife: you are spirit, a soul (that is a human being), who by God's design is male or female. As such, you are co-laborers and joint heirs with Christ. Paul recaps in Galatians 3:28 (MSG):

> In Christ's family there can be no division into Jew and non-Jew, slave and free, male and female. Among us you are all equal. That is, we are all in a common relationship with Jesus Christ. Also, since you are Christ's family, then you are Abraham's famous "descendant," heirs according to the covenant promises.

James 2:12–13 (CSB) provides conclusion to the matter of gender bias in marriage. Here's what James said:

> Speak and act as those who are to be judged by the law of freedom. For judgment is without

---

[21] Romans 2:11

mercy to the one who has not shown mercy. Mercy triumphs over judgment.

In Hebrews 4:13 (CSB), Paul assures us that:

> No creature is hidden from him, but all things are naked and exposed to the eyes of him to whom we must give an account.

The Amplified Classic Version explains further:

> And not a creature exists that is concealed from His sight, but all things are open and exposed, naked and defenseless to the eyes of Him with Whom we have to do.

In that day, all souls will be defenseless. No one is exempt. God holds each one accountable for his or her decisions and actions married and not. Galatians 6:7 (CSB) warns:

> Don't be deceived: God is not mocked. For whatever a person sows he will also reap.

Blessings and consequences will be imposed for deeds we have done on earth. What a day of reckoning it will be for all. Second Corinthians 5:9–10 (TPT) makes this plain.

> So whether we live or die we make it our life's passion to live our lives pleasing to him. For one day we will all be openly revealed before Christ on his throne so that each of us will be duly recompensed for our actions done in life, whether good or worthless.

These are the words of Paul—a servant of Jesus Christ and an apostle who was set apart by God to preach the gospel. Christ may spare us eternal separation from God. Yet and still, our actions in Christ will receive their just due.

Many husbands and wives have forfeited their authority in marriage. This happens when the traditions of men (and women) go unchecked. For instance, when hierarchy is used to exert emotional control over another it will eventually lead to the victim feeling powerless. Recently, I spoke with a client, who for the sake of confidentiality I'll call Tara. Tara, a Christian, was distraught and desperate. Contrary to her Christian beliefs, Tara had been living with a man for nine years. They had four children. Tara had the benefit of staying home to raise their children. Pseudo husband, who I will call Nick, provided food, clothing, and shelter. According to Tara, Nick likes order. He expected the home to be neat, clean, and everything (and everyone) in its place. Early on, Tara felt loved. Nick provided for her and protected her and their children. So to Tara, it seemed like the ideal Christian relationship. Nick was the head. Tara served Nick. Although Nick was content with their arrangement, Tara grew increasingly unhappy. To resolve the conflict between her faith and her lifestyle, Tara wanted to marry Nick. When told by two unlikely, unrelated sources that Nick was not the one, Tara was devastated. That's when she reached out to me.

Tara had two problems. The first and most obvious is her need to resolve the internal conflict between marriage and cohabitation. Since Nick was content with cohabitating, it was Tara's problem. In nine years, Nick hasn't shown the tiniest interest in helping Tara with her problem. Tara suffers and will continue to suffer until she works with God, not Nick, to resolve her problem.

The second problem Tara has is this. The model of their arrangement is hierarchy, not relationship. That Nick provides everything—*food, clothing, shelter, transportation* in exchange for life on his terms, leaves Tara feeling powerless. Moreover, Tara's name is not on the mortgage, the cars, or anything that is considered an asset. Tara has spent the last nine years conforming to the will and wishes of Nick, hoping (and praying) that she would one day get that which she desired: marriage and genuine partnership. Unable to imagine her life apart from Nick and their hierarchical arrangement, Tara stated she felt powerless. She felt trapped and desired more for herself and her children. The first thing Tara did was get her GED. Now she is enrolled in college. Her words to me were, "I am studying so that I can earn what I am worth."

When the traditions of men (and women) usurp our authority and impede us from responding to what the Bible says is right, what we know is right, and what we believe is right, we serve man and not God. We become prisoners, instead of free men and women who happened to be married. In Romans 6:16 (AMPC), Paul writes the following:

> Do you not know that if you continually surrender yourselves to anyone to do his will, you are the slaves of him whom you obey, whether that be to sin, which leads to death, or to obedience which leads to righteousness (right doing and right standing with God)?

Romans 6:16–18 in Eugene Petersen's Message Translation explains the impact upon our freedom.

> So, since we're out from under the old tyranny, does that mean we can live any old way we want? Since we're free in the freedom of God, can we do anything that comes to mind? Hardly. You know well enough from your own experience that there are some acts of so-called freedom that destroy freedom. Offer yourselves to sin, for instance, and it's your last free act. But offer yourselves to the ways of God and the freedom never quits. All your lives you've let sin tell you what to do. But thank God you've started listening to a new master, one whose commands set you free to live openly in his freedom!

The choice is simple. In marriage, we can serve God first, making our spouse the primary beneficiary. Or we can serve our spouse first which may or may not serve God. When it doesn't, in the end, all suffer. Speaking of the generosity that churches in Macedonia showed Paul, he writes in 2 Corinthians 8:5 (TPT):

> They exceeded our expectations by first dedicating themselves fully to the Lord and then to us, according to God's pleasure.

Regaining your authority in marriage begins by acknowledging your freedom, then taking back ownership of your life. That is, what you think, how you feel, and what you do. After we assume ownership, it is then for us to give ourselves to God's pleasure first, as did the churches in Macedonia.

You Were Born for This

Reclaiming your freedom and regaining your authority in marriage is not only possible, but it is also God's will. Speaking to the church at Thessalonica, Paul had this to say about our bodies and sex.

> For this is God's will, your sanctification: that you keep away from sexual immorality, that each of you knows how to control his own body in holiness and honor, not with lustful passions, like the Gentiles, who don't know God.

And if our body and sexual behavior are properly managed, it will be because we have possessed our souls. For the soul, that is the mind, emotions, and will, influence the body's behavior. Therefore, each one must learn to oversee his or her life in a way that pleases God. When we do, others benefit. We can do this. We must. It requires that we change our thinking. Part of this change is recognizing that you are the central figure in the life God created for you. Sadly, Satan has beaten many of God's people to the punch. What I mean is that several years ago and before the Me Too Women's Movement, there was a popular saying. It went like this. "It's all about me." I remember hearing ministers coin this phrase and loosely linking it to scripture. But what it mostly amounted to be was a license to do what one wanted to do. Christians appalled by what was deemed an exploitation of the grace of God, doubled down on the message that Christianity is all about serving others, rather than ourselves. In both cases, partial truths are presented as the whole truth resulting in hostility among Christians.

I took a slightly different approach. I find truth in both positions. It is true that it is all about me. It is all about you. As a Christian, it is about each one possessing his or her life and surrendering it to the Lordship of Jesus Christ. For the Christian, it is not about doing whatever we want, rather what God wants done. Without the element of surrender, we are no different than the non-Christian.

On the other hand, it is about serving others. Our surrender to Christ benefits others. As stated before, when we serve God first, we serve others best. Surrender is key. The truth is we are always surrendering whether to God and His goodness or to the devil. We are free to choose whom we serve. However, God determines the outcome of our service whether blessings or consequence. During the height of the "It's all about me!" trend, I made a T-shirt to sum up my position. On the front it said, "It's all about me…" And on the back it said, "Submitting to Christ!"

All this to say, you are the key figure in God's plan for your life. It is all about you! This is true for married men and women. God creates individuals in His image who can respond to Him. Adam and Eve forfeited this wonderful relationship with the God of the Universe. Jesus won it back. And you and I have the greatest opportunity in the world to know God and take part in His plan to bring all things under the reign of Jesus Christ—beginning with ourselves. Several scriptures inform us that this is an individual pursuit that unavoidably impacts others.

Psalm 139:16 (AMPC) reads:

> "Your eyes saw my unformed substance, and in
> Your book all the days [of my life] were written

before ever they took shape, when as yet there was none of them."

Jeremiah 1:5 says that before we were placed in our mother's womb, God knew us, consecrated us, and appointed us to destiny. God appointed Jeremiah to speak to the nations. God gives each one—*male and female*—a purpose and has a plan He desires implemented. God's purpose is established before He forms us in our mother's womb and before we are born. This means a man and a woman come to marriage each endowed with a unique purpose. Marriage does not change this. It is supposed to aid in our ability to fulfill our purpose.

Jeremiah 29:11 (CSB) adds to the idea that each one is the central figure in God's plan for his and her life.

> For I know the plans I have for you—this is the Lord's declaration—plans for your well-being, not for disaster, to give you a future and a hope.

Psalms 33:11 (NLT) solidifies God's intention.

> But the Lord's plans stand firm forever; his intentions can never be shaken.

God is so committed to His purpose and plan for each life that He says this in Psalm 32:8 (GW):

> The Lord says, "I will instruct you. I will teach you the way that you should go. I will advise you as my eyes watch over you."

I recall Mordecai telling Esther that perhaps she was born for such a time as this.[22] Maybe you too were born for this moment in time. Just maybe you are reading this book at this moment in time

---

[22] Esther 4:14

because God wants to change your paradigm. Like Moses, Esther, Barak (went to war contingent upon Deborah going with him), Joseph (stayed with pregnant Mary despite concerns he was not the father), and every other figure central to God's purpose and plan for his or her life, could it be that owning your place in God's story results in freedom of a nation, a family, or your spouse? All of these possessed their lives, surrendered to God in the face of fear, and triumphed. Each one fulfilled God's purpose and plan for his or her life. Each one possessed soul and body and presented them to God despite fear. God caused each one to prevail. Each one experienced personal success and relational fulfillment.

God's Leading Man: God's Leading Lady

Let me conclude this secret with an analogy. Like many, I like movies. All movies have some things in common. Besides a director, producer, and cinematography, movies have a leading man or woman, supporting actors and actresses, props, and circumstances to navigate. In God's purpose, plan, and playbook for you, you are the leading actor or actress. Everyone and everything else are a supporting actor, actress, prop, or circumstance designed to help you be who God intends and accomplish that which He desires.

Here's a real example. When on earth, Jesus was God's leading man. God's purpose and plan for Jesus becoming a person was to redeem people. The playbook included being born of a woman, teaching, taking part in signs, wonders and miracles, rejection, betrayal, suffering, death, burial resurrections, and ascension. All these things served Jesus. They helped Him become who God intended and to succeed in the work God assigned. In serving God, Jesus served mankind. Everyone and everything in Jesus's life was a supporting actor, actress, prop, or circumstance serving the purpose and plan of God. Mary, Joseph, the disciples, Martha and Mary, the Pharisees, Sadducees, Judas, the Roman soldiers, and the devil advanced the storyline of redemption that was written for Jesus. The difference between Jesus and us is this. Jesus knew it. Oftentimes, we don't! However, Luke 2:52 provides encouragement:

> Jesus grew in wisdom and in stature and in favor
> with God and all the people.

The question for us is not so much whether we know it, rather are we growing in understanding this? You are the central figure in God's purpose, plan, and playbook for your life. Your spouse is a supporting actor or actress that God intends to help you become who He created you to be and do the things He has ordained for you. To see this any other way will lead to certain bondage. Many husbands and wives express feeling trapped, tired, and bored in marriage. The God life is liberating. May I remind you that where Jesus is reigning, there is freedom. The joy and peace that belong to Jesus is present. Therefore, Jesus must reign in you. This is a personal decision, not a marital one. We can know freedom, joy, and peace in the most difficult circumstances when Jesus is in charge. This does not preclude some having to make hard decisions. But such decisions can be done without cruelty.

I am reminded of my friend James. His wife, Emily was a serial adulteress. I know we typically assume it's the husband committing adultery. But in this case, it's the wife. When discovered, Emily apologizes profusely. She was convincing. For weeks thereafter, Emily was attentive to James's every wish. In ten years of marriage, it happened three times. James loved Emily. Though forgiving was hard, each time he forgave her. But it happened a fourth time. James told me that this time was different. He loved Emily, but no longer wanted to work to overcome betrayal. It hurt too much. When asked what he told Emily, this is what he said. "I told her that I love her and that this will never change. And that it was now obvious that her choice to be with other men was more important than her choice and commitment to me. Then I told her that it is best for her and me that we divorce. That way, she could be free too." Several months later, James told me the divorce was final. He was relieved. He looked like a huge burden had been lifted from his shoulders. James was free. And so was Emily.

I really admired how James handled this situation. His decision to divorce was not malicious. It served the freedom of both. It was loving and kind to himself and Emily. Though some may disagree, perhaps James's decision served God best by giving Emily full opportunity for mercy to triumph over judgment.

Who Are You Serving?

It is both easy and complete to assume Jesus did everything for us. After all, that's what scripture tells us. We are told He died for us. He became sin for us. He incurred God's judgment for sin for us. He obtained victory over sin for us. Scripture does support this. One example is Romans 5:8 (NLT):

> But God showed his great love for us by sending Christ to die for us while we were still sinners.

This scripture and many others like it are certainly compelling. They are true. Still, truer is this. Jesus did all for the Father, that is, in response to the Father. Scripture also tells us that Jesus only said and did what He heard and saw from His Father. He did everything for the Father. Humanity, that is you and I, are the primary beneficiaries. In John 5:19 (CSB), Jesus speaks for himself:

> Truly I tell you, the Son is not able to do anything on his own, but only what he sees the Father doing. For whatever the Father does, the Son likewise does these things.

When in the Garden of Gethsemane, Jesus declares His resolve saying the same thing three times.

> My Father, if this cannot pass unless I drink it, your will be done.[23]

---

[23] Matthew 26:42 (CSB)

And then speaking to His Father in John 17:4 (CSB), Jesus says:

> I have glorified you on the earth by completing
> the work you gave me to do.

While Jesus undoubtedly had us on His mind, His attention and allegiance was to the Father. Like Jesus, God had a purpose, plan, and playbook for Paul. In it, Paul was the leading man. All others were supporting actors, actresses, props, and circumstances to help Paul become whom God intended and to accomplish what God planned for him to do. Like Jesus, Paul achieved God's work for him. That work included physical, emotional, mental, and spiritual opposition and hardship. On one occasion, three times Paul asked that a thorn that is a messenger from Satan be removed from his flesh. God's reply is in 2 Corinthians 12:9 (NLT):

> Each time he said, "My grace is all you need. My
> power works best in weakness." So now I am glad
> to boast about my weaknesses, so that the power
> of Christ can work through me.

Paul served God first, including when faced with opposition. While Scripture says that Paul did many things for our sake, in fact, we are the beneficiaries of his allegiance to God and Christ. Paul is credited with writing half of the New Testament that we read.

And then there are many other leading men and women in the Bible. Some familiar. Some unfamiliar. For each one, God had a purpose, plan, and playbook. Some realized it. Some did not. Those that did are some of the mighty men and women of valor with whom we like to identify. At some point, each of these must have known they were the one. And everyone and everything in relationship with them became a supporting actor, actress, prop, or circumstance to fulfill God's plan for their lives. They understood this one thing. If God is for them, then no one and nothing can be against them. Even what is intended for evil, God would use it to His glory and to the benefit of whom they are sent.

This must become our testimony. We are the one in the purpose, plan, and playbook God ordains for our life. Man, you are the one. Women, you are the one. Marriage is one relationship—*a major one as the apex of human relationships*—God intends to help you become what He expects and to do what He assigns you. When we truly understand this, we will ask and answer like Paul did in Romans 8:31, 38–39 (CSB):

> What, then, are we to say about these things? If God is for us, who is against us? For I am persuaded that neither death nor life, nor angels nor rulers, nor things present nor things to come, nor powers, nor height nor depth, nor any other created thing will be able to separate us from the love of God that is in Christ Jesus our Lord.

You are not an afterthought, rather God's first thought. You are not an accident nor are you insignificant. You are here on purpose, with a purpose that only you can fulfill. Therefore, you matter. You are God's unrepeatable miracle. You are born for this moment in time. There is something only you can do. No one has been created to be and do exactly like you! The sooner you get busy being you, your spouse, family, and all God gives you to influence will have opportunity to know Him!

Husbands and wives reclaiming your freedom in marriage enables you to regain your authority. Authority gives you the right to own your life and the power to surrender fully to God. Without freedom, authority, and power, we become servants of man and not God. We become the intended victims of a religious system the seeks to subjugate husbands and wives to gender positions, roles, and needs without regard to God's purpose, plan, and playbook for each one's life. When we serve God's agenda first, we serve each other best.

Zipporah served God by circumcising Moses's son. This occurred after Moses neglected his responsibility and summoned

God's anger. By doing so, Moses's life was spared.[24] Esther served God by confronting her husband concerning Haman's plot to annihilate the Jews. By doing so, many lives were saved.[25] David worshipped God, inciting the anger of Michal.[26] Job refuses to condemn God even though his wife did.[27] Joseph serves God by remaining with Mary despite perceptions.[28] And I have already told you of Abigail, who served God by risking her life to intercede on behalf of her husband.[29] All these were married when proving that serving God first serves their spouse best. Now it is your turn and my turn to do the same! That is to use your freedom to serve God to the benefit of your spouse. This is the nature of God's *Unveiled Love*!

Questions to Learn By

1. Why does the author urge husbands and wives to reclaim their freedom in marriage?
2. A husband or wife commits adultery. Why is it futile for the spouse to ask what the other person had that he or she didn't possess?
3. While each one is free to choose, God retains authority over the outcomes, whether blessing or consequence. What does this mean?

Questions to Grow By

1. Recall a time you exercised your freedom and it resulted in a blessing. Who did your freedom serve?
2. Recall a time you exercised your freedom and it resulted in an unpleasant outcome. Who did your freedom serve?

---

[24] Exodus 4:24–26
[25] Esther 3–6
[26] 2 Samuel 6:14–22
[27] Job 2:8–10
[28] Matthew 1:18–20
[29] 1 Samuel 25:23–35

3. Freedom involves being responsible for your thoughts, feelings, and actions. What are some things you have done to dodge responsibility? Who paid for it?

Questions to Change By

1. The author says that you are the central figure in God's purpose, plan, and playbook for your life. What does this mean to you?
2. Without the aspect of surrendering our freedom, authority, thoughts, feelings, and actions to God, we are no different than those who do not know Christ. Where and/or in what is God inviting you to surrender? What will you do differently? How will you know you have surrendered?
3. Does the area God is inviting you to surrender reflect an aspect of God's glory displayed by your spouse?
4. Since you choose to accept personal responsibility for your thoughts, feelings, actions, and circumstances, you can set your spouse free from duty and obligation. What are some ways you can celebrate their freedom?

Secret 5

Receive Love

> We love because He first loved us. (1 John 4:19 AMP)

The first act of freedom and reclaiming your authority is deciding to receive God's *Unveiled Love*. This Love is the most amazing, awe-inspiring, adaptable thing in the universe. Yet these adjectives do not begin to convey the supreme authority, power, boldness, and versatile nature of this Love. And this Love is neither an it nor a thing. Love is God. And God is Love. Love is Spirit. Love is a Person. This Person has a name—Jesus Christ. That God has given me to write about this Love is both a privilege and an admission of inadequacy. By the grace of God, I write beyond my experiential understanding. Still, I am committed to the struggle of making it so plain that it obliterates what Hollywood portrays as love. Moreover, I fight to reveal this one secret as I believe it is the key to those that follow. Miss this and you might as well close the book and return to life as you know it.

It reminds me of the conversation Morpheus had with Neo in the movie *The Matrix* (1999). Morpheus gave Neo a choice between a red pill and a blue pill. He could choose the red pill and find out the disturbing, albeit life-altering truth about an automated society that makes slaves of men and women. Or Neo could choose the blue pill and stay in the Matrix and go back to life as he believes.

The Matrix movie depicts humanity whose minds are bio-electronically distracted trapping them in a counterfeit reality. Hollywood has duped many and trapped them into thinking that love is a three-letter word—*sex*. On movie screens, love is reduced to sexy lines, hot and steamy looks, and super romantic poses that fit a movie screen. It's all made up. Off screen, we are flooded with celebrity marriages, divorces, re-marriages, and extra-marital affairs, not to mention reports of domestic violence. If we recognize Hollywood's promotion of love as fake, then like Neo, we should opt for the red pill, wake up, and believe the truth about love and marriage. This book, *Unveiled Love,* is a red pill of sorts.

The Church Has Not Helped

While Hollywood distorts and perverts love, the church offers lip service to love. We say things about love that we neither believe nor display in our marriages and families. Isaiah 29:13 (AMPC) renders judgment:

> And the Lord said, "For as much as this people draw near Me with their mouth and honor Me with their lips but remove their hearts and minds far from Me, and their fear and reverence for Me are a commandment of men that is learned by repetition [without any thought as to the meaning]."

Jesus quotes part of this verse in Matthew 15:8 (AMPC):

> These people draw near Me with their mouths and honor Me with their lips, but their hearts hold off and are far away from Me.

Sadly, we the church have delivered a message on God's Love that we have not digested. We make a big show complete with lights, cameras, and smoke, convincing others to receive what we ourselves have not. The show is coming to a theater near you. That being the case, my hope is that you will have taken the red pill and believe the reality of God's Love, marriage, and family. The reality is this. If we have not received God's Love, any attempt to reveal it makes us imposters. No matter our scripture knowledge, gifts, skills, and abilities, we cannot produce God's love on our own.

The Power of God's *Unveiled Love*

God's *Unveiled Love* makes us brave. He inspires us to show up and offer who we are and what we possess to relationships. Alone, this Love overthrows fear, out-muscles opposition, and refuses to be bought. In 2020, Maryland congressional candidate Kim Klacik ran a campaign as the choice who was unboxed, unbought, and unbossed. While she lost the election, her campaign slogan is still applicable. This is the sheer grit of God's *Unveiled Love*—He is unboxed, unbought, and unbossed. And if this kind of love is for us, then who can be our enemy?[30] He will use what the enemy intends for evil for good. Recall what happened when Joseph's jealous brothers sold him into slavery. God used it to place Joseph second in command to Pharaoh. Joseph was over the entire storehouse of Egypt when the famine came. His brothers came to Joseph acknowledged their evil, and here is what Joseph said to them in Genesis 50:20 (CSB):

> You planned evil against me; God planned it for good to bring about the present result—the survival of many people.

Speaking of the authority and power of this love, Paul writes in Romans 8:35 (AMPC):

> Who shall ever separate us from Christ's love? Shall suffering and affliction and tribulation? Or

---

[30] Romans 8:31

calamity and distress? Or persecution or hunger or destitution or peril or sword?

Paul ends the chapter with the verses 38–39:

> For I am persuaded beyond doubt (am sure) that neither death nor life, nor angels nor principalities, nor things impending and threatening nor things to come, nor powers, Nor height nor depth, nor anything else in all creation will be able to separate us from the love of God which is in Christ Jesus our Lord.

Read that again. Slowly. Deliberately. God's *Unveiled Love* provides for us and protects us because He chooses to—*of His free will*. He has no rival. Working with God's Love is imperative if we are to raise marriages from the dead. That's because God's *Unveiled Love* can get things done in marriages that husbands and wives have been unable to do. Consider the changes you would like to see in yourself, your spouse, and your relationship. How many times have either of you apologized for something and promised to never do the thing again? It could be a small irritation or a major breach. You and/or your spouse were sincere. You meant it in the moment. But days, weeks, or months later you find that you or your spouse has been saying and or doing what you vowed not to. Can you relate? God's *Unveiled Love* is the answer.

But how can we work with something or someone we have not received? How can we sit in a chair that we have not accepted as a chair? Or lie in a bed that we do not take as a bed? And even if we do accept these things and sit down and lie down respectively, how does the technology work? How does God's *Unveiled Love* work? An analogy might help.

Water: A Symbol for God's Love

The Bible is full of symbolism. Symbols are naturally occurring phenomena. Symbols are concrete things, events, or people that represent a spiritual reality or truth. Here are a few. Wind is a symbol for the Holy Spirit. A signet ring is a symbol for authority. Doves are a symbol for peace. Fire is a symbol for judgment. All these stand in for or represent a person or thing. Symbols make it easy to understand the intangible. They allow us to get our minds around things. That's why Jesus spoke in parables. It helped people to see what is not readily observable.

The strength of a symbol is determined by the number of characteristics and behaviors it has in common with the real person or thing. Water is a symbol for God's Love. Water reveals the nature and behavior of God's Love. Identifying just some of the many properties, characteristics, and functions of water and comparing them to God's love is a useful way for us to better understand and receive God's Love. And it's worth it because like God's *Unveiled Love*, water is one of the most fascinating, powerful, and versatile resources available to us on planet earth!

To show the extraordinary example between God's Love and water, the following chart summarizes.

Comparison Between Water and God's Love

Characteristic	Water	God's Love
1. Make Up	3 atoms: 2 hydrogen, 1 oxygen	3 Persons: Father, Son, Holy Spirit
2. Form – Exists in 3 states	Solid, Liquid, Gas	Solid – Jesus, Liquid – Holy Spirit, Gas - Father
3. Capacity	Highest heat capacity of any substance, it's range of temperatures makes it virtually indestructible.	Highest authority and power in the universe; its eternal nature make it virtually indestructible.
4. Cohesive/Adhesive	Sticky, elastic, adheres to and climbs up materials like glass, and small tubular objects without breaking the molecule, hold all things together.	God is One. He hold all things together.
5. Universal Solvent*	Can mix with and dissolve more substances than any other resource	Can interact with and/or dissolve all created things.

*Liquid water is an essential requirement for life on earth because it functions as a solvent. It can dissolve substances and enables key chemical reactions in animal, plant, and microbial cells. Its chemical and physical properties allow it to dissolve more substances than most other liquids.[31]

Water makes a worthy symbol, admirably standing in for some choice characteristics of God's Love! But wait. There are more compelling similarities that make water an ideal way to understand God's *Unveiled Love* and what this Love can do for you. Again, a chart will help.

Shared Behaviors Between Water and God's Love

Characteristic	Water	God's Love
1. Promotes Life	Delivers life-giving oxygen to blood and cells	Gives breath of life making each human being a living soul
2. Nourishes	Supplies the cells that make up tissues and organs that make up our bodies.	Supplies the graces of God to our souls that enable us to reflect Christ
3. Hydrates	Lubricates muscles and lubricates joints, facilitating the body's movement	Lubricates mental and emotional muscles improving our willingness to receive and respond to truth
4. Expels Waste	Rids the body of harmful toxins and waste.	Rids the soul of pride, fear, lust.
5. Regulates Climate	Helps manage body temperature.	Helps manage thoughts and feelings

According to the Water Information Program,[32] the human body is about 60 percent water. Blood is 92 percent water, the brain and muscles are 75 percent water, and bones are about 22 percent water. A human can survive for a month or more without eating food, but only a week or so without drinking water. While the body itself is about 60 percent water, the amount of water making up the blood is enormous at 92 percent. And when we consider Leviticus 17:11 that states the life of the flesh is in the blood, it makes water essential to our physical human life.

Just as water is crucial to the body's ability to perform, God's Love is crucial to our ability to perform His will in marriage. Love is not optional. Christian, we may survive for some time spiritually, mentally, and emotionally without study, prayer, and community.

---

[31] https://www.nhm.ac.uk/discover/eight-ingredients-life-in-space.html
[32] http://www.waterinfo.org/resources/water-facts

But immediate is the effect when deprived of God's *Unveiled Love*. We feel it. Our spouse feels it. Our children feel it in outbursts of anger, irritability, strife, intimidation, and graceless interactions. Sadly, this is the state of many marriages today. As the health of our bodies largely depends on water, so the health of our soul largely depends on love—*God's Unveiled Love*. Jesus said that the thief's purpose was to drain us of life, but that He came to fill us with an abundance of life.[33] And that abundant life includes the fulfillment of our hopes and dreams. It includes healthy, vibrant, life-giving men and women married to one another. It includes the opportunity for each couple to create a unique, spectacular relationship where God can show His brilliance in the many aspects of His wisdom. Your husband and your wife are God's creation—a paintbrush, the world is your canvas. Together, you create dazzling art for the world to see that they too may acknowledge God! You are free. You are sovereign. You are unboxed, unbought, and unbossed. Be bold. Have fun! Feel the power!

Our Senses: A Medium for God's *Unveiled Love*

Although God's Love is Spirit and not physical, it uses our bodies and senses. Our physical bodies and senses are what connect us to the physical world and to each other. They permit husbands and wives to relate and connect in the material world. We are connected spiritually and naturally. Our bodies and senses give God's Love the opportunity to express Itself to us and through us. We can see God's Love through our eyes, hear love through our ears, taste love with our mouths, touch love with our bodies, and smell love through our nostrils. When we do, it is not only powerful to us but also for others that experience us. God intends for husbands and wives to feel love in their souls and bodies. Let me say this again, God's *Unveiled Love* is practical. Husbands and wives are supposed to enjoy and make a feast of God's Love. Yet how can they unless each one first receives God's *Unveiled Love*?

---

[33] John 10:10

We Can, Only Because He Did

We can receive God's *Unveiled Love* because He gave love. He made His Love available to us. In every translation of the scripture, "We love because he first loved us." We find the word "because." We can love because He loved us. The word "because" joins two or more thoughts or behaviors. It provides reason for thoughts, decisions, and actions. Jesus said that it is because or for this reason that two human beings can marry and become one—they are male and female.[34] And in many other instances throughout the Bible, we are provided the reason for things taking place. The reason we can choose to receive love is that God loved us first. One of the first scriptures I learned to recite as a child is John 3:16 (MEV):

> For God so loved the world that He gave His only begotten Son, that whoever believes in Him should not perish, but have eternal life.

Later, I learned that God gave His love to us when we were sinful, separated, and rebellious![35] It was not a mutual decision. It was His decision. He made the decision to give us His love freely. He used His authority and a sovereign act of His will. That God gave, we have opportunity. Or because God gave His love, we have opportunity to receive His love. It is only for us to receive or not. It's just that simple. There is nothing else, but to receive God's Love. It sounds too easy, right? And yet it isn't. Now that we have a better understanding of God's *Unveiled Love*, let me offer you a few reasons why it is difficult for so many to receive this love. And I am talking about Christians, men and women, husbands and wives, who struggle to receive God's love. For proof, look no further than our own marriages and families. It is not for love that relationships suffer. Rather, it is the absence of love that causes suffering. Wherever love is missing, fear, pain, and suffering are present. Hosea 4:1–3 (MEV) instructs us concerning

---

[34] Matthew 19:4–6
[35] Romans 5:8

the consequences of a lack of mercy and truth, both of which are intimately tied to love.

> Hear the word of the Lord, O children of Israel, for the Lord has a dispute with the inhabitants of the land: There is no truth or mercy, and no knowledge of God in the land. Swearing, lying, and killing, and stealing and adultery break out, and bloodshed follows bloodshed.

Second Timothy 3:1–4 (TPT) offers a more exhaustive list of what happens when God's *Unveiled Love* isn't working in the souls of men and women.

> But you need to be aware that in the final days the culture of society will become extremely fierce. People will be self-centered lovers of themselves and obsessed with money. They will boast of great things as they strut around in their arrogant pride and mock all that is right. They will ignore their own families. They will be ungrateful and ungodly. They will become addicted to hateful and malicious slander. Slaves to their desires, they will be ferocious, belligerent haters of what is good and right. With brutal treachery, they will act without restraint, bigoted and wrapped in clouds of their conceit. They will find their delight in the pleasures of this world more than the pleasures of the loving God.

All experience the pain and suffering from the absence of God's Love. All have been both perpetrators and victims of the shortage of love. It contributes to our inability to receive God's Love in the places we hurt the most. But also we struggle to receive love because we are taught to work for it. But also shame and guilt convince us to hide from love. Fear of judgment makes it risky to open up and receive love. And pride causes many to forfeit love.

Working for Love

Love cannot be earned, bought, or achieved. We can't work hard enough to get what God intends for us to receive.

Consider the irony. Most are taught that their salvation entirely rests on the shoulders of Jesus Christ. Ephesians 2:8–9 (MEV) explains it this way:

> For by grace you have been saved through faith, and this is not of yourselves. It is the gift of God, not of works, so that no one should boast.

The translation is this: there is nothing, absolutely nothing you or I can do that contributes to our salvation. Moreover, God is love. *Unveiled Love* reveals that it does not rise and fall based on our performance. Speaking of God's omnipresence, David sums it up like this in Psalm 139:7–12 (MSG):

> Is there any place I can go to avoid your Spirit? to be out of your sight? If I climb to the sky, you're there! If I go underground, you're there! If I flew on morning's wings to the far western horizon, You'd find me in a minute—you're already there waiting! Then I said to myself, "Oh, he even sees me in the dark! At night I'm immersed in the light!" It's a fact: darkness isn't dark to you; night and day, darkness and light, they're all the same to you.

Love just is and will always be. That's because love is who God is and what He does and will do. There is nothing you or I can do to get God to love us. He loves us because He chooses.

Sadly, however, once we receive this gracious gift of Jesus Christ, we are instructed, encouraged, and reinforced (by men and women) to work for love. Many adopt a gospel of working and giving love rather than resting and receiving love. This happens despite Jesus's forceful words in Mark 10:15 and Luke 18:17 (CSB):

> Truly, I say to you, whoever will not receive the kingdom of God as a little child will in no wise enter it.

We emphasize "works" despite Paul's words in Ephesians 1 concerning all that God has given to us in Christ. And Peter's words:

> His divine power has given us everything required for life and godliness through the knowledge of him who called us by his own glory and goodness. By these he has given us very great and precious promises, so that through them you may share in the divine nature, escaping the corruption that is in the world because of evil desire.[36]

Some may be able to relate to a time when being at every church service and event proved your commitment to Christ. It seemed that the entire Christian life morphed into giving—*giving time (volunteering), giving money, giving things, giving prayers, giving attention to reading and studying, giving praise, giving thanks, giving devotion.* Feel spent yet? No wonder we burn out! A work mentality (a.k.a. giving) seems to dominate Christian messaging. It is so widespread that when we are unable to give _____ (you fill in the blank), we feel guilty.

In all fairness, the Christian messaging/broadcasting of a work mentality, for many of us, is a mere continuation of what we learned growing up. We don't question the discrepancy between a Christian life based on receiving from the one based on giving.

---

[36] 2 Peter 1:3–4 (CSB)

Instead, we find scriptures that support working *for love*. Scriptures like Luke 6:38 (MEV):

> Give, and it will be given to you: Good measure, pressed down, shaken together, and running over will men give unto you. For with the measure you use, it will be measured unto you.

And 1 Thessalonians 4:10–12 (MEV):

> And indeed, you do have love for all the brothers who are in all Macedonia. But we urge you, brothers, that you increase more and more. Learn to be calm, and to conduct your own business, and to work with your own hands, as we commanded you, so that you may walk honestly toward those who are outsiders and that you may lack nothing.

Paul writing to the Thessalonians has this to say about work:

> For while we were yet with you, we gave you this rule and charge: If anyone will not work, neither let him eat.[37]

Let me be clear. Work is good. It is godly. However, when we place the cart (work) before the horse (receive), it is not good, nor godly. Moreover, it prevents us from receiving the love God has for us.

A Real Example

Growing up, I learned to perform for love. I learned this before I ever became a Christian. I was a swimmer. More than a summer recreational enthusiast, I trained year-round often in the mornings

---

[37] 2 Thessalonians 3:10 (MEV)

and afternoons, six days a week. I was a member of the Amateur Athletic Union (AAU). Competing in AAU-sanctioned swimming meets required membership. There were dues. But not only AAU dues but also local team dues. I swam on the Tigersharks with Coach Malachi Cunningham. Coach Cunningham, along with Jim Ellis's team, dominated Philadelphia swimming in the '70s, introducing competitive swimming to brown-skinned Americans. You might recall the movie *Pride* (2007). It is a biography, loosely based upon the true story of Philadelphia swim coach James "Jim" Ellis. Terrence Howard, Bernie Mac, and Kimberly Elise starred in the movie. The combined efforts of Jim Ellis and Malachi Cunningham were responsible for over fifty brown-skinned Americans receiving swimming scholarships to colleges and universities.

Many swam in national swimming competitions, and several took part in the Olympic trials. I was one that received a swimming scholarship to Howard University as well as swam in national events. I say all this to suggest that if there was such a thing at my age, I was a professional swimmer. So one reason I became so good was that my parents attended every swimming meet, and my mother was at almost every afternoon practice. However, it was my dad who took the most pride in my accomplishments. From coaching me from the bench, and on the way home from a meet, to bragging about my wins to his friends *I felt loved.* The better I got, the more he bragged. Instead of hearing "I love you," I heard "You did great! You'll break the record next time!"

Not only did I learn to perform for love through swimming, but also in school. A's and B's were praised. And getting the chores done just right, the way my mother would have them done, got high marks. I learned it was my responsibility to perform for love and acceptance. The idea of just being myself eluded me. Moreover, I learned to remain connected to my dad and mom by performing for their love and acceptance. During my college years, my parents relaxed their emotional demands for love. But by then, I was well on my way to adulthood as a performer and a fixer. It can look like people pleasing. Though this may be the result, performing and fixing is the high. When I performed or fixed things, I felt loved. When I was not performing or fixing things, I felt no love. I confused love with performance and repairing things. There was always something to do and always something to fix. It was the bread and butter of love *for me*.

It was not long into marriage when my working for love became apparent. I was planned, rigid, and retaliatory. What was lived into me, I was living out with my ex-husband. In both overt and covert ways, I demanded he perform for my love. It was manipulative. I used his performance and follow-through to evaluate his love for me. Sadly, I was a menacing presence and one in which he was not raised to engage. My contribution to our recurring emotional breakdowns was my inflexibility and need to be right for fear of rejection. While this was not the only thing that ultimately led to divorce, it is certain proof that there is no substitute to God's genuine, *Unveiled Love*.

There are other ways people work for love. Unfortunately, this book is not about all the ways we work and vie for love. Rather, it is about that we cannot work for love. We cannot earn it. We cannot buy it. But we can work with God's love. And we can only do this if we first receive it.

Shame and Guilt

Not only does working for love prevent us from receiving love, but shame and guilt do as well. Shame is about what we perceive ourselves to be. When shame is present, we see and experience ourselves as unlovable, unworthy, and/or inadequate. Shame stole the essence of who God created us to be. Jesus reclaimed and restored the essence of humanity to us that believe. God created human beings to be lovable, worthy, and adequate. Imagine not experiencing these things in the core of our being and then being threatened with exposure. It is the feeling we get when our private parts are exposed. I have had clients tell me that they prefer not to undress in front of their spouse. They don't feel comfortable in the flesh of their bodies. Marriage is supposed to be a safe place to relax and work through our discomforts. When shame is compounded by guilt, revealing ourselves can be hard. Guilt has to do with behavior that breaks or is perceived to break a covenant, contract, value, expectation, or belief system.

Shame is an intensely painful feeling that is caused by an awareness that one is not good enough, right enough, pretty, or handsome enough, skinny enough, muscular enough, tall enough, smart enough, and the list goes on! We can experience shame in our bodies, our money, our sex life, our age, race, gender, our education, or our religion. In almost anything, there is the potential for shame to rear its ugly head. Shame attacks our sense of worthiness. It coerces many into believing they do not deserve love. They conclude they are unlovable. Therefore, they are unable to receive love.

Shame is a feeling anchored and reinforced by thoughts and experiences. Everyone including those who are reading these words has experienced shame. And perhaps some of us still do. Not only were we born into sin, but also we were separated from God's love. We were alienated from God. Sin and alienation are always accompanied by shame. Adam establishes this truth. Here are his words in response to God inquiring as to Adam's whereabouts:

> And he said, "I heard you in the garden, and I was afraid because I was naked, so I hid."[38]

God removed Himself from Adam due to sin. Adam was left exposed. He was afraid. Adam experienced the intensely painful feeling of inadequacy. Apart from God, man nor woman were enough then or now. It is noteworthy that neither Adam nor Woman felt shame before choosing themselves over their Creator. Genesis 2:25 (CSB) says, "Both the man and his wife were naked, yet felt no shame." All shame is rooted in the fear of judgment and alienation. First John 4:18 (AMPC) explains it this way:

> There is no fear in love [dread does not exist], but full-grown (complete, perfect) love turns fear out of doors and expels every trace of terror! For fear brings with it the thought of punishment, and [so] he who is afraid has not reached the

---

[38] Genesis 3:10 (CSB)

full maturity of love [is not yet grown into love's complete perfection].

Shame is what we feel on the inside in response to our spouse, family, or friends. We may feel out of place or that we don't fit in. So we withdraw either emotionally or physically. Or we may criticize those we feel are responsible for our feelings. Worse still, we withdraw and decline invitations to interact with God, even though He is the one who loves us best and the most! Moreover, Jesus despised yet endured our shame. In Hebrews 12:1–2 (CSB), Paul writes the following:

> Keeping our eyes on Jesus, the pioneer and perfecter of our faith. For the joy that lay before him, he endured the cross, despising the shame, and sat down at the right hand of the throne of God.

First John 2:28 (NLT) advises us to remain in relationship with Christ, for it is to our advantage.

> And now, dear children, remain in fellowship with Christ so that when he returns, you will be full of courage and not shrink back from him in shame.

Shame causes us to withdraw from love and truth. These are the very things needed to heal our broken, dislocated souls. Shame is felt internally in response to a perceived or actual external experience. That experience might be something that happens to us which may not be our fault or by the guilt of our own behavior. The middle-aged man or woman who was sexually molested when a child bears no responsibility for the actions of the perpetrator. Still, he or she may experience shame and sexual unworthiness in marriage. Instead of being open and fluid sexually, this husband or wife may be fearful of sexual expression and rigid in terms of the conditions in which sex takes place. What happened to these husbands and wives may not be their fault, but it is now their problem.

Shame is subjective. It is what we feel on the inside. Guilt is objective. It's what we do on the outside, that is our behavior. As mentioned before, Adam was not punished because he listened to a woman. Rather, he was punished because his behavior violated the law of life. The consequence was death. Adam was alienated from God's love and suffered guilt and shame as a result. Shame and guilt teach us to hide from God's love. So we pretend to be someone we are not, keep secrets, and stay silent because we fear judgment.

I was acquainted with Jeff and Amanda for several years before they approached me for counseling. Jeff was a faithful blue-collar worker, contributing steady income to the family. He was kind-hearted and helpful. He seemed unsure of himself, frequently glancing at his wife as if seeking a nod of approval.

Amanda was a tenured professor at a local university. She was accomplished and highly motivated. Amanda loved Jeff. It was obvious in the way she spoke to him, as well as the way she spoke about him in and out of his presence. Amanda was a natural nurturer, showing affection with ease and fluidity.

But she was frustrated and complained that no matter how much she told and showed Jeff that she loved him, he didn't receive her love. Unbeknownst to Amanda, he had his reasons. Their conversations rarely reached the depth necessary to produce meaningful change. He just never wanted to talk about emotionally difficult things—not with Amanda, not with anyone.

One on one, Jeff admitted to not feeling adequate. Although he joked about "marrying up," the implications had a far more reaching impact than was obvious to those that chuckled with him. Upon exploring what he meant by "marrying up," Jeff divulged that he did not feel worthy of Amanda. I asked him whether it was Amanda of whom he did not feel worthy or whether in general he did not feel worthy. He admitted generally not feeling worthy of Amanda, of God, of love, and virtually of any good that came to him. Like most parents, Jeff's parents desired the best for him and often told him so. For Jeff, however, these words were like two pieces of bread with years of graceless, critical, condemning words stuffed in between. As hard as he tried, Jeff could not get thoughts of being unworthy out of his head. His parents were brutal, and he lived with the intense feelings of shame. Jeff believed that he was not good enough, right enough, or lovable enough for anyone. Jeff either didn't try or didn't follow through. It cost him jobs and relationships. And it almost cost him his marriage.

Until Jeff accepted the truth, that in Christ God makes him good enough, right enough, and lovable enough, he could not receive love. All efforts to love Jeff would reach an impasse. Amanda confronted this gridlock many times. After ten years of marriage, she admitted wanting to quit. She was tired. Amanda accepted that no amount of love, whether in word or deed, can penetrate a soul that condemns itself unlovable. She could not change that for Jeff.

Jeff needed to agree with God. If at first all he could offer was the willingness to agree that he is lovable, it would be enough. Then he could learn to mentally agree with God that he is lovable and begin thinking this for himself. And with many new experiences over time, Jeff may gradually open more and more of his soul and receive God's *Unveiled Love*. It's the kind of love that would change his life and relationships. This is what happened for Jeff. Instead of thinking Amanda and everyone else was criticizing him and out to get him, Jeff experienced enjoyable and encouraging interactions. He felt worthy. He let down his guard and discovered there are some nice people who genuinely want to help. Most importantly to Jeff was that his relationship with his wife improved. And the best part, it happened without him ever asking her to do anything differently!

Worthy is our birthright in Christ. We are worthy of love—men and women, husbands and wives! Like Jeff, that we too become willing and mentally agree with God that we are lovable. May we decide to receive God's *Unveiled Love* into our souls. And like Jeff, may the outcome be refreshingly different watering the dry places in our lives and relationships.

Fear of Judgment

We have talked about fear earlier in Secret 2. Fear is a real experience. Judgment is also real. There is the judgment of God and the judgment of men and women. They are different. First Samuel 16:7 (MSG):

> But God told Samuel, "Looks aren't everything. Don't be impressed with his looks and stature. I've already eliminated him. God judges persons differently than humans do. Men and women look at the face; God looks into the heart."

Jesus affirms this in Matthew 5:21–22 (MEV):

> You have heard that it was said by the ancients, "You shall not murder," and "Whoever murders shall be in danger of the judgment." But I say to you that whoever is angry with his brother without a cause shall be in danger of the judgment.

Also, in Matthew 5:27–28 (MEV), Jesus speaks:

> You have heard that it was said by the ancients, "You shall not commit adultery." But I say to you that whoever looks on a woman to lust after her has committed adultery with her already in his heart.

In both verses, Jesus's focus is what's happening on the inside—*our hidden parts*. God judges to show mercy. Let me say this again. God judges because He desires to show us mercy and compassion. For a long time, this has been difficult to understand. I mean, if mercy and compassion are the goal, then why not show these things despite how we behave? The truth is, God can't. That's because He is just. He requires justice. He is impartial, ruling based on truth.

The gospel informs us that one man died for all, that all men (and women) might be spared judgment and punishment for sin. Jesus not only died for our sin, but He also became our sin. And He did this so that through Him we can be made right with God.[39] Therefore, God encourages us to come reason with Him in order that we may be cleared of sin and obtain mercy through Jesus Christ. Here's how James 2:12–13 (TPT) sums it up:

> So we must both speak and act in every respect like those who are destined to be tried by the perfect law of liberty, and remember that judgment is merciless for the one who judges others without mercy. So by showing mercy, you take dominion over judgment!

God has judged sin. He is not judging anymore. To do so would be to re-crucify Christ. He died once and for all. He longs to show us mercy. He sent Jesus to prove it. And now He waits for us to come to Him to receive it. It's not the judgment of God that we must fear. He is for us. His desire is to do us good all the days of our lives. But we do need to have regular conversations with God. Sometimes it's what we want to talk about and at other times what He wants to talk about with us.

Fear of Men

But the fear of (judgment from) men and women can prevent us from receiving God's *Unveiled Love*. Our defended souls know all too well what it feels like to be judged and condemned. The pain can be unbearable. David expressed it this way in Psalm 55:12–14 (AMPC):

> For it is not an enemy who reproaches and taunts me—then I might bear it; nor is it one who has

---

[39] 2 Corinthians 5:21

> hated me who insolently vaunts himself against me—then I might hide from him. But it was you, a man my equal, my companion and my familiar friend. We had sweet fellowship together and used to walk to the house of God in company.

When we are hurt by those we love, we are tempted to close our souls. To protect ourselves from reinjury. In some cases, this is both wise and appropriate. As Christians, we are not doormats for others to step on whenever they choose. This is true of the married and unmarried. There are cases when a spouse's untrustworthy, unpredictable, recurring hurtful words and actions demand his or her access be denied to one's vulnerable parts. Verbal and physical abuse are clear examples. Adultery and misuse of finances placing a spouse and children in jeopardy are other examples. Each situation is unique and must be evaluated on its own merits. This book is about receiving God's *Unveiled Love*. When we do, God informs each one according to his or her circumstances. Sometimes sorting it out may require the help of a professional. If you are reading these words and have questions or concerns as to how this may apply to your situation, I encourage you to pray about from whom to seek professional help.

Fear of (judgment from) men and women is a trap. It discourages us from choosing to receive God's *Unveiled Love*. Proverbs 29:25 (MEV) reads:

> The fear of man brings a snare, but whoever puts his trust in the Lord will be safe.

Judgment can look like rejection, abandonment, or any number of things. Regardless, it contributes to many not wanting to use their willing and choosing muscles to open and receive God's *Unveiled Love*. They simply do not want to experience the hurt and pain again! I get it. But God, the Father, is not a man and is incapable of loveless actions. Yet and still, His love belongs to truth and truth to love. They are inseparable. In 2 Thessalonians 2:8–10 (MEV), Paul emphatically writes:

> Then the lawless one will be revealed, whom the Lord will consume with the breath of His mouth, and destroy with the brightness of His presence, even him, whose coming is in accordance with the working of Satan with all power and signs and false wonders, and with all deception of unrighteousness among those who perish, because they did not receive the love for the truth that they might be saved.

Paul links our believing what is false to our unwillingness to receive love for the truth. Another translation reads "love of truth." God's *Unveiled Love* is combined with and belongs to truth. Though we may try, we can't have one without the other. That's because both love and truth are aspects of God's nature and essence. It's who He is. They work together to bring about the plans and purposes of God in our lives. Love without truth enables sin. But truth without love is repelling.

Here's the thing.

For love and truth to work together to heal us and make us whole, both must touch us at the site of injury. The place we have been hurt is the place from which God begins healing. Said another way, the place in which we were taken advantage of is the same place from which we are taken to freedom. Either way, we must be taken. And the first step to God taking us somewhere new and exciting is to receive His *Unveiled Love*. It's daring and risky, but the only way to move from hurt to healed is to open and receive love and truth where it hurts most. A wife who has been sexually molested may have difficulty with sex for fear she will be taken advantage of and hurt again. But what if in that place and posture of hurt, she received the tender love of a husband. What if instead of experiencing a forceful, unwanted advance she experienced a self-controlled, gentle, patient lover. What if he listened to her, felt her fear, and responded with this kind of love? What if, at the same time, she could talk about what happened with him, a trusted friend, a pastor, or a professional? What if this experience with God's *Unveiled Love* was for her the beginning of healing, wholeness, and sexual freedom? And what if, for him, it brought a deeper understanding of God's *Unveiled Love* as a husband? And what if God's Unveiled Love led to a more satisfying and fulfilling sexual experience for both husband and wife? It would it be a convergence of love and truth for two wounded souls. One person working with God's *Unveiled Love* can do all this and more!

Pride

Receiving God's *Unveiled Love* is humbling. It disembowels pride. The *Merriam-Webster Dictionary* defines pride as deep pleasure or satisfaction derived from one's own achievements. By extension, in whatever we place reliance on or confidence in that supports us, advances us, and preserves our lives can be a form of pride. It could be our education, skills, possessions, work, ministry, a position, and even a person. Pride can be blatant and overt or subtle and covert. It can be nice or nasty. Pride opposes humility. Humility is the ability to receive and manifest the will of God with whomever He assigns. The Bible has much to say about pride. James 4:6 (TPT) summarizes:

> But he continues to pour out more and more grace upon us. For it says, God resists you when you are proud but continually pours out grace when you are humble.

The Message Translation amplifies the meaning:

> You're cheating on God. If all you want is your own way, flirting with the world every chance you get, you end up enemies of God and his way. And do you suppose God doesn't care? The proverb has it that "he's a fiercely jealous lover." And

> what he gives in love is far better than anything else you'll find. It's common knowledge that "God goes against the willful proud; God gives grace to the willing humble."

Pride makes it impossible to receive from God and others. I know Christians that admit with a badge of honor that they have difficulty receiving from others. I am talking about some of the kindest, most God-fearing people, married and not. They are generous—first to give, last to receive if they do at all. These must always be on the giving end of the relationship. What makes it hard for others is that these sincerely believe that giving is the whole of Christianity. And others do as well. Therefore, the pride that prevents them from receiving goes undetected. Although their giving is sincere, it is a form of godliness that lacks the substance of one having received. Whatever Jesus said or did was a direct result of what He received from the Father. He says so in John 5:19 (CSB):

> Truly I tell you, the Son is not able to do anything on his own, but only what he sees the Father doing. For whatever the Father does, the Son likewise does these things.

In John 12:49 (GW):

> I have not spoken on my own. Instead, the Father who sent me told me what I should say and how I should say it.

In His lengthiest recorded prayer to the Father, Jesus speaks in John 17:6–8 (TPT):

> Father, I have manifested who you really are and I have revealed you to the men and women that you gave to me. They were yours, and you gave them to me, and they have fastened your Word firmly to

their hearts. And now at last they know that everything I have is a gift from you, And the very words you gave to me to speak I have passed on to them. They have received your words and carry them in their hearts. They are convinced that I have come from your presence, and they have fully believed that you sent me to represent you.

Here's the point. Jesus only gave what he received. We can only truly reveal what we have received. Pride or the refusal to receive God's love invalidates our witness in marriage, family, and among those God gives us to influence. This is true despite our knowledge and memory of scripture, our ability to teach, preach, and explain Christian concepts to others. While these things might invite honor among people, it wins disapproval from scripture. Proverbs 16:18–19 (MSG) states the following:

> First pride, then the crash—the bigger the ego, the harder the fall. It's better to live humbly among the poor than to live it up among the rich and famous.

Philippians 2:3 (TPT) instructs:

> Be free from pride-filled opinions, for they will only harm your cherished unity. Don't allow self-promotion to hide in your hearts, but in authentic humility put others first and view others as more important than yourselves.

Among many other things, God's *Unveiled Love* is genderless and positionless. This means it applies to husbands and wives. There is not a separate love for men and another for women. There is One Love, just as there is One God and Father of all. One Savior and Lord. God's *Unveiled Love* cannot be divided, only multiplied. It's in partaking and sharing in this love that husbands and wives deepen their connection. God's *Unveiled Love* is Spirit that must be taken into the soul to manifest in our lives and relationships.

Whether we refuse God's *Unveiled Love* because we have been taught to work for it, shamed, and guilted into hiding from it, fear of judgment, or pride, one thing is clear. Unless we take in this love, we cannot show it. Any other method used to display this love produces artificial results. These methods merely imitate and thereby mock God.

Receiving Love

All giving and displaying of God's *Unveiled Love* is an outgrowth of having received it. Paul's prayer to the church at Ephesus underscores the point:

> I pray that he may grant you, according to the riches of his glory, to be strengthened with power in your inner being through his Spirit, and that Christ may dwell in your hearts through faith. I pray that you, being rooted and firmly established in love, may be able to comprehend with all the saints what is the length and width, height and depth of God's love, and to know Christ's love that surpasses knowledge, so that you may be filled with all the fullness of God.[40]

We must be rooted and grounded in love if we hope to understand it, share in it with other believers and experience the fullness of God. Paul adds in Galatians 5:22–23 (CSB):

> But the fruit of the Spirit is love, joy, peace, patience, kindness, goodness, faithfulness, gentleness, and self-control. The law is not against such things.

---

[40] Ephesians 3:16–19 (CSB)

Paul calls love fruit. This means there is a seed that gets planted, takes root, and produces fruit. God planted the seed. It's up to us (the soil) to receive the seed into our souls and accept the water, heat, and minerals that cause it to take root and produce fruit. God intends for His love to grow continuously inside of us. Perhaps therefore, Paul says there is no limit to how much love and the other fruits of the Spirit we can experience. That's amazing! The supply of God's *Unveiled Love* never runs out. We cannot exhaust it. We can have as much as we desire.

Water plays an integral part in the soil that holds a seed. It provides oxygen, nourishment, and hydration to seed and plant life. Combined with excreting waste and regulating internal temperature, water helps transform a seed to a plant to tree that reproduce each one after its kind. Likewise, God's *Unveiled Love* is essential to the soul's transformation from baby to adolescent to a mature Christian.

The astonishing thing about water and God's *Unveiled Love* is that they do these things all by themselves. Let me say it this way. The soil or soul's job is to receive. How well this occurs depends on the number of pores or holes in the soil and by extension your soul. The holes in the soil hold the water and oxygen necessary for life. A soul without holes has no place to hold God's Love. Therefore, it cannot grow mentally and emotionally. God has many ways of making holes and supplying life-giving oxygen to our souls. Some we find pleasant. Others not so much. Many of us have no holes, that is no space to receive love. We are busy. Almost every waking hour is filled with children, work, church, ministry, social media, social events, video games—all things technology and a host of other things. I was on my way to church one Sunday, and God said to me, "So what day will be your day of rest?" I hadn't planned to go to church that day, opting instead to work, and then decided to go with intention to come home and work. You can see God's question to me was well-placed. I did not work that Sunday. After church, I had lunch, then took a long walk. It was good and refreshing! I needed it. It was a hole, a space, an opportunity to receive His love, and I did. Let's make some holes for God's Love to fill. Let's acknowledge we have worked far too long for love, and we have felt way too unworthy of love. Let's admit that we have feared love and that pride has kept us from seeing our need to receive God's magnificent love.

One of the most pleasant ways to take in God's *Unveiled Love* is by choosing to receive Love. We can decide to receive God's Love just like that. We are free. We can think for ourselves. We can believe what we want. We can decide for ourselves. I dare you to make it your mission to receive God's Love on purpose. That's it! Receive His Love in the area that troubles you in your relationship. Receive His Love in the area that hurts you the most. Better still, ask God in what area of your life He would like you to receive His Love.

I want to make one final point about receiving God's love. To do this, I want to give two more illustrations using water, the symbol of God's love. First, water is essential to all life. In the human, it is part of all bodily functions! How do you get water to do its part in the nourishment of the tissues and organs in your body? What must you do for water's hydration to lubricate your muscles and joints enabling you to move? What must you do for water to help expel the toxins and waste from your body? What do you do for water to regulate your body's temperature? If your answer is "drink it," you are right! The thing we must do is ingest it. Water does the rest, what it is designed to do, all by itself. It neither asks your permission nor waits for your gratitude.

Second, what do you think of when you see brown, dry grass on a lawn? It needs water! Or wilting house plants? They need water. In each of the illustrations, the nourishment of the body, and the dry grass, and house plants, the water is just received. They don't *do* anything but just take in the water. This is how it is with God's *Unveiled Love*. You don't have to do anything but take it in. Each one must decide to receive God's Love into your soul. That's it! God's Love does not require your help. God's *Unveiled Love* does what is best for you by breathing life and nourishment into your soul, supplying you with His grace, oiling your mental and emotional muscles for better responsibility, ridding your soul of pride, fear, and lust, and helping you to manage your thoughts and feelings. All this and all we do is receive. It's time for husbands and wives to experience a new level of freedom and power inside marriage. When they do, the temptation to step outside of marriage becomes much less appealing. Wouldn't you agree?

Questions to Learn By

1. After reclaiming your freedom and authority in marriage, what does the author say we must do next?
2. How does Hollywood portray love? Do you think Christians buy into this portrayal without realizing it? Give some examples.
3. Scripture says that our ability to receive love is only because God gave love. What does this mean to you?

Questions to Grow By

1. What has been your experience with God's *Unveiled Love* through the church?
2. What characteristic or behavior of water most reflects God's Love to you? Why?
3. Which of your senses has God used to express His Love to you? Give an example when this happened.
4. Which of your senses is it most difficult for you to recognize God's Love?

Questions to Change By

1. The author says working for love, shame, guilt, fear of judgment, and pride prevent us from receiving love. Which of these prevents you from receiving God's Love? (Questions 2 through 5 pertain to your answer in question 1).
2. Ask God to show you what this looks like (i.e., what does pride do, how does it behave?).
3. How do you think your spouse experiences your behavior (i.e., how do you think your spouse experiences you when you are being proud?)?

4. What and/or who has contributed to your struggle to receive God's Love?
5. That you admitted these things, are you ready to make an intentional decision to receive God's Love? Pray. Below is a sample prayer that you may choose to use or modify to your language.

Prayer to Receive God's *Unveiled Love*

Father, you already poured out your love into my spirit by the Holy Spirit. I am invoking my right as your child and heir to receive this love into my soul. I willfully open my soul that includes my mind, emotions, as well as all the details of my life to the love that only comes from You. Now fill my soul with Your love. Flood my soul with the love that was in the soul of Jesus Christ. Like Jesus, cause this love to overflow from me into the lives of those You have given me. You said that there is no limit to how much of Your love my soul can receive, so I keep on intentionally asking and receiving. I thank you for hearing me and answering me. And now I pause and wait quietly to demonstrate my availability, faith, and receipt of Your love with thanksgiving. In Jesus's Name![41]

---

[41] *Face It with Love: The Guide to Conquering Fear* (2016) by Kim Moore

Secret 6

Rely on God to Meet Your Needs

> My God will richly fill your every need in a glorious way through Christ Jesus. (Philippians 4:19 GW)

God's love unveils His faithfulness to us as He provides answers to our every need known and unknown. Jesus does not offer us a trouble-free world. Instead, He gives us the answers to every problem we face. John 17:15 reads:

> I do not pray that You should take them out of the world, but that You should keep them from the evil one.

All human relationships encounter problems. In no relationship is this more apparent than in marriage. Problems are needs turned inside out. Think about a T-shirt printed with your favorite cause, sports team, or business. Few, if any of us, would intentionally hide the print by wearing the T-shirt on the wrong side. Yet in marriage, we hide our needs. We wear our problems externally as if they had no connection to what is taking place internally—*in our souls*. I know this is the case because we repeat our problems. Recurring relationship breakdowns are proof. We keep our problems because we wrongly believe they meet our needs. That we don't associate our problems with our needs dooms us to recreating our problems. It's the husband and wife who have the same argument on a different day. Year after year, the triggers may be different, but the problem is the same—*the need remaining unaddressed.*

Ron and Dina's Example

Ron and Dina have been married for almost twenty years. Ron enjoys sex and wants more. Dina tolerates sex in between the increasing demands and routines of daily living. The first few years, it was pregnancy and children. Then it was work. Then it was her health. Then it was caring for her parents. Then it was "I'm tired." There always seemed to be a legitimate, albeit frustrating reason to decline Ron's invitations for sex. Since Dina did not initiate sex, they were rapidly becoming a sexless couple. Sex was a problem for Ron. Sex was a problem for Dina. And sex was a problem for their relationship. The simple answer is to have more sex, right? After all, that would solve the sex problem. Or would it? What if sex were not the problem? What if Ron and Dina's problem persisted because an underlying need remains unaddressed? If so, imagine how ineffective, at best, and damaging at worst, solutions focusing solely on the sexual act itself, could be. I often hear of couples scheduling sex dates. There is certainly nothing wrong with this. However, if there are underlying needs that require addressing, scheduling sex is futile.

Jennifer's Experience

A former client, Jennifer, admitted that she enjoyed sex. She initiated sex. She brought fun and creativity to their sexual encounters. At first, her husband, Tom, was willing, but uneasy. Increasingly, he had reasons for not taking part, and like Dina, they seemed rational. So they agreed to schedule date nights that included sex. Later, Jennifer had this to say about scheduling sex with her husband. "It worked at first. We both showed up, though sometimes it was awkward. It didn't last. It's been three to four weeks since we have had sex." And then Jennifer said this, "I can't help or be understanding about the situation if he isn't going to be honest about what's really going on." What's really going on are underlying needs which may be unknown to her husband.

Communication, money, and sex round out the three most cited problems couples experience. Couples cite these as problems, rather than needs. Problems are a result of decisions and actions having taken place. These decisions are comprised of unpleasant and pleasant past experiences with others and our learned responses. All human beings share common needs. They are common to men and women, husbands and wives. We begin experiencing these needs as children. Our primary caregivers and those in authority address these needs whether properly and adequately or not. In either case, we learn responses that become habits that eventually characterize how we relate to others. Sadly, many husbands and wives painfully learn that how they coped as children doesn't work in marriage. That's because marriage is one of our last opportunities to grow up emotionally. God has the supernatural ability to take us back to the place of the emotional breach.

Connecting the Dots

Most husbands and wives do not connect their emotional limitations with the unpleasant experiences in childhood. We may not even view childhood experiences as negative or unpleasant. That's because children are wired to remain connected to family to survive. No matter how dysfunctional a family may be, children make it work, until they can't. When they can no longer reconcile the emotional discomfort they feel in remaining attached to family, they become more overt in their efforts to get out.

It could be the teen that joins a fringe social group or a gang. It could be the teen that resorts to drugs. Today, it could be the teen that tries out different genders or variant sexual encounters. It could be the teen that chooses to take his or her life or perhaps that of another.

But it could also be the young adult who is now married and has one or more college degrees or several. Or the young adult now married who has a successful career, owns a business, and is financially stable. It could be the young adult now married who is a well-respected church or community leader. It could be otherwise responsible parents advocating what is in the best interest of their children. Easily, it could be you or me.

We don't link our present responses with past experiences for a few reasons. First, we are adults now. Whatever we experienced growing up was then and not now. We think we can divorce ourselves from the pain of the past. But we can't. Unfortunately, religion supports this idea. One of the most cited scriptures that leads us to believe we can cut off our past is 2 Corinthians 5:17 (CEV):

> Anyone who belongs to Christ is a new person.
> The past is forgotten, and everything is new.

Various translations use different words, but they all convey the idea that our past is irrelevant. There is also the idea of the finished work of Christ. Scripture provides a lengthy explanation of the finished work of Christ in Romans 6. The emphasis is Christ's death to sin once and forever. This is the reason God can spare us eternal judgment. But also Paul says that because Jesus overcame sin, so can we. Romans 6:1–4 (CSB) tells us how this is possible.

> What should we say then? Should we continue in sin so that grace may multiply? Absolutely not! How can we who died to sin still live in it? Or are you unaware that all of us who were baptized into Christ Jesus were baptized into his death? Therefore, we were buried with him by baptism into death, in order that, just as Christ was raised from the dead by the glory of the Father, so we too may walk in newness of life.

By reason of Jesus Christ, we that believe have been born into the family of God. John 3:3 and 7 use the words "born again" to convey what happens when we believe in the finished work of Christ.

Our spirit has been recreated into the image of God. God's Holy Spirit now can reside in us as it was before Adam and Eve sinned.

Many erroneously think that their soul was born again at this same time. That all their past experiences (especially the unpleasant, hurtful ones) housed in their mind, emotions, and members are gone and forgotten. Moreover, there is no need to reconcile our past and present. No matter what has happened to us, we can simply behave as if it never happened. We don't have to talk about the hurt and pain that continues to undermine our relationships.

Our spirit was recreated once and for all time. Our souls are being recreated continuously. Here is Paul speaking to the Philippian church:

> And I am convinced and sure of this very thing, that He Who began a good work in you will continue until the day of Jesus Christ [right up to the time of His return], developing [that good work] and perfecting and bringing it to full completion in you.[42]

Now there is the finished work that addresses our position and standing with God through Christ, and there is a progressive, completing work in which we take part. If the finished work addressed the soul life, then why is Paul encouraging the Philippians in this manner? There are many other scriptures that inform us concerning the work that remains to be done with our souls. In Philippians 2:12–13 (CSB), Paul writes the following:

> Therefore, my dear friends, just as you have always obeyed, so now, not only in my presence but even more in my absence, work out your own salvation with fear and trembling. For it is God who is working in you both to will and to work according to his good purpose.

---

[42] Philippians 1:6

If everything concerning our salvation is finished, then why is Paul advising the church to work with God as He works in them? And to the Colossian church, Paul writes these words:

> Therefore, as God's chosen ones, holy and dearly loved, put on compassion, kindness, humility, gentleness, and patience.[43]

To put on something requires intention and action. If these qualities were already functional and mature in our souls our marriages would tell a different story. In fact, it is the absence of these qualities that contribute to the breakdowns between husbands and wives. Whether Paul advises us to "put on" or "put off," it is work that involves the soul—necessarily the mind, will, and emotions.[44] Upon salvation, our spirit was recreated, our souls are being recreated. In Romans 12:2, Paul argues that we do not conform to the ways of the world, rather change our mind so that we can discern and fulfill God's will. Again, Paul speaks concerning the soul—*the inner man.*

If these few scriptures are neither compelling enough nor provoke us to reconsider the mental and emotional work before us, then consider Jesus's words in Matthew 23:25–26. Jesus distinguishes our spiritual work from our soulish work:

> Woe to you, scribes and Pharisees, hypocrites! You clean the outside of the cup and dish, but inside they are full of greed and self-indulgence. Blind Pharisee! First clean the inside of the cup, so that the outside of it may also become clean.

Connecting the dots requires that we understand and are open to exchanging our thinking about the experiences we had while

---

[43] Colossians 3:12
[44] Colossians 3:9–14

growing up. It means be willing to embrace truth in our soul. David offers language in Psalm 51:6 (MEV):

> You desire truth in the inward parts, and in the hidden part You make me to know wisdom.

The truth may sometimes hurt, but wisdom adds knowledge as to how to use the truth to your advantage. But first, we must connect the dots. Religion has taught some that there is no requirement or benefit to connecting the dots. The past is a weapon Satan uses against genuine believers. God is a master at turning weapons into tools. But he only works with what is given into His hands.

But Wait, I'm in Charge

Another hindrance to connecting the dots is that we believe we are in control. That we do what we want to do, when we want to do it, and how we want to do it. Isn't this an often underlying, unexpressed thought? We all have our methods of trying to control our relationships. Whether actively or passively, we are adept at stopping emotional threats. Pam uses work to escape vulnerable conversations. John uses humor and sarcasm to avoid feelings of inadequacy. Tonya uses the children to get out of sex. Endless is the creativity of men and women in sidestepping what they find hard to confront. Still, we legitimize our avoidances adding to the belief that we are in control. But we are not.

Recurring conflict between husbands and wives is proof. Paul speaking concerning himself in Romans 7:15–20 (TPT):

> I'm a mystery to myself, for I want to do what is right, but end up doing what my moral instincts condemn. And if my behavior is not in line with my desire, my conscience still confirms the excellence of the law. And now I realize that it is no longer my true self doing it, but the unwelcome intruder of sin in my humanity. For I know

that nothing good lives within the flesh of my fallen humanity. The longings to do what is right are within me, but willpower is not enough to accomplish it. My lofty desires to do what is good are dashed when I do the things I want to avoid. So, if my behavior contradicts my desires to do good, I must conclude that it's not my true identity doing it, but the unwelcome intruder of sin hindering me from being who I really am.

Now that's a mouthful. Let me help with an example. Recall the last time you and your spouse experience conflict. Suppose that you were genuinely at fault and courageous to admit it. Somewhere in the discussion, you promised to never let it happen again. You were sincere. You really meant it and had every intent on upholding your word. And you did…it just didn't last. Eventually, your word fell to the ground, and you ended up doing the very thing you vowed not to do. Be kind to yourself. And if you are recalling a promise your spouse made to you, be kind to him or her. It is not their fault. Like most who believe they are in control of their behavior, we underestimate the power of the law. Though some like to believe, no one is above the law. When you or your spouse repeats something, they vowed not to do, it is not them, rather sin that lies within their soul and body. The law of sin has one outcome—*death and destruction*. Only the law of life in Christ Jesus overcomes the law of sin and death.

The law of sin and death is true. That means it applies to all and in whatever area we have not overcome by the law of life. The law of sin and death shows brazen disregard for age, gender, roles, born-again status, positions, title, and even needs. When sin is in control, we are not. This is true despite beliefs to the contrary. Sin results in needs. When real needs go unaddressed, they become armed bandits that steal, kill, and destroy our lives and relationships. Sadly, this is when many learn that they are not in charge.

Only when we connect the dots can the law of life in Christ Jesus overcome the law of sin and death. Here is Paul speaking in Romans 8:1–2 (TPT) summarized:

> So now the case is closed. There remains no accusing voice of condemnation against those who are joined in life-union with Jesus, the Anointed One. For the "law" of the Spirit of life flowing through the anointing of Jesus has liberated us from the "law" of sin and death.

I like the way the Message Translation lays out the case.

> With the arrival of Jesus, the Messiah, that fateful dilemma is resolved. Those who enter into Christ's being-here-for-us no longer have to live under a continuous, low-lying black cloud. A new power is in operation. The Spirit of life in Christ, like a strong wind, has magnificently cleared the air, freeing you from a fated lifetime of brutal tyranny at the hands of sin and death.

In and of ourselves, we are powerless to exert control over the law of sin and death. Superior knowledge, the strongest will, the best intentions, and the most passionate efforts to uphold our word will inevitably cave to the force of the law of sin and death. Paul tells us why in verse 3:

> For God achieved what the law was unable to accomplish, because the law was limited by the weakness of human nature.

In other words, the law was unable to transform the soul of men and women because they (not the law) are weak—*and not in control.* Jesus personally took on our human condition. He didn't address our need remotely. He entered our lives, our mess, our struggle, our pain, and working from the inside out, He set us free from the law of sin and death. Jesus changed us. Now this Jesus, through the Holy Spirit, resides in our spirit.

> Now we have this treasure in clay jars, so that this extraordinary power may be from God and not from us.[45]

Paul acknowledges this power in sharing God's reply to his request to remove the thorn in his flesh. Second Corinthians 12:9 (CSB) reads as follows:

> My grace is sufficient for thee: for my strength is made perfect in weakness. Most gladly therefore will I rather glory in my infirmities, that the power of Christ may rest upon me.

God's strength, that is His transformation power, is revealed to us in weakness and need.

The law does not change men and women, married or not. Romans 4:15 indicates that the law brings about the anger of God. The law judges and condemns them. That's because the law does not prevent sin, instead it provokes sin. Similarly, the law does not satisfy the needs of men and women, married or not. The law exploits the needs of people bringing them into bondage. The law is powerless to free husbands and wives, meet their deepest needs, and fulfill their God-given desires. The law is based on external compliance to rules. Grace is based on internal responsiveness to the truth—*no matter through whom it may come.*

Let me offer a few final thoughts about connecting the dots. The Old Testament and the New Testament are internally connected and consistent. Jesus is the theme and central figure of both Testaments. When speaking to the Jews, to whom the law was given, Jesus said

---

[45] 2 Corinthians 4:7 (CSB)

that He did not come to destroy the law but to fulfill it.[46] After giving the two greatest commands, that is to love God first and with all, and then to love your neighbor as yourself, Jesus made it clear in Matthew 22:40 (CSB):

> All the Law and the Prophets depend on these two commands.

Keep in mind, Jesus was speaking to the Jews. In this verse, He speaks to their past, present, and future all at the same time. God does not have to take you to your past to address your past. That's because whatever is left unresolved from your past will show up in your present relationships. God is so committed to freeing us, healing us, restoring us, and making us whole that He will allow us to experience the same problem repeatedly. He allows this until we come to our senses, like the prodigal son, and admit our real need. Only then are we open and available for God to satisfy us with answers.

If we respond to our spouse the way we responded to our parents when growing up, our past is our present. We have not changed. Likewise, if we continue to initiate these responses with our children, our past is our present. We have not changed. Unless there is intervention, what our families of origin live into us, we live out in marriage and with our children. We say things to our spouse like, "You act just like your mother (or father)" or "You always..." "You never..." These kinds of statements are not typically meant to be positive. When we make these and similar statements, we verify that our spouse's past is very much present, alive, and well. It is also an indication of the need for deliverance, sanctification, and healing. Listen, my friend. Most of us do not require psychotherapy or *years* of counseling. We require our actual needs to be addressed—*now*. I'm not talking about what religion has decided are your needs as husbands and wives. I am also not talking about pre-assembled, mass-produced, and recycled answers to your needs. I am talking about unique, genuine needs that can be deeply known and answered

---

[46] Matthew 5:17

in marriage and covenantal relationships. I want to show you how this is possible. But first, I would be careless if I did not address the hurt inflicted upon husbands and wives by religion.

Need Theology

I am a writer. I know the time and effort that goes into writing a book. It is hard and focused work. This is my third or fourth rewrite of this one secret alone. This book has been two years in the making. I was trying to find a way not to challenge anyone nor elevate the content in this book by upending the content of other books. So far, I think I have done well. However, on the topic of what I call "need theology," I am at an impasse. I have firsthand knowledge of the damage caused by some popular marriage material widely used in the church. I have ongoing experience in coaching husbands and wives who are discouraged and desperate for understanding and practical answers to their frustrations in marriage. That said, I must talk about the concept of "need theology."

Need theology is the theory that husbands and wives' emotional and physical requirements fall along prescribed gender lines and each one is suited to meet the other's needs. Needs have been stereotyped as male or female. The mixture of psychological and religious literature based on need theology has permeated and influenced the church's marriage teachings. These teachings define gender needs by ascribing behaviors to these needs and then prescribing how to address them. Sadly, this concept has achieved widespread acceptance as dogma by the church. Two well-known books, which can be fairly grouped into the need theology category are: the psychology-based Revised and Updated Edition of *His Needs, Her Needs: Making Romantic Love Last* (Dr. William F. Harley, 2022) and the Christian psychology–based *Love and Respect: The Love She Most Desires; The Respect He Desperately Needs* (Dr. Emerson Eggerichs, 2004).

Dr. Harley is a renowned licensed clinical psychologist, marriage counselor, and author. Among other books is his best-selling, classic first edition of *His Needs, Her Needs: Building an Affair-Proof Marriage* (1986). The book has been republished with the later editions having different subtitles, *His Needs, Her Needs: Building a Marriage That Lasts* (2012), and *His Needs, Her Needs: Making Romantic Love Last* (2022). In his books, Dr. Harley says that men and women have five needs they bring to marriage. For ease of reading, see the chart below. The needs are listed in the exact order Harley presents them in his book.

His Needs, Her Needs: Building an Affair Proof Marriage
(Dr. Willard Harley, 1986)

Husband - His Needs	Wife - Her Needs
1. Sexual Fulfillment	1. Affection
2. Recreational Companionship	2. Conversation
3. An Attractive Spouse	3. Honesty and Openness
4. Domestic Support	4. Financial Support
5. Admiration	5. Family Commitment

Harley suggests husbands and wives can make themselves irresistible to one another by simply meeting each other's five emotional needs. Harley writes, "Couples start out irresistible and only become incompatible as they leave each other's basic needs unmet. When someone outside of the marriage offers to meet those needs, an affair starts."

What Harley calls an affair, the Bible calls adultery. Adultery does not begin with the lack of sex or a wife failing to be a recreational companion to her husband. Nor does adultery begin with his failing to meet his wife's need for affection or conversation. Jesus says adultery begins in the heart.[47] Peter refers to one's eyes being full of adultery.[48] And James says that each one of us are enticed by the desires raging within us.[49] We cannot blame our behavior on our spouse. Jesus makes this clear when He says that it is not what hap-

---

[47] Matthew 5:27–28
[48] 2 Peter 2:14
[49] James 1:13–15

pens to us, that is, it is not what we get or don't get that defiles us, rather it is what we do. Jesus speaks in Mark 7:20–22:

> And he said, "What comes out of a person is what defiles him. For from within, out of people's hearts, come evil thoughts, sexual immoralities, thefts, murders, adulteries, greed, evil actions, deceit self-indulgence, envy, slander, pride, and foolishness."

Still, years of clinical experience, observation, a handful of scriptures, and references to God continues to pin back the ears of the most learned Christians. After all, Harley's solution is simple—*simple enough, right?* The fact that the book has topped the bestselling charts time after time and has been a top shelf, go to reference book for church leaders and laity alike, makes it hard to dispute its universal appeal.

But does universal appeal equate to universal answers? The big question should be is a book based on need theology really the answer? Is it your answer? What about your problems? Have you or others you know embraced Harley's assessment? If so, have you made earnest efforts to comply with Harley's prescription? Have you or others you know upheld your end of the deal? And if so, has your spouse become irresistible to you? Has it prevented pornography, adultery, sexless marriages, divorce, et.al.?

The two most problematic issues I find with the content of *His Needs, Her Needs: Building an Affair Proof Marriage* are the implication that a wife is responsible if her husband has an affair and that husbands and wives can transact needs. I have already pointed out that what Harley calls an affair, the Bible calls adultery. However, adding to the popularity of the thinking that a wife can control her husband's behavior (or vice versa) are the words of Pat Robertson. On his television show, *The 700 Club* (2013), a wife asked Mr. Robertson concerning her husband committing adultery. Incidentally, I heard his reply firsthand. At the time, it was quite the headline in some Christian circles. However, when for this book I attempted to provide proof of Mr. Robertson's statement, I only find trace information. Here's what Mr. Robertson said to the wife—*the victim.*

> "Here's the secret," 83-year-old Robertson said. "Stop talking about the cheating. He cheated on you. Well, he's a man. Does he provide a home for you to live in? Does he provide food for you to eat? Does he provide clothes for you to wear? Is he nice to the children…is he handsome? Males have a tendency to wander a bit, and what you want to do is make the home so wonderful that he doesn't want to wander."

Robertson's statement drew backlash then, and yet Harley's book still remains one of the top-selling Christian books on marriage. Husbands and wives are not responsible for each other's behavior. They can make it easier or harder to engage in ungodly and godly behavior. However, God will require each one to account for his or her behavior.

The second problem I have with Harley's book is that it advertises love and sex as products that can be sold and bought. And while this may be so in the world, God's *Unveiled Love* is not so. In the Kingdom and family of God, *Unveiled Love* may cost the giver, but never the receiver. Treating love and sex as merchandise that can be bought and sold might result in temporary wins and some good times. However, when change and lasting change is indicated, God begins from the inside out. Harley's list focuses on the physical life of husbands and the emotional life of wives. Neither address the innermost needs of a man or a woman. A gospel that does not go deep down into the inner recesses of our being, that is the seat of our willing and choosing parts is powerless to achieve lasting change. Among other things, a gospel that doesn't include us bringing our physical and emotional lives to the cross is not the gospel of Jesus Christ. By employing Harley's approach, couples may experience positive, superficial, temporary changes. However, the real underlying emotional needs and the fears that accompany them will surface again and again until properly answered. Lastly, I want to ask you these questions with all due respect to Dr. Harley. Could a prospective reader of the book *His Needs, Her Needs* wonder why the subtitle has changed twice? Certainly, one might ask why? After all, the subtitle goes from *Building an Affair-Proof Marriage* (1986) to *Building a Marriage That Lasts* (2012) to *Making Romantic Love Last* (2022). You might ask yourself, "Has the content or meaning changed?" "Is it more progressive over the years?" Or "Has the author's views changed?" Or "Is the title changing just a marketing tool?" I suppose to really know, one would have to examine all three renditions of the book. So what's my point? You don't have to ask yourself these questions about the Holy Scripture. The Bible. Its title doesn't change. Its content and meaning haven't changed nor has it become more progressive over the years. This book *Unveiled Love* is not based on need theology or psychology. God's *Unveiled Love* is based on timeless truths in God's Word. That means the truths are just as relevant today as they were yesterday and as they will be tomorrow. *Unveiled Love* is impervious to the fleeting minds of husbands and wives as well as the ever-changing circumstances that confront them. Moreover, these truths can be applied to virtually all relationships.

Love and Respect

Award-winning author, teacher, and pastor Dr. Emerson Eggerichs specializes in male-female relationships. Eggerichs has a PhD in Child and Family Ecology. He also has three master of arts degrees in Biblical Studies, Communication, and Divinity. Dr. Eggerichs pastored a church for twenty years before embarking on a speaking ministry promoting the idea that women need love and men need respect. Recall, need theology is the theory that men and women and, by extension, husbands and wives have different unique needs. Supposedly, when husbands and wives transact the emotional business of their relationship along these lines, then a happy marriage is inevitable.

Dr. Eggerichs's book, *Love and Respect: The Love She Most Desires; The Respect He Desperately Needs* has sold millions of copies.

Like Harley's book, *Love and Respect* is one of the most referred to books on Christian marriage. Surely a PhD, three masters' degrees, including one in Divinity, international acclaim as a speaker and a best-selling author, means Dr. Eggerichs must be right. Right? Let me share a few quotes directly from the book and see what you think.

> My theory says that the wife has a tendency to react in ways that feel disrespectful to her husband—thus the command to respect—and the husband has a tendency to react in ways that feel unloving to the wife—thus the command to love. (p.319)
>
> I am still only a man, and the flesh can be weak. (p.107)
>
> My wife, Sarah has accepted that her disrespect is equal to my lack of love. (p.103)
>
> Wives don't need a lot of coaching on being loving. It's built into them, and they do it naturally. However, they do need help with respect because this is foreign to many women. (p.183)
>
> Men are sensitive. Men are more vulnerable to criticism. (p.209 and 211)
>
> How should a wife act if she strongly disagrees with her husband about some issue? I Timothy 2:12 has some advice. Paul writes, "I do not allow a woman to exercise authority over a man but to remain quiet." (p.220)

What kinds of feelings do these passages from the book; *Love and Respect* evoke for you? Honestly, I was provoked by this book, as I am certain, so were others. Here are a few reasons why I cannot endorse the book. First, like Harley, Eggerichs reduces needs to gender. Wives need love. Husbands need respect. Both scripture and my work with clients support the truth that human beings need love and respect. In his own words, Eggerichs commands women to (unconditionally) respect their husbands. And he commands husbands to love their wives. When asked what the greatest commandment is, Jesus replied in Matthew 22:37–40 (CSB):

> Love the Lord your God with all your heart, with all your soul, and with all your mind. This is the greatest and most important command. The second is like it: Love your neighbor as yourself, All the Law and the Prophets depend on these two commands.

Nowhere in Jesus's words to the Pharisees do we find a direct or indirect command for wives to respect their husbands. But we do find the command that we—male and female, husbands and wives—ought to love each other as ourselves. Jesus adds to the command to love others in John 13:34 (CSB).

> I give you a new command: Love one another just as I have loved you, you are also to love one another.

And in John 15:13, Jesus explains that the strongest kind of love and affection is to give up his (or her) life for his friends. Love, then, is giving up something we value for something of greater value—*while maintaining our freedom and authority*. Jesus is our example.

As Christian men and women who happened to be married, we are not only called but also commanded to love one another. In fact, twenty-three times in the New Testament (CSB), we are instructed to love one another. And if, according to Eggerichs, women are naturally loving and don't require coaching, then why does Jesus not leave them out when commanding us to love one another? Today, there are many women and wives that grew up in loveless and unaffectionate homes. Love and affection are not native to these wives. They, too, must learn how to receive and give love.

Unconditional Respect

A second reason I cannot endorse the book, *Love and Respect*, is because scripture does not advise us to unconditionally respect any human being. Jesus never gave up his right and responsibility to yield, defend, and stand by truth nor His responsibility to oppose evil. Therefore, Jesus would not ask us to give up these rights and responsibilities. I do not recall in scripture where Jesus called for, commanded, or coerced His disciples to respect Him. That Eggerichs admonishes wives to respect their husbands is out of step with God's Word. Who should we believe?

Respect

For the truly sincere, it may help to clarify. According to the *Merriam-Webster Dictionary*, the word "respect" means "to give attention to or high regard for." Synonyms include "esteem" and "admiration." The word "reverence" means "devotion." It implies a sacredness. Esteem, admiration, and gratefulness are implied. However, that one respects another does not imply devotion or sacredness. We can respect people that we do not agree with or perhaps even like based on their performance or success. I respect Dr. Harley's and Dr. Eggerichs's successes with their books, *His Needs, Her Needs* and *Love and Respect*. Writing a book is an accomplishment and a respectable one at that! However, I do not agree with the premise of either of their books. I know neither man, so I have no disrespect or dislike for them personally.

Reverence

We cannot reverence a person without esteeming them and even admiring them. Here's why. Respect is about what a person does, while reverence has to do with who God says someone is to us. I reverenced my parents while living and now cherish memories as they have passed. It's who God made them to me. Sadly, it wasn't until later in life that I realized how much I admired them. The challenges they overcame to provide me a quality of life far better than their own were incredible. That they were able to do this and maintain their integrity is my legacy.

In marriage, there are times when the behavior of a husband or wife is sinful, wrong, and/or hurtful. When it is, we have a responsibility to appeal to each one's relationship with God. Paul goes over this in Ephesians 5:6–17. He tells us (men and women, husbands and wives) to pay attention and walk wisely, rather than unwisely. Right before this, twice he tells us not to partner or participate in evil. That we should test what is pleasing to the Lord and expose that which is not. A wife can disrespect her husband's behavior and still reverence who God says he is. Let me say it another way. I cannot think of a reason God would give a wife a reason to act irreverently toward her husband. But, I can think of reasons why God would have her disregard his behavior. Reverence is bestowed. Respect is earned. To husbands who desire more respect, I challenge them to "up their game." In other words, either change the way you are doing something, improve your consistency, and/or follow through and see what a difference it will make. Not only will you have greater respect for yourself, but you will also win the respect of others, including your wife. Before anyone might suggest hearing overtones of feminism, let me suggest that "upping your game" can just as easily apply to wives. That's because we all require love and respect! It's not a gender thing.

Unlike Drs. Harley and Eggerichs, I do not believe the answer is "need theology"—*the gender stereotyping, gender-based, transactional solution for meeting needs in marriage.* Need theology is an exchanged based formula that says, "If you do this, I will do that." And "If you don't do this, then I won't do that (at least not with, or for you)." This ideology, which many have grown to idolize is anti-Christ. According to Paul, God's exchange system works this way:

> Be not deceived, God is not mocked; for whatsoever a man soweth, that shall he also reap. For

he that soweth to his flesh shall of the flesh reap corruption; but he that soweth to the Spirit shall of the Spirit reap life everlasting.[50]

On that day when the works we have done in Him are judged, we won't be able to say, "The devil made me do it," "My spouse made me do it," "My children made me do it," "That pastor made me do it." "That pastor made me do it." Are you tracking with me? One day, we will answer to God. Our motives will be on full display. We will reap the motive by which we sow. If a wife is only having sex with her husband to gain access to his wallet, then the sex is about her, not him. If a husband brings home flowers, takes his wife out to dinner, and later that evening harasses his wife for sex, then the flowers and dinner were likely less about her and more about him. Something to keep in mind is this. We sow words and actions. But also sown is the motivation behind these things. That's why scripture says that God doesn't judge the way man does. He is keenly aware of and interested in our motives. First Samuel 16:7 says it this way:

> But the Lord said to Samuel, "Don't judge by his appearance or height, for I have rejected him. The Lord doesn't see things the way you see them. People judge by outward appearance, but the Lord looks at the heart."

That's one reason *Unveiled Love* focuses on those truths and scriptural principles that apply to men and women—married or not. When approaching the topic of needs, not only does "need theology" interfere with husbands and wives getting their needs met, but also it tends to confuse needs with wants, desire, and lust as well as believing what we seek is what we need.

---

[50] Galatians 6:7–8

Needs, Desires, Lusts

As discussed, a need is something that is required to live on earth, in relationship to God and others. This means it is essential. We must have it. When we do not get it, we will react, often in unhealthy ways. All have needs that have been neglected, abused, or exploited. The severity of which is different from person to person. And our acceptance of counterfeit answers to real needs is as numerous as the scenarios from which we arrive to marriage. We have a spiritual need for God. Our physical bodies need food, water, and shelter. Our heart and mind do not only need meaning and discipline to realize our purpose, but we also require the emotional benefit of acceptance, significance, authority, and reconciliation of our past hurts with our present experiences. These needs are answered in relationship to other human beings. Marriage, family, friendship, work, church, and recreational relationships, which all contribute to our emotional well-being. I add sex as a need for reproduction of human beings. Sexual intercourse between a husband and wife is God's sanctioned method for achieving this. Sex in marriage also serves a God-given desire for couples to experience the delight and fulfillment of oneness.

Wants, Desires, Lust

A want is something that we would like to have, but is not essential to sustaining our life. I have a home. I want a home on a lake, inlet, or the ocean. While I need a home, there is no requirement that it must be on the water. Despite all the reasons that I can come up with *(and I have a lot—smile)*, I will not die spiritually, mentally, emotionally, or physically if I never have a home on the water in my lifetime. It is what I want. It is a compelling desire.

A want or desire is something we crave. We develop an appetite for it. We hunger for it. We look for it. We see it. We admire it. We see ourselves in it, enjoying it. When we feed our wants and desires, we strengthen them. Think about a time you may have been looking to purchase a new car. Once you decided on the kind of car you wanted, you began to see it everywhere. You couldn't help it. And each time you saw the car, it reinforced your desire for it. As I write wants and desires, I am reminded of Philippians 2:13 (NLT):

> For God is working in you, giving you the desire
> and the power to do what pleases him.

God gives us certain desires. Some are spiritual. Others are natural. Together, these enable us to fulfill His purpose for our lives. Psalm 37:4 adds the following:

> Find your delight and true pleasure in Yahweh,
> and he will give you what you desire the most.

By these verses, I am not trying to make the case for a home on the water. Rather, I'm simply saying that desires, in and of themselves, are not always wrong. God has a hand in some of our most natural desires. When God is involved, He continuously adds twigs to keep the fire burning. This enables us to endure as we wait and work with Him toward fulfillment.

Lust is the unreasonable desire for something. Temptation is very real and very powerful. James explains the strength of a desire turned lust and the temptation that follows:

> When you are tempted don't ever say, "God is tempting me," for God is incapable of being tempted by evil and he is never the source of temptation. Instead, it is each person's own desires and thoughts that drag them into evil and lure them away into darkness. Evil desires give birth to evil actions. And when sin is fully mature it can murder you! So, my friends, don't be fooled by your own desires![51]

---

[51] James 1:13–16 (TPT)

This is what the scripture means when it says your wants become as an armed robber.[52] When wants and desires overpower us, lust gains opportunity. When this happens, we lose objectivity and the freedom to choose what is in our long-term best interest. Instead, we settle for the pleasure of sin for a season. When lust hijacks our mind and flesh, we become so preoccupied that we look for ways to indulge it. We build lifestyles that include lying, cheating, and stealing for the gain of pleasure. But it is a deceptive pleasure. Moses, when he became a man, refused to be called the son of Pharaoh's daughter. Hebrews 11:25 (CSB) explains his decision:

> And chose to suffer with the people of God rather than to enjoy the fleeting pleasure of sin.

As the son of Pharaoh's daughter, Moses had access to the wealth and liberties of the palace. But he refused. In Mark 4:19 (AMPC), Jesus refers:

> Then the cares and anxieties of the world and distractions of the age, and the pleasure and delight and false glamour and deceitfulness of riches, and the craving and passionate desire for other things creep in and choke and suffocate the Word, and it becomes fruitless.

When lust gains a foothold in our lives, it steals our affections, kills our appetite for the things of God, and weakens our ability to honor God in decision making. It's what the Bible calls an inordinate affection. Paul writes in Colossians 3:5–6 (MEV):

> Therefore put to death the parts of your earthly nature: sexual immorality, uncleanness, inordinate affection, evil desire, and covetousness,

---

[52] Proverbs 24:34

which is idolatry. Because of these things, the wrath of God comes on the sons of disobedience.

Whether it is lust for power, money, things, or sex, we are giving up control of our lives. We do so not because sin is at the forefront of our minds. Rather, we sincerely believe yet are deceived into thinking that what we lust after is a real answer to our needs. In Proverbs 27:7 (MEV), Solomon adds his understanding:

> The full soul loathes a honeycomb, but to the hungry soul every bitter thing is sweet.

When we conflate wants and lust with needs, we almost always decline God's invitations to meet our deepest, most genuine needs. *Unveiled Love* is about relying on God to meet our needs, no matter how long it takes and no matter how He chooses to bring about the answer. When we refuse to take matters into our own hands, but remain open, available, and responsive to God, there is no limit to what He is willing to do, nor length He is willing to go on our behalf. This is, in part, what the scripture we often quote says in Jeremiah 29:11:

> "For I know the plans I have for you"—this is the Lord's declaration—"plans for your well-being, not for disaster, to give you a future and a hope."

When we confuse needs with desires and lust, we are liable to pursue things that are unable to satisfy. Consider the spouse who desires more sex for pleasure purposes. There is nothing wrong with this. Sex is a deeply satisfying way to experience oneness. It's at the top of the list of ways we can experience the unity of the Godhead on earth. Incidentally, Satan also knows this too. And for what does Satan lust, other than to be worshipped as God. Sexual perversion is one of the primary methods Satan uses to gain the worship of men and women. So then, what is the case of the spouse that is always demanding more sex and variation to sexual encounters? Could it possibly be this spouse has brought an unrestrained sexual appetite to the marriage? What then? Do we shame his or her spouse with scriptures like in 1 Corinthians 7:3–5?

> A husband should fulfill his marital duty to his wife, and likewise a wife to her husband. A wife does not have the right over her own body, but her husband does. In the same way, a husband does not have the right over his own body, but his wife does. Do not deprive one another—except when you agree for a time, to devote yourselves to prayer. Then come together again; otherwise, Satan may tempt you because of your lack of self-control.

Or, in the case of a husband with an insatiable sexual appetite. Do we remind this wife of his need (Harley, 2004) and her responsibility to meet it? Or could it be that more sex is not the underlying need, rather there is a need for restraint? What if God were cultivating the fruit of the Holy Spirit called self-control?[53] Could it be that this husband (or wife) is sexually out of control and God through his or her spouse's lesser appetite is providing a unique opportunity to gain control over the flesh? Challenging? Yes. All discipline is for a season. But also it may be hard to accept because there is nothing in "need theology" that advises such an *Unveiled Love* approach.

The Disguises We Wear

Disguises hide our deepest needs. We reach adulthood heavily cloaked with a self-love that is anything but healthy. Many of us are sanctified versions of what we detested growing up. As mentioned before, your strengths are not who you are. These sanctified versions of ourselves often show up as strengths and praiseworthy traits. Strengths are what you've learned to think and how you've

---

[53] Galatians 5:22–23

learned—the real you—*the weak, vulnerable, unloved parts of yourself.* Strengths and weaknesses are two sides of the same coin. Life in some ways reminds me of a coin toss. Heads we win. Tails we lose. We win with our strengths. We lose with our weaknesses. That's what we learn growing up. So we develop our strengths and hide our weaknesses. Isn't this the meaning behind the mantras, "Never let them see you sweat" and "Fake it till you make it"? Take heart, we are not the only ones that hide. Adam hid when he realized he was naked. He was always naked. But sin made him afraid of God and, at the same time, recognize his need for covering. So he sewed fig leaves to provide clothing for himself. Adam and Eve disguised themselves because they were naked, afraid, ashamed, and vulnerable (Genesis 3:7–10). Jeroboam improved upon Adam's strategy of hiding his vulnerability. He used his wife instead of himself.

In 1 Kings 14:33–34, we learn that Jeroboam I was the first king of Northern Israel. He was an evil king who refused to repent. He was cut off from the face of the earth. But before this, his son became deathly ill. Jeroboam neither had standing nor favor with God. He knew it and therefore, enlisted his wife to seek the blessing of the prophet. In 1 Kings 14:2–3 (CSB), Jeroboam speaks to his wife.

> Go disguise yourself, so they won't know that you're Jeroboam's wife, and go to Shiloh. The prophet Ahijah is there; it was he who told about me becoming king over this people. Take with you ten loaves of bread, some cakes, and a jar of honey, and go to him. He will tell you what will happen to the boy.

God alerted Ahijah, the blind prophet, and here is how the conversation began in verse 6.

> When Ahijah heard the sound of her feet entering the door, he said, "Come in, wife of Jeroboam! Why are you disguised? I have bad news for you."

Fatefully, it didn't go well for Jeroboam's family. They were destroyed from the face of the earth. The entire account can be found in 1 Kings 14. We cannot get what we need and want by pretending to be someone or something we are not. It didn't work for Adam and Eve. It didn't work for King Jeroboam. And it won't work for us.

The Undressing

God uses marriage to undress you—*in every way*. Every shred of clothing is removed physically, mentally, emotionally, and spiritually. Marriage removes the gloss, the paint, the veneer from husbands and wives one layer at a time. No one that dares to enter escapes the hand of God. If willing and cooperative, each one is reduced to nakedness of body, nakedness of thought, nakedness of feeling, and nakedness of motive. Nothing is left to chance. Marriage is full frontal, unrelenting attack on pride, and selfishness. And it doesn't stop, lest one opts out. But why? Why would anyone subject themselves to such a fatal attack?

I can think of two reasons. God is preparing a bride for His Son. Ephesians 5:25–27 provides one answer.

> Husbands, love your wives, just as Christ loved the church and gave himself for her to make her holy, cleansing her with the washing of water by the word. He did this to present the church to himself in splendor, without spot or wrinkle or anything like that, but holy and blameless.

Christ gave Himself to His bride. He didn't hold back. He had no disguise nor pretense. His nakedness made her holy. His humility made her clean. All this so that He could experience her splendor without pretense. That through His actions, she was made holy and blameless. Jesus was naked and not ashamed being in relationship with us, then or now. Hebrews 2:11 (AMPC) reads:

> For both He Who sanctifies [making men holy] and those who are sanctified all have one [Father].

For this reason, He is not ashamed to call them brethren.

One reason God is stripping us bare is that we become the bride of Christ without spot or wrinkle and without one drop of pretense. Covenant relationships do this exposing and stripping like no other. And the marriage relationship is the apex of covenants between God, one man, and one woman. There is no superior human relationship.

Another reason, I believe, is that God desires husbands and wives to experience oneness on earth. The kind of oneness that happens when two are naked, undefended, unconcerned for themselves and fully aware of the other—*caught up in a moment.* Think sex. Recall a time when both you and your spouse were fully present and connected through and through, finding a rhythm that brought each of you to a climax. Once the adrenaline subsided, you entered a rest, a peace, a presence that neither of you created on your own. In that moment, there was no fear, just pure love. Two people, a man, and a woman, naked and not ashamed. If you and your spouse have yet to have such an encounter, then I hope and pray you do.

When our dress (a.k.a. disguises) prevents us from getting our real needs answered, God is committed to our disrobing. That's because when needs are unaddressed, we act out. Sometimes, we react in admirable ways. They look Christian. They may be morally upright. For instance, a stellar employee, a respectable businessman or woman, helping the homeless, giving time and money, volunteering at your children's school—*the list of good things we can do to cover up our weaknesses is endless.* But then there are also the hurtful things we do that reveal unanswered needs. Some may use drugs, alcohol, pornography, masturbation, adultery, lying, overeating, stealing, and any number of other behaviors used to avoid addressing our real need.

Whether our disguises are acceptable or unacceptable, God sees the motive behind each one. He shows us to others and to ourselves, so that we may find help in time of need and be empowered to choose differently. Each one must decide for him or herself.

Seeking What We Want, Rather than What We Need

Honestly, we often believe that what we seek is what we really what we need. In the above example, the spouse who pursues more sex for pleasure believes it is a need and a right on the grounds he or she is married. After all, in 1 Corinthians 7:2, Paul writes the following.

> But because sexual immorality is so common, each man should have sexual relations with his own wife, and each woman should have sexual relations with her own husband.

Let's face it. Some men and women primarily get married in order not to sin by having sex outside of marriage. When they do, and sex wanes, trouble is inevitably on the horizon. Despite Harley listing sexual fulfillment as a man/husbands' number one need and Eggerichs's alluding to sex as part and parcel with men's need for respect, Jesus doesn't see it that way.

Jesus emphasizes our need to be accepted and belong, as well as our need for significance. He does not assign a gender to these needs. They are human needs. He demonstrates the need to belong through His relationship with Peter. In the gospels, when listing the names of disciples, Peter's name came first. Peter was important to Jesus, and everyone knew it. When Jesus made inquiries of the disciples, He either directed them to Peter, or Peter was the first to respond—*right or wrong*. God gave the revelation of who Jesus is to Peter.[54] The only record of a disciple openly opposing Jesus involves Peter.[55] Even then, Jesus did not demand Peter respect Him. Jesus distinguished His Father's will from Satan's will, helping Peter to see of what spirit he spoke. Jesus won the admiration and devotion of Peter.

In Luke 5:1–11, we observe Peter move from a master-servant relationship with Jesus to a more intimate personal relationship with

---

[54] Matthew 16:16–17
[55] Matthew 16:21–23

Him. After fishing all night and catching nothing, Peter and the other fishermen began cleaning their nets. So Peter was annoyed when Jesus suggested they go out cast their net again. Reluctantly, Peter did. When they began pulling the net into the boat, it was so full of fish, the net tore. Peter fell at Jesus's knees. Here's what he said to Jesus:

> Go away from me, because I'm a sinful man, Lord!

Peter was wrecked by Jesus's love and regard for him. He didn't want to offer the only thing he had to give Jesus, that was his sin. Still, love convinced him otherwise. We know because Peter no longer calls Jesus Master (Luke 5:5), but Lord. Lord is intimate and implies a personal relationship. Peter is a man. And no, this wasn't about sex. Peter had a deeper need—*a need to belong and be accepted.* Luke 5:10–11 (CSB) is Jesus's response to Peter and what happened afterward:

> "Don't be afraid," Jesus told Simon. "From now on you will be catching people. Then they brought the boats to land, left everything, and followed him."

Peter left everything for love and acceptance, not sex. Finally, Peter belonged. Jesus and Peter's story does not end there. Jesus predicted Peter would deny Him three times before the rooster crows.[56] When it happened, all gospel accounts say that Peter wept bitterly. He was a broken man who learned he was not who he presented himself to be. But that's not the end of the story. Peter still needed love and acceptance—*not sex.* He needed to be reminded to whom he belonged, and that in and of himself, he could do nothing. Jesus restores Peter's love for him and the brothers in John 21. Three times, Jesus establishes the foundation of His relationship with Peter. What is that foundational need—*love, acceptance, belonging, community.*

---

[56] Matthew 26:34, 75; Mark 14:30, 72; Luke 22:34, 61

Oftentimes, what we seek is not what we need. And when left to our own creative minds, we are easily deceived. That's why relationships are so important. That's why marriage matters. Your spouse helps you see who you are and who you are not. Peter thought he was many things until Jesus unseated him from his own throne. Your spouse displays an aspect of God's glory, that is, a light that shines in your darkness. Your spouse is salt to season you, salt to cleanse and deliver you, and salt to preserve you to the Day of Jesus's return. When we celebrate the aspect of God's glory revealed in our spouse, we receive some of the answers to our needs. But also we enjoy the benefits of truth and grace. Truth frees us. And grace enables us to yield to new ways of thinking and acting. Isn't this the transformation to which we are called?

God always supplies our needs. He promised to do so. He does not lie. He gives us an analogy in Matthew 6:25–33:

> Therefore, I tell you: Don't worry about your life, what you will eat or what you will drink; or about your body, what you will wear. Isn't life more than food and the body more than clothing? Consider the birds of the sky: They don't sow or reap or gather into barns, yet your heavenly Father feeds them. Aren't you worth more than they? Can any of you add one moment to his life span by worrying? And why do you worry about clothes? Observe how the wildflowers of the field grow: They don't labor or spin thread. Yet I tell you that not even Solomon in all his splendor was adorned like one of these. If that's how God clothes the grass of the field, which is here today and thrown into the furnace tomorrow, won't he do much more for you—you of little faith? So don't worry, saying, "What will we eat?" or "What will we drink?" or "What will we wear?" For the Gentiles eagerly seek all these things, and your heavenly Father knows that you

need them. But seek first the kingdom of God and his righteousness, and all these things will be provided for you.

Let me repeat. God always supplies our needs whether physical, mental, emotional, or spiritual. He uses relationships to accomplish this. That's why our relationship with Him, ourselves, and others matter. This is how He supplies our needs. Our failure to experience the satisfaction of our needs being met is not for lack of supply nor for shortage of people. When we lack emotional and/or physical fulfillment it may be that we have confused what we need with what we want. God meets needs. So, if we misunderstand our true need, then it can lead us to think God has not answered us.

Disguises further prevent us from identifying the opportunities God provides to meet our needs. We cannot pretend to be someone or something we are not, to get what we need and want. It is dishonest. Sometimes, we are deceived into thinking that what we seek is what we need. Finally, while we may have identified a real need, there could be a greater need which God is answering. We perceive this as God not answering us, when in fact He has already. For example, consider the husband or wife, either of whom grew up as the center of attention at home, the teacher's pet at school, and the star of the sports team. Many years later, they marry. They feel like they are suffering from the lack of attention from their spouse. To hear them tell it, their spouse is being cruel, insensitive, and uncaring. That's because, being the center of attention, they sincerely believe that their primary need is for attention.

Does this spouse require attention? Yes, it's part of feeling accepted and connected in marriage. But might they also need to learn how to be alone without constant attention from others? Perhaps, the lack of attention from a spouse serves this need. This does not mean the spouse's reasons for being inattentive are right. But we are not talking about why he or she is inattentive. We are talking about God isolating and answering the higher need to be alone and okay. To retain our freedom and maintain our authority, we must have the ability to be alone and okay.

Knowing What You Really Need

Here's where you must make a choice. You can continue to believe "need theology." That is, your needs are fixed by gender. Religion uses an exchange formula as the basis for getting these needs met. If you and your spouse fit these gender stereotypes, then this model may work well for you. If so, carry on.

For those of you that don't fit gender stereotypes or the exchange theory of meeting your needs isn't working and you are tired and wasting away from thirst for an alternative, there is hope. The wait is over. *Unveiled Love* is the thirst quencher. It's about using your freedom and authority to rely on God to meet your needs. It's about learning how to identify your need and/or the highest priority need that God is faithfully answering.

But first, give yourself permission to not fit the gender stereotype. You are no less of a woman or man because you defy the labels and behaviors traditional marriage approaches assign you. As a group, men are similar. Within the group, each one is unique. The same is true for women. As a group, they are similar. But within the group, each one is different. You are not a stereotype or a label. You are a person. You are God's unrepeatable miracle. There is no one exactly like you. It's also true of your spouse. He or she is a person and God's unrepeatable miracle. There is no one exactly like your spouse. Therefore, there is no other marriage exactly like the one you create together. You are free. Reclaim your freedom and use your authority to declare your freedom from a religious marriage.

Now set your spouse free. Keep in mind, when you do, you are letting go of all the expectations religion has assigned. You can no longer hold your spouse hostage to perform to these expectations. Nor can you retaliate when your spouse doesn't live up to what you think is right and best. Freeing your spouse means accepting them as they are, forgiving them when their actions harm you, and, at times separating yourselves to ensure the health and safety of all. This is *Unveiled Love*.

Identifying Your Highest Need

There are many ways to identify the main thing God is answering for you. The main thing today, hopefully, is not the main thing next year or the year after that. When we exercise the answer to our need by continuously responding, something amazing happens. Eventually, the answer exercises us. When this happens, we no longer think about it. We just do it. It has become a habit and finally a way of life. It's who we are, that is who we become. A simple example will suffice.

With help from the Holy Spirit, I decided that I needed to be more kind. So I prayed for kindness. I received the kindness of God. Then I began to declare the words, "I am kind." I did this for some time. Then one day, the Holy Spirit started showing me when I was kind to someone. It made me happy. But what made me even happier was when others voluntarily began to tell me how kind I was. I wasn't trying to be kind. I was kind. I am kind. I am the kindness of God.

It is important to note that while others benefit from my kindness, I didn't become kind for them nor to get something from them. I needed to be more kind because this reflects my Father and God. The Holy Spirit helped me to see my need for kindness through the response of others. I have been told that I can be unkind. That I speak as a matter of fact can push others away. And my silence can come across as unkind and judgmental. Instead of refuting other's experiences of me, I asked God about it. I concluded that I needed to be more kind to others. It worked together for the good of all! Now I am free to talk to God about the next need He is answering. You see, He and I have a running dialogue.

We will have many needs over the course of our lives. All All need to cultivate all the fruits of the Spirit found in Galatians 5:22–23 (CSB). Kindness is only one of them. In addition to the fruits of the Spirit, we also have some core emotional needs.

Core Emotional Needs

Core emotional needs are those needs unique to all human beings everywhere, all the time, regardless of gender or marital status. They are top shelf needs, meaning they are the highest emotional needs we possess. They include the need to belong, the need for significance, the need for authority, and the need to reconcile good and bad. When we belong, we experience acceptance, approval, affirmation, and others advocating on our behalf.

We also need to feel significant, that is that our lives mean something. We need to mean something to ourselves and others. Experiencing significance depends on our freedom and ability to act independently, apart from others. To mean something requires that we do something. We need to be able to think and act independent of others. It also involves being able to establish boundaries—*even in marriage*. Townsend and Cloud wrote an excellent book on establishing healthy boundaries in marriage. It is called *Boundaries in Marriage* (1999). Boundaries protect and preserve the freedom and authority of each one to govern his or her life. We need healthy boundaries to develop and become who God created each one to significantly be.

This leads to the next core emotional need: authority. Each of us has the right to make decisions for ourselves. When appropriate, we also have the responsibility to yield to decisions made by others. In marriage, this looks like submitting one to another. Ephesians 5:21 (CSB) reads:

Submitting to one another in the fear of Christ.

How we respond to take authority and how we receive authority matters. Authority is spiritual and emotional. We feel good when we take authority, follow through, finish, and succeed at something. We feel hurt and suffer when others abuse their authority in relationship with us.

A final core emotional need is reconciling our past and present, our goodness and badness, our lovely and unlovely part. Emotional health and wholeness require the integration of the fragments of our lives. I like the way scripture says it. After feeding the five thousand to their fill, Jesus told his disciples the following in John 6:12–13:

> "Collect the leftovers so that nothing is wasted."
> So, they collected them and filled twelve baskets
> with the pieces from the five barley loaves that
> were left over by those who had eaten.

Nothing of your life will be wasted in the fulfillment of your God-given purpose. All must work together for the good of them that love God and have been called according to His purpose.[57]

How these needs are addressed by our parents, teachers, and church leaders matter. How we respond also matters. How we respond eventually becomes the way we address these needs when presented by others. So getting our core emotional needs answered in healthy ways plays a central role in who we are, who we will become, and how we interact with.

Typically, emotional needs are downgraded, disguised, or ignored altogether. Still, our core emotional needs drive much of our behavior. That we do not see it, admit it, or simply refuse to address it interferes with our ability to experience personal and relational fulfillment. Unavoidably, we suffer as well as those in relationship with us.

Our best hope is in identifying our core emotional needs and engaging the opportunities God provides (and allows) to answer them. So how can you learn more about your core emotional needs?

Feedback

When we get information from others about our behavior, we experience feedback. Whether requested or not, feedback is import-

---

57. Romans 8:28

ant to growth and change. Solomon offers us a reason why in Proverbs 16:2 (CSB), repeating himself in Proverbs 21:2:

> All a person's ways seem right to him, but the
> Lord weighs motives.

In other words, our ways or patterns of interacting with others seem clean, innocent, and pure to us. But our motives can betray our behavior. We can be doing what seems right, yet our motives, our true self will land us in the plot of destruction. Proverbs 14:12 (CSB) agrees:

> There is a way that seems right to a person, but
> its end is the way to death.

Sometimes, we do the right thing with the wrong motives. Others may not have a clue and even benefit from our actions. But God sees. In Hebrews 4:12–13, Paul shares just how deeply God examines into us:

> For we have the living Word of God, which is full of energy, like a two-mouthed sword. It will even penetrate to the very core of our being where soul and spirit, bone and marrow meet! It interprets and reveals the true thoughts and secret motives of our hearts. There is not one person who can hide their thoughts from God, for nothing that we do remains a secret, and nothing created is concealed, but everything is exposed and defenseless before his eyes, to whom we must render an account.

God is not fooled by us confusing our needs with wants and desires, nor is He deceived by our disguises. He certainly knows that what we seek is very often just the opposite of what we need.

Accepting and asking for feedback from others is one way God helps us to see what He sees in us, whether good or bad.

Our spouse is a valuable source of information. That's because our spouse sees and experiences us like no others. I have often said that our spouse is our sobriety program. That's because all young couples in age or emotional maturity come to marriage full of themselves, *intoxicated if you will.* A husband and wife effortlessly facilitate the other's withdrawal experience. In marriage, God uses our spouse to break our dependence on our emotional survival skills. The degree of withdrawal we suffer depends on the severity of our emotional attachment to impure motives. How we respond when our spouse gets close to an impure motive is telling.

Every time Sharon brought up anything having to do with spending money, Ray would cringe. Though not present, I could almost hear him saying, "What now?" Ray and Sharon had recurring breakdowns around money. She was a spender, he was frugal. Sharon, my client, told me that Ray became visibly distressed whenever kids' clothing needs, house repairs, or the word "vacation" came up. Ray preferred to eat at home, recreate at home, and save money. When it got intense, Ray wouldn't eat and had trouble sleeping. Sharon recognized his anguish. Ray would become irritable, critical of her and the kids, and unable to take part in pleasurable social activities.

Sharon triggered Ray's discomfort. She wasn't trying to make him uncomfortable. Growing up, she had a different experience with money. Money was always available when needed. Seldom did she hear the word "No" when it came to spending money. Unlike Ray, Sharon's attitude about money is that it's plentiful. Ray grew up differently. There never seemed to be enough money for basic needs. His parents scrimped and scrounged to make ends meet. So Ray decided the answer to this dilemma was to save money at all costs. It cost him personal enjoyment, friendships, and it was undermining his marriage. Ray believed that he would not have enough money to make ends meet. Therefore, if he was going to survive, then he must save all the money he can.

The problem for Ray is that Jesus Christ does not advocate keeping ourselves alive. Here is what Jesus did say:

> If you truly want to follow me, you should at once completely reject and disown your own life. And you must be willing to share my cross and experience it as your own, as you continually surrender to my ways. For if you choose self-sacrifice and lose your lives for my glory, you will continually discover true life. But if you choose to keep your lives for yourselves, you will forfeit what you try to keep. For even if you were to gain all the wealth and power of this world—at the cost of your own life—what good would that be? And what could be more valuable to you than your own soul?[58]

Much of Ray and Sharon's recurring conflict revolves around their competing beliefs and motivations about money. Money is not the problem. It can do nothing on its own. Rather, the problem is their rival responses to money. Beneath their problem is the need for each one to develop more godly ideas and motivations about money and how to use it effectively—*to the benefit of their family*. Until they do, Ray and Sharon will continue to experience conflict about money. That's because recurring conflict happens when we refuse to change our mind and grow up emotionally. Toward the end of the most renown chapter on love, Paul has this to say:

> When I was a child, I talked like a child, I thought like a child, I reasoned like a child; now that I have become a man, I am done with childish ways and have put them aside.

Both Ray and Sharon were living and relating to each other the way each was raised. Marriage is an invitation to live the way we were created and made.

---

[58] Matthew 16:24–26

Without even trying, Ray and Sharon were giving each other useful feedback to evaluate their own behavior. They could continue blaming one another and advance no further in their relationship or they could use feedback to change their minds. George Bernard Shaw, playwright and political activist said:

> Progress without change is impossible and he that cannot change his mind cannot change anything.[59]

Feedback is vital. Our spouse sees what we don't see about ourselves. Some of what they see is good, like those glory aspects of God we possess. Some of what they see isn't so good, but helpful. What irritates your spouse about you? What does your spouse think you do too much or too little? What beliefs and attitudes do you hold that contend with your spouse?

Feedback helps us to get below the surface. Core emotional needs are buried and must be dug up. The impure motive behind your spouse's feedback does not sway the truth. Your spouse's motive may be self-serving, even hurtful. Their motive is not your concern. The information is what you require. It's the information that's valuable in identifying core emotional need.

Whenever and from whomever we are given information that impacts us (whether praise or criticism), it is advisable to talk with God about it. God will always confirm truth in the mouth of two or three or more witnesses. If two or three or more unrelated people share the same unpleasant experience with you, it is fact. Second Corinthians 13:1 (CSB) establishes this truth:

> This is the third time I am coming to you. Every matter must be established by the testimony of two or three witnesses.

---

[59] https://www.brainyquote.com/quotes/george_bernard_shaw_386923

Our spouse, parents, children, siblings, friends, employers, coworkers, church leaders, and church family, virtually anyone can be a valuable source of information in assisting you in identifying your core need.

Without requesting feedback, we can simply pay attention to how others respond to us across environments. With only shades of difference, how we are at home is how we are at church is how we are at work. That's because wherever we go, there we are and will be. For the cleverest among us, it's only a matter of time before you show up in all your pride and man-made glory.

Our Conscience

Our conscience is also an important mediator in revealing need. Our conscience alerts us to right and wrong and truth and error. Paul speaking about the Gentiles in Romans 2:15–16 (CSB) has this to say about our conscience:

> They (the Gentiles) show that the work of the law is written on their hearts. Their consciences confirm this. Their competing thoughts either accuse or even excuse them on the day when God judges what people have kept secret, according to my gospel through Christ Jesus.

The Bible uses various words to describe the many states of conscience. Here are a few adjectives: good, clear, weak, defiled, as belonging to you, seared, clean and evil.[60] All suggest the various possible conditions of our conscience. Albeit there is overwhelming scripture support that we maintain a clear conscience.

Still, God and Christ are the final authority in all. Paul says even though he may have a clear conscience, it is still up to God to decide all matter concerning him. First Corinthians 4:4 (CSB) explains it this way:

---

[60] Acts 23:1, 24:16; 1 Corinthians 8:7, 10; 2 Corinthians 2:12; 1 Timothy 4:2; Titus 1:15; Hebrews 9:12, 10:22.

> For I am not conscious of anything against myself, but I am not justified by this. It is the Lord who judges me.

That's why taking all things to God in prayer, conversation, and then sitting silently is vital. God gave us a conscience so that we could learn what pleases Him from that which doesn't. If we watch and listen, our conscience is a wonderful aid in identifying our need. We all have had the experience of saying or doing something we shouldn't and then feel bad. That's our conscience at work. And if we are still enough in that moment, we can learn the reason for our behavior.

Aside from feedback, taking note of others' responses to us and paying attention to our conscience, consequences, and recurring conflict also expose needs. Repeated distasteful consequences have a way of slowing us down that we may evaluate what we are doing and why. Penalties are informative. They give us the opportunity to make changes. Spouses are ill-advised in using rewards, punishments, and ultimatums to control each other. It may work but ultimately to the demise of the relationship. Naturally occurring consequences are far more effective and sustainable than anything manufactured.

Recurring Conflict

Conflict is God's request for your disguise so that He can reveal more of Himself in you. Recurring conflict is the refusal to give God that which he desires. That a conflict is repeated suggests there is an underlying unanswered need. While refusing, neither our best prayers nor our most earnest efforts will bring about the change we desire to see. Only by yielding to truth do we gain freedom to change and experience lasting personal and relational fulfillment. When there is recurring conflict, both husband and wife contribute. Each one brings a problem that hides a need. How this works, along with the questionnaires to identify core emotional needs, is the subject of another book. But for those that can't wait, counseling and coaching can help cut to the chase.

The goal is not to change your behavior. The goal is to heal the mind and emotions that produce the undesirable behavior. It's the difference between addressing the roots of conflict and the fruit of conflict. While the latter may result in temporary change and improvement, it seldom lasts. If this interests you, then visit www.kimmoore.org and sign up for one-on-one coaching or consider taking part in a seminar or workshop.

The Big Idea Here Is This

God meets needs. Therefore, relying on God to meet our needs is safe, secure, and most effective. He is faithful and never forsakes those in right standing with Him.

When we rely on God to meet our needs, we maintain our freedom. When God does use our spouse to meet a need or desire we possess, gratefulness is our natural response. That's because we have relinquished expectation. Our spouse is free to answer or not. Who we are neither rises or falls on what our spouse chooses to do or not do for us or with us. And when they do supply our need or fulfill our desire, we can receive it with a clear conscience. Ironically and miraculously, it is freedom from your spouse that brings you closer to your spouse. When God is our provider, we are free!

Questions to Learn By

1. The three most cited problems in marriage are communication, sex, and money. But the author says problems are unaddressed needs. Do you agree? Why or why not?
2. What is the difference between a problem and a need?
3. What are some reasons it is difficult to connect the dots between present behavior and past experiences?
4. How does the author define a core emotional need?

Questions to Grow By

1. In the example of Ron and Dina's sexual problem, what underlying needs could be in play? (There is no right or wrong answer; be creative.)
2. What are some reasons you or your spouse might be resistant to exploring emotional needs?
3. The author writes about connecting the dots. Can you identify and trace your present unhealthy reactions to past experiences? Explain.
4. Dina always had something to do when Ron invited her to have sex. Do you observe any patterns in your responses when invited to be intimate and sexual?

Questions to Change By

1. What feedback have you received from your spouse? What irritates your spouse about you? When you break down, what is the one thing they say repeatedly? How have you responded?
2. Examine a recurring conflict in your relationship and answer the following questions. *
    a. What triggered the conflict?
    b. What was your spoken expectation?
    c. What was your unspoken hope?
    d. Did you feel defensive? Why?
    e. What did you fear?
    f. What disguise might you have worn?
    g. What might all this tell you about your real need?

*These questions are intended to assist you in digging deeper into what really is taking place in your relationship. No one answer establishes an emotional need. But together, they are intended to provide you with information valuable in identifying your core emotional needs. If you desire help in processing your answers and desire to go further, please visit www.kimmoore.org

Part III—Go!

The swimmer dives in and swims when the horn sounds. Through countless hours of practice the athlete has learned to "live" in the water, allowed all the coaching to guide every stroke, endured the forces of the water acting against every movement, and finally touching the wall at the finish. In Part III, we will learn to live in Christ let God do the correcting, endure the forces of contradiction, and celebrate the victory of finishing the race.

> Don't you realize that in a race everyone *swims*, but only one person gets the prize? So *swim* to win! All athletes are disciplined in their training. They do it to win a prize that will fade away, but we do it for an eternal prize. So I *swim* with purpose in every *stroke*. I am not just shadowboxing. I discipline my body like an athlete, training it to do what it should. Otherwise, I fear that after preaching to others I myself might be disqualified (1 Corinthians 9:24-27, personal paraphrase of the verse, adapted by author to portray a swimmer rather than a runner).

Secret 7

Live in Christ

For in Him we live and move and exist [that is, in Him we actually have our being], as even some of your own poets have said, "For we also are His children." (Acts 17:28 AMP))

I remember a difficult lesson I learned about living in Christ and honoring God before my ex-husband. We were having a series of hard conversations about some of the internal challenges we were facing in our relationship. We needed to make some tough decisions. The conversations were emotionally charged and ended before we could agree on a way forward. I decided to pray and ask God to intervene. I asked God to cleanse me of the need to be right, the temptation to blame, and any other hindrance to us finding a solution. A few days later, I approached him to have a conversation. Although he obliged me, talks inevitably broke down again. He left the house, and I ran to our bedroom, threw myself on the bed and cried. I prayed. I asked for help. And it didn't work out! So I asked God what I should do. I believe God told me to make his favorite meal, and I did.

I let him know what I had made. He replied that he was not hungry and did not know when he would be home. Upon hanging up, I ran to our bedroom and hurled myself on the bed again! I cried even harder. I was beside myself. I did not understand.

Then I heard the Father's voice gently say to me, "Kim, who told you to make his favorite meal?"

I said, "You did, Father."

And then He said these words to me, "I am well pleased, My good and faithful servant."

I was startled because I expected that when I followed God's instructions, everything would turn out all right between us. And then I heard these words, "Kim, sometimes what you do for me must be enough—especially when you don't get the outcome you desire."

Our response in marriage must be to please God first and foremost. Sometimes, it will work out in our relationships. But when it does not, our peace is in knowing we responded to God in the name of Jesus Christ, our Lord. This is what I learned "living in Christ" meant. Rather than living in and at the whim of my spouse, I was to live as unto God and Christ. Colossians 3:17 (AMPC) clarifies.

> And whatever you do [no matter what it is] in word or deed, do everything in the name of the Lord Jesus and in [dependence upon] His Person, giving praise to God the Father through Him.

No matter how much we may try, we will not be able to please our spouse all the time and in every situation. What I learned that day was this: my greatest need is for communion with God, by living in Christ. Moreover, that I am welded together with Christ in an ever-growing, unbreakable bond of trust.

I once heard it said that men and women marry to become one, then fight over which one of them they are going to become. Though we might like to think this, God had neither you nor your spouse in mind. Husbands and wives' best hope and opportunity to experience ongoing oneness is to live in Christ. We can only experience true unity by living in Christ. The goal of living in Christ is that each one might experience unity with God, self, and others. Unity affords each one rest, as well as an opportunity to work together.

Living in Christ requires each one to surrender his or her emotional weapons to God and allow Him to turn them into building tools. In the process, we become undefended souls, maturing as we face fear, focusing on commonalities and celebrating differences. To do this each one of us must reclaim freedom and authority taking responsibility for our own life. When we receive God's love, we grow in confidence that He will meet our needs. Then we are available to fully live in Christ. When we are living in Christ, our mind, will, and emotions are governed by God's Holy Spirit. That Paul was persuaded of these things nourished and perfected his ability to respond to God and others. When expressing gratitude to the Philippians for their care and support, Paul had this to say:

> I don't say this out of need, for I have learned to be content in whatever circumstances I find myself. I know how to make do with little, and I know how to make do with a lot. In any and all circumstances I have learned the secret of being content—whether well fed or hungry, whether in abundance or in need. I am able to do all things through him who strengthens me. Still, you did well by partnering with me in my hardship.[61]

We have already discussed Paul's plea and God's response to removing the thorn from his side. God said that His grace was sufficient. The thorn remained. Whatever Paul's highest need, it was not to be thornless. I say this to assure you that I realize marriage is not always a walk in the park. Sometimes, it is difficult and painful. But it doesn't have to be easy, just possible. And it is possible that two similar and, at the same time, dissimilar people can become one in Christ. Jesus said so in Matthew 19:5, 26 and Mark 10:8, 27 (CSB).

> And the two will become one flesh. So they are no longer two, but one flesh. With man this is impossible, but with God all things are possible.

---

[61] Philippians 4:11–14 (CSB)

Admitting His soul was overwhelmed with anxiety, suffering to the point of feeling like He was dying, Jesus appeals to His Father in Mark 14:36 (TPT).

> Abba, my Father, all things are possible for you. Please—remove this cup of suffering! Yet what I want is not important, for I only desire to fulfill your plan for me.

Husband, wife, it doesn't have to be easy, only possible. Someone must go first. Learning to live in Christ is the way to true unity in marriage. It is the only way to experience the unity known to Father, Son, and Holy Spirit. In Jesus's long appeal to the Father, four times, He requests and declares that we may be one. John 17:11 (CSB) makes plain God's intention for us that believe whether married or not.

> I am no longer in the world, but they are in the world, and I am coming to you. Holy Father, protect them by your name that you have given me, so that they may be one as we are one.

Verses 21–23 (CSB) read as follows.

> May they all be one, as you, Father, are in me and I am in you. May they also be in us, so that the world may believe you sent me. I have given them the glory you have given me, so that they may be one as we are one. I am in them and you are in me, so that they may be made completely one, that the world may know you have sent me and have loved them as you have loved me.

Jesus said that we, inclusive of husbands and wives who believe, are in the Father and in Him. He also says that He is in us, as the Father is in Him. This is how we can be made whole and one. Husbands and wives can be made whole and experience unity in so much as they each live in Christ and surrender to God's Word and the Holy Spirit within. God's life-transforming glory is revealed in each one to the degree of their surrender. It may be that one spouse is not living in Christ. Still, the spouse that is living in Christ and surrendering to God's Word and the Holy Spirit within can experience unity with God. This means it only takes one to surrender completely to facilitate change in his or her spouse. This is the power of *Unveiled Love*. It takes one person working together with God to enable change.

That's why I found it puzzling when a Christian wife in a Facebook group asked how to approach a husband engaging in pornography. Here are her words and my response: "Please don't ask me to leave him. I have had plenty I could have left him for over the years, but I am committed to working this out with him." [sic] She goes on to say, "He denied it. He gets angry to the point of sleeping on the couch. He has no remorse. As far as I know, he is not in a good place spiritually—I just don't know how to approach him on it. I don't want to let it just fly."

In my response, I first quoted her words beginning with "He denied it." And then offered this: So you want to know how to approach someone who is neither listening to you nor choosing you, because you don't want to let it fly? I went on to suggest that she did not need to leave him, even though it sounded like he had virtually left her. Since he is not listening to her, stop talking to him and instead talk to God. A better course of action would be to ask the question, "Father, how would you have me conduct myself given his choices?" Then I explained that when she loves God first, she will love him best—*whatever that looks like.*

When this wife fully surrenders to God at whatever cost to her or the marriage, she will serve her husband best. Moreover, living in Christ by answering God is her best hope in salvaging her relationship and experiencing unity with her husband. But first, she would do well to come into unity with God. So what does true unity look like? What is false unity, and how exactly do we live in Christ?

True Unity

True unity is when at least two fully functioning, self-contained, self-sustaining units rest and work in conjunction with one another. *Unveiled Love* primarily focuses on the spirit and soul of each unit. Our spirit, mind, will, and emotions make up the brain and guts of human life. In marriage, you might think that the unit of one man and one woman would be equal to the sum two units added together. Yet the secret of living in Christ is that husband and wife together are greater than the sum of their units. It is a synergy that forms a unity. Marriage is the richest, most creative, and productive human relationship available to men and women. For true unity to occur each unit must be able to independently think, feel, decide, act, and respond of his and her own free will. Of course, there are circumstances in which one unit might be impaired and require more help from the other. When *Unveiled Love* is present, the grace of God makes this possible.

Christopher Reeve and his wife, Dana, immediately come to mind. They are a couple; one had a chronic illness which required greater dependency on his wife. You may remember Christopher Reeve as the star in the movie *Superman (1978)*. In 1995, after just three years of marriage to Dana, Christopher broke his neck in an equestrian competition and was paralyzed from the neck down. A beautiful relationship was observed in the aftermath of the accident. Dana assumed the burden for his care, remained with Christopher, and continued that care until his death in 2004, almost a decade later.

Christopher and Dana found a way to make their relationship work despite drastic changes in his ability to interact normally. That's what love does. It finds a way. The way may look very different from marriage to marriage. It did for Christopher and Dana. Two units, one of which was impaired, the other a devoted spouse. A synergism and unity greater than the sum of two individuals became a grassroots movement. That movement eventually became the Christopher and Dana Reeves Foundation after the untimely death of Dana in 2006.

True unity is healthy. And it can look different from couple to couple. Many will not face such catastrophic circumstances as the Reeves. Still, Christopher and Dana, each did what they could, and from this a unity was formed. The key to unity is that each unit accepts personal ownership for initiating and responding in the relationship as unto the Lord. Paul makes this plain in Colossians 3:23–24 (TPT).

> Put your heart and soul into every activity you do, as though you are doing it for the Lord himself and not merely for others.
>
> For we know that we will receive a reward, an inheritance from the Lord, as we serve the Lord Yahweh, the Anointed One!

Unity requires us to be all in. Unity is not 50-50. Nor is unity always fair. Unity demands equal sacrifice—giving all that one possesses. And since the measure God gives each one is different, husbands and wives should not expect measures given to be equal. It is only that we give all the measure God gives us.

I like author and founder of the Ancient Hebrew Research Center, Jeff Benner's explanation of unity. We tend to see a person or a thing as one, as in one solid piece. However, Jeff suggests that a man (or woman) is not one. Rather, each person is a collection of body, bones, flesh, organs, and blood, and that together these units form a unity.[62] Benner gives the example of a tree. He says that a tree is the sum of what we see. However, a tree is a unity of roots, branches, leaves, and trunk.

Paul supports Benner's explanation of unity in Romans 12:4–5 (AMPC for emphasis). The explanation follows his warning to us not to conform to this world, but rather to be transformed by the renewing of our minds (verses 1 and 2). And then in verse 3, Paul warns us that thinking more highly of ourselves than appropriate shows a lack

---

[62] Jeff Benner, "Living Words Volume 1," Virtual Bookworm Publishing 2007, https://www.virtualbookworm.com

of understanding and good judgment. Here's the reason Paul gives in verses 4–5.

> For as in one physical body we have many parts (organs, members) and all of these parts do not have the same function or use. So, we, numerous as we are, are one body in Christ (the Messiah) and individually we are parts one of another [mutually dependent on one another].

Just as a tree is a unity of units—roots, trunk, branches, and leaves; so is the Body of Christ of whom each unit is a member. Marriage also is a unity of units, one male and one female. The husband is one fully functioning unit as is the wife. Together, they form a remarkable unity.

Marriage is a relationship of equal units. They are equal in their capabilities to function both independently and together. Despite the erroneous belief that marriage completes us, each unit—male and female—is already complete. We are complete, albeit imperfect. Both husbands and wives have beliefs, attitudes, and behavior that have yet to conform to Christ. This will be the case until we are no longer in these earthly suits and contend with the flesh. Yet and still, marriage has the god-like supernatural ability to host and respond to an unlimited number of variables, circumstances, and outcomes.

Consider that there are just three primary colors. These three colors produce every other color we know and enjoy and even the ones we don't. Here's is the kicker: to make a new color, two or more of the primary colors must surrender their color to the palette. Each color gives up its color to the palette to become a new color. The colors surrender, but not always in equal amounts. Hence, there are variations in shades, tones, and intensity of each new color. Sometimes, these differences are subtle, almost imperceptible. But all new colors arise from just three primary colors.

So it is with marriage. Two fully functioning human beings—male and female that become husband and wife. Each one retaining freedom and the authority to lay down their respective lives only to take them up again. Daily, each one deciding to surrender or not. When we do, we become what Paul calls a living sacrifice.

> Therefore, brothers and sisters, in view of the mercies of God, I urge you to present your bodies as a living sacrifice, holy and pleasing to God; this is your true worship. Do not be conformed to this age, but be transformed by the renewing of your mind, so that you may discern what is the good, pleasing, and perfect will of God.[63]

What is required of each one may be different, but the surrender and sacrifice will be felt the same. For example, an extrovert may give up some socializing with others to the marriage. An introvert may give up time alone to the marriage. Each one will feel the discomforting withdrawal from his or her usual manner and way. That's because marriage is a life for a life. One finds life and renewable energy in being around others. Another finds life and renewable energy in being alone. It's what makes each one come alive. If we did not feel the loss of our life, then we could not know God's life.

Like the three primary units of colors, each husband and wife give up a life to make a brand-new life—*something that never existed before*. Each one still retains his and her identity. Think of marriage as three pieces of paper. There is your piece of paper, your spouse's piece of paper, and then there is a piece of paper called "Us." Every day, each of you decides how much of you, that is your time, your mind, emotions, resources you give to the piece of paper called "Us." Some days, it's more. Other days, it's less. And some days, it may be nothing at all. Whatever each of you places on the paper called "Us" forms a unity of units.

Truth is the only viable, sustainer of unity. The truth is, in marriage, each one is free to govern him and herself. The forming of a

---

[63] Romans 12:1–3 (CSB)

unity occurs as each one surrenders to the Person of Jesus Christ. He is truth. First John 1:6 (CSB) offers this to the conversation.

> If we say, "We have fellowship with him," and yet we walk in darkness, we are lying and are not practicing the truth.

Verse 7 adds:

> If we walk in the light as he himself is in the light, we have fellowship with one another, and the blood of Jesus his Son cleanses us from all sin.

Fellowship is the Greek word, "koinonia." It means community, communion, joint participation, and even intercourse. All these words express individual units forming a unity. True unity is more than externally agreeing with another. Forming a unity is an internal experience that manifests in outward behavior. This kind of unity can handle the irrefutable differences between husbands and wives. Not only can true unity handle these differences but also capitalizes on them to produce something far more magnificent than husband or wife can alone.

Unity in marriage is experienced when each one is accepted and respected as an independent unit, taking part of his and her own free will—*a decision as changeable as the weather*. And this is what makes marriage a scary proposition. All attempts to control this decision erode each other's freedom.

But even as fickle and unfaithful as we all can be, God leaves the choice up to us. He did so when He planted two types of trees in the Garden of Eden. And He does so, each time a man and a woman say, "I do." Despite all, marriage is a beautiful, splendid mixing of colors to produce an infinite number of new color variations! That husbands and wives aren't coloring and making new and beautiful variations of love and life is sad. Even more heart-breaking are the many forms of false unity of Christian marriage that litter the landscape.

False Unity

When we do not possess truth, we are prone to lie. That's because we become the prey and victims of the Father of lies. When speaking to the Jews, this is what Jesus calls the devil in John 8:43–45 (CSB).

> Why don't you understand what I say? Because you cannot listen to my word. You are of your father the devil, and you want to carry out your father's desires. He was a murderer from the beginning and does not stand in the truth, because there is no truth in him. When he tells a lie, he speaks from his own nature, because he is a liar and the father of lies. Yet because I tell the truth, you do not believe me.

When we do not have the truth, we tend to make up things that appear true. This is not new. We inherited this inclination from Adam and the Woman. After losing the true covering of God, they made up what appeared to be a covering. Genesis 3:7 explains.

> Then the eyes of both of them were opened, and they knew they were naked; so they sewed fig leaves together and made coverings for themselves.

Aware of their spiritual nakedness and need for cover, they attempted to conceal their bodies with fig leaves. The only ones deceived by this charade were Adam and Woman. God's response to their pretense is recorded in Genesis 3:21 (CSB)

> The Lord God made clothing from (animal) skins for the man and his wife and He clothed them.

God never intended something dead or artificial to replace living and genuine. Like many today, Adam and Eve failed to understand this one thing. No external human effort, no matter how clever or emotionally and physically satisfying will ever meet our internal requirement for God, Himself. God is holy and unyielding to pretense. Here's what Hebrews 10:1–4 (TPT) says about external efforts to satisfy His holiness.

> The old system of living under the law presented us with only a faint shadow, a crude outline of the reality of the wonderful blessings to come. Even with its steady stream of sacrifices offered year after year, there still was nothing that could make our hearts perfect before God. For if animal sacrifices could once and for all eliminate sin, they would have ceased to be offered and the worshipers would have clean consciences. Instead, once was not enough so by the repetitive sacrifices year after year, the worshipers were continually reminded of their sins, with their hearts still impure. For what power does the blood of bulls and goats have to remove sin's guilt?

We seldom hear these verses as it relates to marriage. However, I suggest that whenever we try to accomplish unity by external activities alone it is forced and false. Any method to achieve unity in marriage, other than living in Jesus Christ and surrendering to His cross, is false unity. True unity is brought about from the inside out. Sadly today, many husbands and wives feign unity. Here are some of the ways they do.

Peacekeeping

In Secret #6 we spoke about the disguises we wear, that is, how we pretend to be something or someone we are not to get what we want. Jackie wanted to maintain peace and harmony in her marriage.

Toward this end, Jackie avoided confrontation. Earlier in life and before marriage, Jackie learned that disagreements triggered rejection. It was something she watched repeatedly growing up. When Dad disagreed with Mom, her mom became caustic, then silent and emotionally unavailable. Jackie empathized with her dad. She learned that opposing those you love is costly. She believes that keeping the peace with her husband, Ted, is the best way to maintain his affection and harmony in their relationship. Even when Ted's actions result in mental, emotional, physical, and financial hardship, Jackie goes to great lengths to avoid confrontation. She minimizes her pain by refusing to admit when Ted hurts her feelings. But this simply relieves Ted of taking responsibility for his actions and the wake he leaves.

This scenario could just as easily be reversed. For example, consider the husband who avoids conflict. He assumes responsibility for his wife's feelings by managing and adapting his own. He apologizes first and often. He avoids the emotional discomfort of his wife being angry with him. Both husbands and wives can be devout peacekeepers. At the risk of losing relationship, these are unwilling to show up, say what they think or feel. Husbands and wives need not be doormats for their spouse. Saying "No," objecting, and disagreeing with a spouse does not mean the relationship is over. Healthy relationships require boundaries to protect the sanctity of each unit. Each unit must retain his or her freedom and authority to think, decide, and act independently. When a husband or wife engages in peacekeeping, otherwise known as people-pleasing, they forfeit their freedom and authority to govern their life.

Peacekeeping is false unity because it requires the person to be disloyal to God, dishonest to self, and others. True unity requires two fully functioning, independent units willfully converging in Christ. True unity not only welcomes diversity of thought, but it also manages opposing opinions. A friend once asked for prayer that God would save her marriage. I told her that God had not abandoned her marriage. And instead, we might ask God to show us all the ways He could restore her husband to their marriage. Moreover, what role God might have her play. Sometimes, we must go to war to make peace. That means we must become peacemakers, rather than peacekeepers. Peacekeeping undermines the sincere and godly desire for unity in marriage—for this reason it is false unity.

Hierarchy as the Foundation

When husbands and wives organize their relationship around positions, ranks, and roles, they may appear united. We use positions, ranks, and roles to conduct business and go to war. And indeed, Christian marriages must engage the business of God and often find themselves engaged in war on behalf of God. Business and war require agreement and the alignment of those taking part to accomplish objectives. Effectiveness relies on what each one will do to ensure the success of all. But neither business nor war require emotional attachment. In fact, emotional vulnerability in business and war is a sure way to defeat. I am aware that a trending topic in business is emotional intelligence. The purpose of such intelligence is to connect with those a leader desires to influence. Emotion and motivation are related forces that drive behavior. Though relatively new to business, the importance of emotions is not new to God.

First, marriage is about who each one will become in relationship to the other. We are spirit beings. We are also human, living souls.[64] As souls we are made up of mind, will, and emotions. We think, feel, and decide. It's who we are and what we use to become. Who we become in marriage is equally, if not more important than what we do through marriage.

Troy, a client tells me the following: "We get along, rarely argue. We go to church and volunteer—me with the youth, Jill with the choir. We attend the kids' baseball and soccer practices and games. But basically, we live as roommates." Troy and Jill's interactions revolve around tasks associated with typical positions and roles. Troy provides the lion share of income. Jill does work part-time while their children are in school. She buys the food, prepares the meals, cares for the clothing and the house, as well as their children's needs. I

---

[64] Genesis 2:7 (KJ21)

only spoke with Jill on one occasion. She seemed tired, but dutiful. Jill stated her desire to please God in marriage. She reads books on marriage and occasionally talks with their pastor's wife.

According to Troy, they do have sex, albeit not often enough for his wife. He says that their sex life is boring and routine. But he was quick to admit that he puts forth little effort or creativity into their sex life. Pressed further, Troy admitted that he is no longer emotionally or physically attracted to his wife. In the same breath, he also stated that he was neither willing nor ready to explore these feelings further. During our brief work together, I did learn that when idle, Troy liked watching sports and playing virtual video games with people he has met online.

Troy and Jill represent a marriage organized around hierarchy—positions, ranks, and roles. From the outside looking in, they appeared united. Fellow churchgoers say as much. No doubt, both are committed to marriage and their children. However, Troy seems questionably committed to Jill. He showed little interest in showing up and connecting with Jill emotionally. Troy seemed more committed to the effort of staying the way he was than putting forth effort to grow and change. As of this writing, Troy remains married, dutiful in providing for his family, and emotionally unattached to Jill. Jill continues to support her husband by providing domestic help and caring for their children. Troy and Jill's marriage is based on duty. Each one faithfully carries his and her assigned responsibilities. Neither one is happy nor are they united.

Hierarchy as the foundation, instead of Christ, can result in the maintenance of routines of daily living in marriage. It can even result in husbands and wives accomplishing some amazing things together. However, hierarchy will never produce the emotional intimacy required for unity. Only when each one surrenders his and her vulnerability to Christ and each other is true unity in marriage possible. That's because true unity is about who the husband and wife are becoming in relationship to each other. Who you are becoming requires God and your spouse to explore your thoughts and feelings to ultimately influence your actions. This is how we grow and change. When marriage is based on a relationship of equals, husbands and wives have the greatest opportunity to experience healing, wholeness, and unity in Christ.

Hierarchy as a foundation for marriage is false unity because it focuses on the work husbands and wives do together, rather than who they are being together. When laboring together is effective and successful, husbands and wives can appear united. It is also false because Paul makes it clear that Jesus Christ is the foundation of our relationship with God and fellow believers. In 1 Corinthians 3:10–11 (CSB) Paul writes:

> By the grace God has given me, I laid a foundation as a wise builder, and someone else is building on it. But each one should build with care. For no one can lay any foundation other than the one already laid, which is Jesus Christ.

Pursuing Equality

The word "equality" comes from the word "equal." Pursuing equality is promoting the idea and related activities that suggest men and women are interchangeable. They are not. In the natural, a mother will never become a father nor a father a mother. A woman and mother can perform tasks that are routinely assigned to a man and father and vice versa. But this neither makes her male nor him female. God designed us to be human, that is, male and female. Men and women are different.

Husbands and wives are equal. However, the pursuit of interchangeability does not bring about unity. Unity is the result of living in Christ. Humanity is one, made up of male and female. This same principle appears in the Godhead. Deuteronomy 6:4 (CSB) states the following:

> Listen Israel: The Lord our God is one.

In John 17:11, Jesus petitions the Father to make us one as He and the Father are one. The entire book of Ephesians is about the unity available to us in Christ. The first three secrets provide the doctrine and basis of unity. And the last three secrets address the practice of unity. In Ephesians 2:13–14, Paul speaks truth as it applies to the Gentiles and the Jews' relationship. As you read these verses, keep in mind truth transcends all relationships, gender, and marital status. It is true on every level for those that enter Christ through His cross. So while Ephesians 2:13–14 (TPT) focuses on Gentiles and Jews, the truth of Paul's words equally applies to men and women, husbands, and wives.

> Yet look at you now! Everything is new! Although you were once distant and far away from God, now you have been brought delightfully close to him through the sacred blood of Jesus—you have actually been united to Christ! Our reconciling "Peace" is Jesus! He has made Jew and non-Jew one in Christ. By dying as our sacrifice, he has broken down every wall of prejudice that separated us and has now made us equal through our union with Christ. Ethnic hatred has been dissolved by the crucifixion of his precious body on the cross.

That we are equal means we need not make striving for equality our goal. Striving for equality is any variation of making men and women externally the same. Neither outward sameness nor uniformity make husbands and wives united. But proving women can do anything a man can do and vice versa is pointless. There are many things that both men and women can do. There are also some things only men can do. And there are some things only women can do. Women do not carry sperm and men do not carry babies. Women do not ejaculate sperm. Men do not express milk. No amount of wordsmithing, Photoshopping pictures, or prosthetic genitalia will change this. Those that try to persuade otherwise, kick against God's unchangeable truth. All attempts to alter this truth will inevitably fail.

That said, authority and power are spiritual forces. Authority is the right to do something. Power is the ability to do something. Authority and power can be received, engaged, and manifested through men and women, husbands, and wives. As spiritual forces, authority and power are always present—*both the right to do something (or not) and the ability to do something (or not).*

In marriage, typically authority is assigned to husbands and power has been assigned to wives. Husbands lead and declare. Wives follow and do. It is inflexible. However, when true unity is present, a wife might just as easily display the authority, confidence, and expertise in a matter. And a husband may yield his power or skills and abilities to get it done. This flexibility is called submitting one to another. Ephesians 5:21 (CSB) informs us.

> Submit to one another out of reverence for Christ.

Donna and Mike have been married for fifteen years. Both are strong-willed and opinionated. Mike is an attorney and Donna is a tenured professor at a university. The argued—a lot—and in front of me. Neither relented. Neither one was able to self-reflect or had space for the other's concerns. It was like listening to two-year-olds fighting over a toy. Seriously. I was taken aback because both are respected in their careers, their church and among their extended family. Others saw them as a united force with which to reckon. I didn't. Yes, they had money and lived well, but they had zero respect for each other. Did I mention that Mike and Donna profess to be committed Christians? For as educated and successful as they were, Donna and Mike displayed gross disunity. No doubt they were equal—*equally unyielding.* Striving to maintain their equality eroded their ability to trust each other. Moreover, their uniqueness to each other became commonplace and distasteful. Mike and Donna's story ended in disunity and finally divorce.

Of Jesus, Paul says that equality with God was not something worth pursuing.[65] When we seek unity by striving for equality, we erode trust and fail to appreciate the differences that make each marriage unique. Pursuing equality results in false unity because it tends to focus on external uniformity. And uniformity is not unity.

The goal of marriage is not equality, rather unity. This requires equal sacrifice, not equal gifts, talents, skills, abilities, or responsibilities. Equal sacrifice means that the cost of conforming to the truth is the same for husband and wife. Marriage is a life for a life. Anything less tips the scales of justice.

Understandably, some couples experience a lack of equity. Unlike equality, equity is the ideal of justice. There are husbands and wives who take as much as they can, while offering very little of themselves to the marriage. These take advantage of and exploit their spouse for selfish gain. It's the husband who uses provision to control his spouse. A Facebook friend who is Christian and married had this to say: "I am struggling with my husband to be fair with me in the finances. I homeschool our two boys. I have no say in how money is spent. We do not share checking accounts. When I ask for something, it's an automatic 'We can't afford that right now.' I have talked with him about getting a part-time job. All he tells me is that we are doing fine, and I don't need to work. He comes home with new tools and is planning a trip with his side of the family and is very excited. In my heart, I just don't want to go. He doesn't trust me, and I don't feel respected. When I try to tell him how all this makes me feel, he walks away from the conversation. He seems to enjoy the control."

Can you hear her despair? Her spoken desire is for fairness in the use of their money. However, what I hear underneath this is a desire to be included, trusted, and respected in relationship with her husband. This husband and wife are emotionally disconnected and experiencing disunity. Equity or justice can improve how they handle their finances. But true unity is formed where inclusion, trust, and respect are present. Unity recognizes each independent, fully functioning, contributing unit.

---

[65] Philippians 2:5

Pursuing equality as the means to unity is false because it is based on men and women being interchangeable. They are not. Husbands and wives are both equal and unequal. Both possess authority and power to use in the creation of the marriage God desires for them. Flexibility is required as each marriage is different. Each marriage's assignment is different.

Religion

I have written much about the adverse impact of religion on marriage throughout this book. However, it bears repeating here that religion emphasizes outward conformity to rules and regulations. Paul had something to say about this in Ephesians 2:14–16 (CSB).

> In his flesh, he made of no effect the law consisting of commands and expressed in regulations, so that he might create in himself one new man from the two, resulting in peace. He did this so that he might reconcile both to God in one body through the cross by which he put the hostility to death.

The goal of religion is uniformity, not unity. To achieve this, gender-prescribed positions, needs, and roles are assigned to husbands and wives. The difficulty occurs when scripture is used to coerce compliance. When scripture is taken out of context and presented as doctrine rather than instruction, couples feel compelled. A good example of this is sermons on marriage beginning with Ephesians 5:22–26 (CSB).

> Wives, submit to your husbands as to the Lord, because the husband is the head of the wife as Christ is the head of the church. He is the Savior of the body. Now as the church submits to Christ, so also wives are to submit to their husbands in everything. Husbands, love your wives, just as

> Christ loved the church and gave himself for her
> to make her holy, cleansing her with the washing
> of water by the word.

First, let's agree. Doctrine is unchangeable truth. Instructions are changeable. Jesus Christ is the one and only mediator between mankind and God.[66] There is no other name under heaven given whereby men and women are saved.[67] These two statements are doctrines of Christianity. They were, are, and will always be true and unchangeable.

Instructions change depending on situations and circumstances. For instance, Paul instructed Timothy to stop drinking water and instead drink a little wine for his chronic infirmities.[68] However, in Romans 14:21, Paul advises against drinking wine if it offends or weakens a fellow believer. In both scenarios, circumstances impacted Paul's instructions. Unlike doctrine, instructions apply in some cases and not in others. Religion is dismissive of circumstances when promoting the submission of wives to an unruly husband. Ephesians 5:22 is not doctrine. It is not an unchangeable truth. Jesus said that upon the resurrection, no one will marry or be given in marriage.[69] Therefore, the human relationship we call marriage is temporary and not eternal. Doctrine is eternal, instructions are not.

To appreciate the verse Ephesians 5:22, we must zoom out and consider the purpose of the epistle to the Ephesians and then the twenty-one verses that precede verse 22. Ephesians was written by Paul to the faithful believers in Christ, then located in Ephesus. Paul further qualifies this by saying those that believe in Christ and have love for all believers.

The purpose of the epistle to the Ephesians is to establish the basis for unity in Christ and the practicality of unity. The finished work of Jesus Christ is both doctrine and the foundation of unity.

---

[66] 1 Timothy 2:5
[67] Acts 4:11–12
[68] 1 Timothy 5:23
[69] Matthew 22:30; Luke 20:35

Paul lays out the doctrine in Ephesians 1–3. Ephesians 1:9 reveals God's purpose.

> He made known to us the mystery of his will, according to his good pleasure that he purposed in Christ as a plan for the right time—to bring everything together in Christ, both things in heaven and things on earth in him.

Verse 11 says that God works out everything in agreement with this purpose and plan. There is no separate plan for men and another for women. God is gathering all in Christ. And then in chapter 4:1–3 (CSB), Paul tells us that we ought to behave appropriately to the call to unity. He even tells us what this looks like.

> Therefore I, the prisoner in the Lord, urge you to walk worthy of the calling you have received, with all humility and gentleness, with patience, bearing with one another in love, making every effort to keep the unity of the Spirit through the bond of peace.

In verses 4–6 (CSB), Paul emphasizes the origin, foundation, and ongoing basis of unity. Here are his words.

> There is one body and one Spirit—just as you were called to one hope at your calling—one Lord, one faith, one baptism, one God and Father of all, who is above all and through all and in all.

Religion would have husbands and wives believe that unity is the result of fulfilling our positions, titles, adhering to gender roles and meeting each other's gender-based needs. But there is nothing in the above scriptures or in Ephesians 1–4 that directly or indirectly promotes this ideology. The foundation of unity is Christ alone. Living in Christ makes us one. Acts 17:28 says that it is in Christ that we live, move, and exist. Husbands do not live in their wives and wives do not live in their husbands. Who each one is does not rise and fall on the other. Each one is free to think, feel, and decide for him or herself. And when this freedom is surrendered to Christ, it looks like Ephesians 5:1–21.

These are the twenty-one verses before Paul instructs wives to submit to their own husbands. In them, Paul lays out the practical basis for unity. He provides measurable grounds for instructing wives to submit to their own husbands. Note, verses 1–21 apply to all believers—*male and female, husbands and wives.* However, we are addressing these scriptures as related to verse 22 that is, wives submitting to their own husbands. Paul establishes the kinds of behaviors worthy of a wife's submission to her husband. Husbands displaying these behaviors serve as the basis for instructing wives in verse 22. Some of these behaviors include imitating Christ, walking in love, being truthful, thankful, and living sacrificially. But also Paul condemns sexual immorality, greed, rudeness, belittling, crude jokes, drunkenness, and lying among other things. When a husband is practicing the latter behaviors, a wife is under no compulsion to submit to her husband.

Unfortunately, religion has and continues to contribute and perpetuate the abuse of women and wives by insisting they submit to unruly husbands. Religion tells women to pray, trust God, and cover for their husbands, for after all they are only human. But Paul offers this advice in Ephesians 5:8–11 (CSB).

> For you were once darkness, but now you are light in the Lord. Walk as children of light—for the fruit of the light consists of all goodness, righteousness, and truth—testing what is pleasing to the Lord. Don't participate in the fruitless works of darkness, but instead expose them.

In verse 1–20, Paul has some weighty things to say before instructing wives to submit to their own husbands. No human being is perfect. This includes husbands. I do not believe verses 1–20 are meant to be a check-off list. Rather, they provide guidance to evaluate each other's fruitfulness. In marriage, when fruit is either lacking or ungodly a wife (or husband) must decide how to respond. There is no one way to respond. Let us count the ways God might have us respond. Unlike us, God takes everything and everyone into consideration. What may work in one situation may not work in another. In each case, the response could be different yet orchestrated by the same Spirit. Sadly, religion does not permit for such nuances. Verses 18–21 cannot be overlooked as true unity involves these things too.

> And don't get drunk with wine, which leads to reckless living, but be filled by the Spirit: speaking to one another in psalms, hymns, and spiritual songs, singing and making music with your heart to the Lord, giving thanks always for everything to God the Father in the name of our Lord Jesus Christ, submitting to one another in the fear of Christ.

After laying all this groundwork, then Paul says:

> Wives, submit to your husbands as to the Lord, because the husband is the head of the wife as Christ is the head of the church. He is the Savior of the body.

Religion, regardless of the denomination, has no intention of making husbands and wives one. Religion offers false unity. It confuses uniformity with unity. By compelling all husbands and wives to behave the same, they appear unified. True unity develops from the inside out and cannot be regulated by external rules.

Living in Christ

The epistle to the Ephesians provides us the biblical foundation of unity in marriage and shows us what living in Christ looks like.

It is interesting that when John addressed the church at Ephesus in Revelation 2, he praised their work, their effort, and their endurance. He also said that these believers exposed evil and persevered through hardship and remain strong. John commended how well they adhered to some of the groundwork Paul laid out in Ephesians 5:1–21.

Despite this, John condemned their abandonment of the love they had for Christ at first. Here's what John said in Revelation 2:4–5 (TPT).

> But I have this against you: you have abandoned the passionate love you had for me at the beginning. Think about how far you have fallen! Repent and do the works of love you did at first. I will come to you and remove your lampstand from its place of influence if you do not repent.

True unity in marriage requires that we live in Christ. To love Him is to live in Him. That's because when we really love someone, we care about what they think. But not only what they think but also how and why they think as they do. Therefore, if we are going to live in Christ and experience unity in marriage, then His mind must become our utmost concern.

The Mind of Christ

We mature as men and women as we adopt the mind of Christ. Husbands and wives grow deeper, more connected, and intimate with one another as they embrace what Christ thinks, how He thinks, and why He thinks a certain thing. God may not always provide us the how or give us to understand the why, but knowing Christ intimately is worth the asking. It becomes our life-long pursuit, that is, to know *Him—I mean really know Him.* To the extent we know Christ, we are transformed. Paul explains in Philippians 2:5–8 (NIV).

> In your relationships with one another, have the same mindset as Christ Jesus: Who, being in

> very nature God, did not consider equality with God something to be used to his own advantage; rather, he made himself nothing by taking the very nature of a servant, being made in human likeness. And being found in appearance as a man, he humbled himself by becoming obedient to death—even death on a cross!

If we are going to be successful in marriage, then we must change our mind. We must abandon all forms of false unity and embrace this one thing—*the mind of Christ*. We must hold on to, wrestle with, and in all ways engage Christ's mind. And not only His mind but also who He is—*the essence of His being*. He is bread, the way, the truth, the life, the light, a door, and he is human. To live in Christ is our best hope to experience unity in marriage. And to live in Christ, we must hear, receive, and conform to truth.

When we wholeheartedly embrace the mind of Christ, that is truth, we grow, change, and mature. We experience the value and benefit of waiting on God to bring our spouse into this same mind. But this waiting isn't passive. It's active, engaged, and deliberate. But *Unveiled Love* is not forceful. It does not lie, manipulate, cheat, or steal to get what it desires.

Jesus's Example

In the same verses that urge us to adopt the mind of Christ, Paul reveals how Jesus waited and interacted with His disciples as God brought them to truth. These would ultimately not only receive the truth but also proclaim it and give their lives for it. Imagine a marriage in which a husband and wife take in the truth for personal use, then proclaim it in the way they live and interact with each other, their children, and others. What if love motivated them to give up something of value for something or someone of value for something or someone of greater value? I wonder what power God might display through them, what miracles might they perform? What might living in Christ do for our spouse and all God gives us to influence?

No doubt when both husband and wife make the decision to live in Christ, a unity is formed.

Each disciple, except for Judas, did make this decision. Together, twelve independent male units formed a unity that brought the Kingdom of God to earth in dramatic fashion. They performed miracles, signs, and wonders. The disciples' unity came as each one chose to receive truth. Even more remarkable is that the strength of unity survived disagreement.

Jesus provided the opportunity. How? What strategy did He employ to bring a bunch of independent, self-willed, ambitious, proud, fickled human beings to believe in Him? The same strategy Jesus used is the same strategy those working with *Unveiled Love* use. It is how we facilitate others coming to believe in Him and live by truth. When He is wholeheartedly received, Jesus provides an unshakable bond of unity. So let's unpack Philippians 2:5–8 (NIV) to understand Jesus's strategy. Because He is on earth as are we, this strategy belongs to us as well. Here are the verses again, spaced wider for enhanced clarity.

> In your relationships with one another, have the same mindset as Christ Jesus: Who, being in very nature God, did not consider equality with God something to be used to his own advantage; rather, he made himself nothing by taking the very nature of a servant, being made in human likeness. And being found in appearance as a man, he humbled himself by becoming obedient to death—even death on a cross!

Boast in Your Spouse

First, Jesus Christ is in the very nature and image of God. Therefore, He did need not seek to be equal with God. Jesus did not seek to be the Father nor did the Father try to be the Son. Their essence is the same. The Father boasts of the Son and the Son boasts about the Father. Neither one brags about Himself. This eliminates competition.

Since our spirit has been recreated in the nature and image of God, we need not seek to be gods. Husbands and wives that receive Christ share God's nature and image. The wife boasts about her husband and the husband boasts about his wife. Neither boasts about him or herself. If they do, comparison and competition are sure to follow. We boast of ourselves when we must be right, the best, the first, and the only. We boast when our worth is anchored in positional power, titles, money, possessions, intellect, or any other inanimate object or person other than Jesus Christ. Paul has a lot to say about boasting and it isn't favorable. In one verse, he writes the following:

> Love endures long and is patient and kind; love never is envious nor boils over with jealousy, is not boastful or vainglorious, does not display itself haughtily.[70]

Boasting in self is a form of pride and adversarial to the mind of Christ. Jesus drew the disciples' affections by not speaking much of Himself, rather He spoke about the Father, about life, about things that mattered to others. One way we can draw our spouses' attention is to consider and talk about the things that matter to them.

Jesus understood He was the nature and image of God. Living in Christ means settling this truth. You are the nature and image of God. Since husband and wife share this truth, they are free to celebrate the aspects of God's glory most prevalent in each other. Husbands boast of their wives and wives boast of their husbands, eliminating the tendency to compare, strive, and compete. This is how Jesus thought about His relationship with the Father and we ought to as well.

---

[70] 1 Corinthians 13:4 (AMPC)

Be Human

Free from comparing, striving, and competing with God, the Pharisees, and Scribes and even His disciples, Jesus was completely available to become the servant of all. Philippians 2:7 (CSB) tells us how Jesus did it.

> Instead, he emptied himself by assuming the form
> of a servant, taking on the likeness of humanity.
> And when he had come as a man.

Rather than pursuing equality with God, Jesus emptied Himself by taking the form of a servant. That means Jesus gave up all the rights and privileges belonging to Him as the Son of God. Some believe that Jesus emptied Himself of His essence, who He is, that is His Deity. However, I do not agree. Jesus cannot stop being who He is, but He can refuse to use or rely on His rights, privileges, and perks as God in the flesh. Who Jesus is will never change. What did change is how He would accomplish His Father's will. Paul tells us exactly how Jesus does it and informs us on how we are to accomplish God's will in our relationships.

Jesus took the form of a servant. His form was in the likeness of humanity. And His appearance was that of a male. On earth, Jesus not only identified with humanity, but also He became human and lived the human experience. Jesus did not deny, dismiss, nor disown his humanity. He showed up. He experienced community, love, rejection, betrayal, and exploitation. Jesus was tempted in every way we are today. He contended with lust of the flesh and lust of the eyes and pride, and He prevailed, unscathed by all (Matthew 4:1–11). In thirty-three years, it is safe to say that Jesus experienced many cold, lonely, dark nights of the soul, suffering to maintain adherence to His Father's will (Hebrews 12:4). Jesus engaged the human experience by the power of the Holy Spirit.

The key to living in Christ is taking on the form of a servant, in the likeness of humanity appearing as male or female. This means embracing the weaknesses of humanity—*our own weaknesses and limitations*. Husbands and wives, it means shedding the pretense. It means owning and offering what each one thinks and feels to the conversation. It means showing up and being yourself in the moment. It's about being honest, open, and transparent. Jesus didn't hide His tears, His pain, or His suffering. Others saw Him at His most vulnerable moments in life. Husbands and wives would do well to learn from Jesus. Jesus showed up fully to the degree His audience could handle. He showed up to the scribes and Pharisees one way. He showed up another way to the seventy. And another way to the twelve. And still another way to the Peter, James, and John. Each time Jesus showed up fully, albeit differently depending on the nature of the relationship.

In marriage, each one must assess and determine what fully showing up means. Jazmine writes me: "He emotionally, and mentally abuses me. Gaslights, degrades, and devalues me. I have been trying so hard to make things work but the stress from this marriage has caused me some health issues. He is against seeking professional help for our marriage." Jazmine's experience of her husband does not sound like he is someone with whom Jazmine can show up vulnerably. From what Jazmine writes, this is anything but a marriage relationship. Jazmine needs help for herself. When she changes the way she shows up with her husband, the relationship will inevitably change. Hopefully, this will be for the better, but there is no guarantee. Jazmine's situation is loaded with many unknown variables. Proper professional help can help navigate these details and advise Jazmine accordingly. For our purposes here, Jazmine's story is a gross example of an unsafe relationship in which to show up vulnerably. In this case, showing up fully might mean offering just the facts.

It's amazing how much of the human experience we try to avoid, deny, and escape. This is particularly so when it comes to experiencing loss, hurt, pain, and suffering. We compartmentalize the aspects of our lives to prevent such feelings from seeping at unwanted times and places. And then there are those of us that try to faith out what God would have us walk out. I have been told by more than one respectable Christian that they do not get offended. Moreover, that mature Christians don't get offended. But this was not one of them. In Matthew 18:7 (CSB), Jesus speaks about offenses. Here's what He says.

> Woe to the world because of offenses. For offenses will inevitably come, but woe to that person by whom the offense comes.

Offenses are unavoidable. They will occur. Husbands and wives know this all too well. It's part of the human experience. Jesus does not tell us that we should not get offended. Nor does He measure our maturity on whether we experience offense. We will. Jesus tells us how to respond to offense in Matthew 6:14 (CSB).

> For if you forgive others their offenses, your heavenly Father will forgive you as well.

This is especially important in marriage because husbands and wives often offend each other. It's part of the human experience. And if we are going to embrace our humanity fully, then we must acknowledge when offended. It's not even that your spouse must fix it or change to your satisfaction. It just means making it known and deciding how God would have you respond. This is what it means to show up in marriage.

Jesus became like those His Father wanted to redeem. He did so without engaging in their sinful conduct. He was able to distinguish the pain that led to sin and the pain caused by sin from sin itself. Jesus lived among the people He most desired to influence—the seventy, the twelve, the three, and then there was Peter.

Of all the disciples, Jesus's relationship with Peter was most prominent. It is Jesus's most written about human relationship. If Jesus had a best friend, it would certainly be Peter. Or at least the gospel writers must have thought so. Peter is always first in any listing of the disciples. Jesus's interactions with Peter were a recurring subject of conversation. Peter is the only disciple who walked on water (Matthew 14:29). And the only one who rebuked Jesus (Matthew 16:22). Jesus loved Peter, with God's *Unveiled Love*. By observing

Jesus engage Peter's humanity, we see the breadth and depth of what it is to be human. But also we see the effectiveness of Jesus's strategy in bringing Peter to truth. Jesus entered the messy unpleasantness of Peter's life to show Peter the kind pleasantness of His Father. Jesus clothed Himself in a manner that Peter could relate with Him.

In marriage, husbands and wives enter the messiness of each other's lives that each has an opportunity to see and experience the grace and glory of God. But this can only happen when a husband or wife lives in Christ. They do this by taking on the form of a servant, showing up as a human being, that is either male or female and relying on Holy Spirit to do the rest of the work. Jesus did not work or even try to be spiritual. He is spirit, therefore a spiritual being. He did not practice being spiritual. However, Jesus worked very hard to be human and subject His humanity to His Father. Hebrews 5:7–9 (CSB) clarifies.

> During his earthly life, he offered prayers and appeals with loud cries and tears to the one who was able to save him from death, and he was heard because of his reverence. Although he was the Son, he learned obedience from what he suffered. After he was perfected, he became the source of eternal salvation for all who obey him.

Becoming real and human requires a lot of work and lots of love! But if husbands and wives are going to experience unity, this is required. One of my favorite children's books is *The Velveteen Rabbit* by Margery Williams. In it, the rabbit asks the Skin Horse how toys are made real. The Skin Horse explains:

> "Real isn't how you are made," said the Skin Horse. "It's a thing that happens to you. When a child loves you for a long, long time, not just to play with, but really loves you, then you become Real."

> "Does it hurt?" asked the Rabbit.

"Sometimes," said the Skin Horse, for he was always truthful. "When you are Real you don't mind being hurt."

"Does it happen all at once, like being wound up," he asked, "or bit by bit?"

"It doesn't happen all at once," said the Skin Horse. "You become. It takes a long time. That's why it doesn't happen often to people who break easily, or have sharp edges, or who have to be carefully kept. Generally, by the time you are Real, most of your hair has been loved off, and your eyes drop out and you get loose in the joints and very shabby. But these things don't matter at all, because once you are Real you can't be ugly, except to people who don't understand."

Be Sacrificial

The final aspect of Jesus's strategy to redeem us was to surrender His humanity to His Father. That's how Jesus used His freedom and authority to govern His life while on earth. He didn't live for Himself. He lived for God. Philippians 2:7–8 (CSB) inform us.

> And when he had come as a man, he humbled himself by becoming obedient to the point of death—even to death on a cross.

Jesus yielded to the authority and will of God when it meant death to His physical being. But before this fatal decision, Jesus surrendered many other things including His maleness, His strengths, weaknesses, and vulnerabilities. He gave His thoughts, feelings, and actions to God. He withheld nothing. As a human being, all of this could not have been easy. In fact, in Hebrews 12:2–4 (CSB), Paul says it was anything but easy.

> Let us run with endurance the race that lies before us, keeping our eyes on Jesus, the pioneer and perfecter[b] of our faith. For the joy that lay before him, he endured the cross, despising the shame, and sat down at the right hand of the throne of God. For consider him who endured such hostility from sinners against himself, so that you won't grow weary and give up. In struggling against sin, you have not yet resisted to the point of shedding your blood.

Surrendering to the will of God can be difficult, unpleasant, and even undesirable. Jesus never lost, gave up, or handed over His freedom and authority to respond to God. Though He endured unimaginable pain, He never became the slave of sin.

In marriage, we are called to surrender ourselves to God and each other. However, like Jesus, we must retain our freedom and authority to respond to God. God never asked Jesus to give up who He is nor His right to respond to His Father's will. Jesus never handed over His authority to be who He is to Satan or any human being. We are well advised to do likewise. Toward the very end of our marriage, I remember telling my ex-husband that I desired to listen to him and support him. But that he did not have the authority to decide who I will be. This right and responsibility belonged to me. Thirty years of religious influence made those words difficult to say and difficult for him to receive.

To live in Christ is to surrender all that pertains to you to God. This includes your humanity—*your soul and body*. This is husbands and wives best hope to form a unity of units. And that necessarily means adopting the mind of Christ. We must think what he thinks. We must think how He thinks; that is His strategy. We must believe that we will understand His why, perchance God permits. Paul sums it up this way in 1 Corinthians 13:11 (TPT).

> When I was a child, I spoke about childish matters, for I saw things like a child and reasoned like a child. But the day came when I matured, and I set aside my childish ways.

Paul's Example of Surrender

Paul also had to learn to embrace the mind of Christ. It didn't happen all at once. On the road to Damascus, God confronted Paul with truth. Over many years, God dealt with Paul through circumstances, and people. Second Corinthians 6:4–10 (CSB) gives a summary of some aspects of Paul's training.

> Instead, as God's ministers, we commend ourselves in everything: by great endurance, by afflictions, by hardships, by difficulties, by beatings, by imprisonments, by riots, by labors, by sleepless nights, by times of hunger, by purity, by knowledge, by patience, by kindness, by the Holy Spirit, by sincere love, by the word of truth, by the power of God; through weapons of righteousness for the right hand and the left, through glory and dishonor, through slander and good report; regarded as deceivers, yet true; as unknown, yet recognized; as dying, yet see—we live; as being disciplined, yet not killed; as grieving, yet always rejoicing; as poor, yet enriching many; as having nothing, yet possessing everything.

In next three verses (11–13, TPT), Paul appeals to the Corinthian believers.

> My friends at Corinth, our hearts are wide open to you and we speak freely, holding nothing back from you. If there is a block in our relationship, it is not with us, for we carry you in our hearts with great love, yet you still withhold your affections from us. So, I speak to you as our children. Make room in your hearts for us as we have done for you.

Paul not only shared the gospel with the Corinthians, but he also opened his life to them—his hardships, his emotions, and amid all, his desire to remain true to God. Paul was honest and vulnerable. He gave them his humanity by indicating he had withheld nothing from them. On another occasion, Paul prevented the people from worshipping him and Barnabas, emphatically declaring they were not gods, but rather human beings, just like them.[71]

And then Paul gives us more insight into his training in 2 Corinthians 11:24–27 (CSB).

> Five times I received the forty lashes minus one from the Jews. Three times I was beaten with rods. Once I received a stoning. Three times I was shipwrecked. I have spent a night and a day in the open sea. On frequent journeys, I faced dangers from rivers, dangers from robbers, dangers from my own people, dangers from Gentiles, dangers in the city, dangers in the wilderness, dangers at sea, and dangers among false brothers; toil and hardship, many sleepless nights, hunger and thirst, often without food, cold, and without clothing.

This is Paul's story. It is horrible and unwelcomed. Take courage, most of us will never endure all that Paul did. Paul informs us that

---

[71] Acts 14:11–15

much of what we call Christianity here in the West is far from the life Jesus and disciples experienced. It is not easy to be Christian—*especially sometimes in marriage.*

Paul's experiences and his response to them transformed him. During various stages of his journey in surrender, Paul made four statements. Consider Paul's attitude as God turns him into a servant, in the likeness of humanity in the appearance of a man. We meet Paul in Galatians 1:12 (CSB), boasting of receiving the gospel from God and not man. He says that he consulted no one. And in verse 14, speaking of his former life, Paul boasts about being superior to his colleagues and contemporaries, because he was studied and obsessed with the traditions of his ancestors.

> For I did not receive it from a human source and I was not taught it, but it came by a revelation of Jesus Christ. I advanced in Judaism beyond many contemporaries among my people, because I was extremely zealous for the traditions of my ancestors.

Sometime later, Paul meets the apostles. Here's what he said afterward.

> For I am the least of the apostles, not worthy to be called an apostle, because I persecuted the church of God.[72]

Then there were more trials, tests, and temptations. Consequently, Paul has this to say in Ephesians 3:8 (CEV).

> I am the least important of all God's people. But God was kind and chose me to tell the Gentiles that because of Christ there are blessings that cannot be measured.

---

[72] 1 Corinthians 15:9 (CSB)

Finally, Paul rests his case with these words in 1 Timothy 1:15–16.

> This saying is trustworthy and deserving of full acceptance: "Christ Jesus came into the world to save sinners"—and I am the worst of them. But I received mercy for this reason, so that in me, the worst of them, Christ Jesus might demonstrate his extraordinary patience as an example to those who would believe in him for eternal life.

Paul decreased that Christ might increase in Him. This is the result of embracing the mind of Christ. Paul understood, what Jesus understands, and it became the basis of their full and complete surrender. Paul expressed it in Romans 11:36 (CSB)

> For from him and through him and to him are all things. To him be the glory forever. Amen.

There is nothing that can happen to you that you and God can't manage together—*absolutely nothing*. If husbands and wives are to live in Christ and become a unity of units, it will require each one's full surrender and nothing less. Each one must choose to engage the training God assigns to develop the mind and way of Christ. Marriage, then, is not for the faint of heart.

Questions to Learn By

1. What most resonated with you in this secret?
2. In what ways have you and your spouse tried to become one? Has this worked? Why or why not?
3. What is false unity? Give an example.
4. What does to live in Christ mean?

Questions to Grow By

1. Read Philippians 2:5–8 with a person willing to discuss it with you. What was Jesus's strategy of reconciliation?
2. Think about the last major decision you made as a couple, in which you started out on different pages. Make a list of what you did to get on the same page and arrive at a joint decision.
3. Pray and ask God in what area of your life is He requesting greater surrender. What does this look like? When will you surrender? How will you surrender? Who might hold you accountable in your surrender?
4. Do you find yourself comparing, striving, and competing with your spouse? If so, how?

Questions to Change By

1. What change in your thinking are you taking away from this secret?
2. How will you apply this new way of thinking in your marriage? What will you do differently?
3. Since offense is unavoidable, how do you plan to address offense going forward?
4. List at least three things you can boast about your spouse and then tell him or her.

Secret 8

Let God Do the Correcting

> Our parents corrected us for the short time of our childhood as it seemed good to them. But God corrects us throughout our lives for our own good, giving us an invitation to share his holiness. (Hebrews 12:10 TPT)

As an introduction to Secret 8, here's an account of a situation that really happened during my marriage. We had been associate pastors of a fast-growing church for a little over a year. At the time, our oldest daughter was eight and the same age as the senior pastor's daughter. The two had become friends. The pastor's daughter stayed with us one weekend. My mother was also coming to visit that weekend. My mother was beautiful, detailed, and articulate. My mother never went camping. But if she did, it wouldn't have been in a tent. Rather, a glam camper with its own private shower and toilet. You get the picture.

That Friday, a cold shower and a forgetful husband convinced me the gas bill had not been paid. Normally, when he was forgetful in paying the bills, I would bite his head off, followed by a long silence. But that day, a strange calm came over me. When I asked him whether he knew what was going on, he immediately called the gas company and paid the bill. However, it was Friday, and it would be Monday before the gas would be turned back on. I could not explain the calm I felt; it wasn't me. My mom was scheduled to arrive Saturday morning. I insisted that he pick her up from the airport, so he could inform her of the hot-water situation. I did not want to incur her displeasure. To my surprise, when they arrived home from the airport, both were laughing and carrying on. I wondered whether he had said anything to her at all. He assured me that he did. And again, I was puzzled.

Since there was no hot water, showers were out. But my husband found a solution. And it worked marvelously! That Saturday night, he began heating pots of water on the electric stove. He used this approach to ensure four ladies had a hot bath that Saturday night. He went up and down the steps, carrying more pots of hot water than I could count. His kind and thoughtful actions went above and beyond anything I could have imagined. It was endearing.

That was not the first time he forgot to pay a bill. It was a source of conflict throughout our marriage. The fact that it happened while our pastor's daughter and my mother were guests in our care increased my anxiety. I feared their reaction and what others might think about how we managed our home. Even though my husband's forgetfulness was not new. God prevailed.

By remaining calm and unable to fix it, God showed up and showed out to the benefit of all. I held my peace. My husband found a solution. And four ladies received hot baths. What could have been a disaster turned out to be a success! In that one experience, God dealt with all of us. I learned that I could not fix my spouse. I couldn't even fix the circumstances caused by my spouse. It was still my problem. However, the peace of God held my soul through to the solution. Moreover, I was emotionally drawn to my husband. God did the correcting, not me.

I will say this. Watching him go up and down the stairs as many times as he did elicited compassion. Moreover, I experienced a humility in him that I had not known before. He seemed sorrowful that this happened. His commitment to engaging a solution was proof. We continued working through how to best manage the bills.

As for the kids, they just thought it was fun! They made a game out it. And Monday morning, "Voila!" the gas was back on!

Our best work pales in comparison to God's ability to deal with, change, and fix our spouse. God's *Unveiled Love* has a feature that is autocorrecting. If we let Him, God will do the correcting. What this means is that you can stop trying to change your spouse—*forever!* God's *Unveiled Love* can take over from here on out. It just requires you and I to use our freedom and authority to receive His love, allow Him to meet your needs and commit to becoming the people He would have us be. It means that from now on, who you are neither rises nor falls on your spouse's behavior. When you are free from your spouse in this manner, God uses you best to facilitate changes in your spouse. Perhaps less appealing than more overt ways to get your spouse to behave differently, albeit infinitely more effective.

Autocorrecting

Autocorrection is a term with which most are familiar. Using a word processor or texting on a cellphone are prime examples. Misspell a word, the device makes the correction for you. It's built into the software. On our phones, this feature can be a real pain. That's because sometimes we hit Send, then realize the device's chip brain, to our dismay, changed an entire word from what was typed, texted, or dictated to something totally different. Has this happened to you?

God's *Unveiled Love* is autocorrecting. This means that it adjusts to the information, situations, and circumstances unique to each husband and wife. God takes into consideration absolutely everything about you and your spouse. Every shred of information is known to God and His *Unveiled Love*. It is never caught off guard or thrown for a loop. God's *Unveiled Love* adjusts to every nuance or inconsistency presented.

"Machine learning" can help us get our minds around *Unveiled Love's* autocorrecting function. A machine "learns" by storing and searching for patterns in large amounts of data. Filters can be placed around the search input so that a certain set of data is examined for repetitions. Once a pattern or repetition has been isolated, an algorithm updates the stored data for recall. If people can program a machine to do this, then we can safely assume that it is native to God. To say that God's *Unveiled Love* is autocorrecting is to say that it adjusts to each husband and wife's unique information, habits, and patterns. *Unveiled Love* never fails in this manner.

It never malfunctions. It is impervious to viruses or hackers. There is no glitch that it can't handle. There is no missed intention. Nothing escapes the notice of *Unveiled Love*. Our thoughts and intentions are always and accurately understood—*if only to God*. Sometimes, we don't even understand the underlying reasons for our attitudes and behaviors. But God does all the time and in every situation. Paul writes concerning this in Hebrews 4:13 (CSB).

> No creature is hidden from him, but all things are naked and exposed to the eyes of him to whom we must give an account.

Not only does God see and know all, but also He is committed to you and your spouse. Paul offers assurance.

> He who started a good work in you will carry it on to completion until the day of Christ Jesus.[73]

Moreover, Paul writes in Philippians 2:13 (CSB):

> For it is God who is working in you both to will and to work according to his good purpose.

God is working in you both. And because it is Jesus to whom each one will give an accounting of the deeds done in the flesh, Paul says:

> Therefore, my dear friends, just as you have always obeyed, so now, not only in my presence

---

[73] Philippians 1:6 (CSB)

but even more in my absence, work out your own salvation with fear and trembling.[74]

Paul tells us exactly how to do this in verses 14–16 (CSB):

> Do everything without grumbling and arguing, so that you may be blameless and pure, children of God who are faultless in a crooked and perverted generation, among whom you shine like stars in the world, by holding firm to the word of life.

Finally, Paul says this is how we can know our work will be rewarded. That's because it will not have been done in vain. Are there times when husbands and wives passionately disagree? I would hope so. For if not, how will they know what is of God and what is not. When disagreements reach an impasse, we are likely confronting a spirit and not the person. We will never be able prevail against the spirit operating through a spouse by human intellect or emotional intelligence. Spirit must address spirit.

Unlike texting malfunctions, God's *Unveiled Love* is a foolproof, fail-safe system. This ensures each of us has every opportunity to choose to align with God's will and plan for our lives. God's System of *Unveiled Love* is flawless. It is always precise, always timely, and always effective. *Unveiled Love* is always successful; it transcends all possible variables. To paraphrase, Proverbs 19:21 says that man makes many plans, but the God works all things according to His will. God's *Unveiled Love* is unaffected by the whims of our flesh. Speaking to the Ephesians, Paul writes the following.

> In him we have also received an inheritance, because we were predestined according to the plan of the one who works out everything in agreement with the purpose of his will, so that we

---

[74] Philippians 2:12 (CSB)

who had already put our hope in Christ might bring praise to his glory.[75]

God works everything, which includes those things that concern you in agreement with His purposes. Think about this for a moment. Even when you or your spouse mess up, derail, and behave in ways that oppose grace and truth, God still uses it to establish His will. May I remind you when Jesus fed the five thousand. All those present ate to their fill. He instructed His disciples to gather the remains. Twelve baskets of bread remained. The reason Jesus gave for collecting the uneaten bread was so that nothing would be wasted![76]

Husband, wife, there is nothing that you nor your spouse has done that God will not use to bring you into agreement with His will. God shares your desire to see your spouse grow and change in mind, manner, and way. In fact, He desires this more than you. But also God desires you to grow and change. After all, He created both you and your spouse for Himself—*that is for His pleasure!*[77] This applies whether your spouse is Christian or not.

Engaging in repeated arguments on different days should be seen as proof of God's commitment to correcting husbands and wives. It is God's unrelenting, unveiled invitation for each one to make different choices. The fact that we don't just leads to more conflict and "wandering in the wilderness". God doesn't give up on us. He wants for His Son—*a bride without flaw.* The fact that He invites us to take part in His vision is magnificent!

The Bride without Blemish

Certainly, none of us will be spotless until God rids us of these physical bodies and completes the transformation of our souls. Still, this is the plan and progression of consecration. The more dedicated to Christ a husband or wife is, the more holy he or she will become.

---

[75] Ephesians 1:11–12
[76] John 6:10–13
[77] Revelation 4:11

The more committed to Christ we become, the less vulnerable we become to temptations.

Here's another actual real-life example: A husband explained his wife's adultery as being due to his lack of attention. He admitted working all the time. When home, he recharged best by himself. From his viewpoint, it made sense. He reasoned that it may have made it easier for her to succumb to temptation. However, for him to conclude that his spouse's faithfulness is dependent on his attention of the other spouse is not the right paradigm. Ultimately, faithfulness is a decision that one makes of his or her own free will. The authority to abide by this decision, a marriage vow, a covenant of faithfulness, resides with the individual, with help from God's grace. When unfaithfulness is in the heart of a husband or wife, external factors serve only to hinder or expedite infidelity but will not permanently prevent it. That's because whatever is stored within us eventually makes its way out of us. Jesus uttered this truth when he rebuked the Pharisees in Matthew 12:34 (GW):

> You poisonous snakes! How can you evil people say anything good? Your mouth says what comes from inside you.

Again, to the Pharisees in Mark 7:15, Jesus reiterates that what comes out of a person defiles him or her. Finally, in Matthew 5:28 (TPT) Jesus has this to say.

> However, I say to you, if you look with lust in your eyes at a woman who is not your wife, you've already committed adultery in your heart.

Whether it is a husband lusting after a woman who is not his wife or a wife lusting after a man who is not her husband, adultery has occurred. What remains is only when lust is acted upon. It is not surprising that the husband in the above example assumes responsibility for neglecting his wife, but adultery is her sin and burden to bear.

Jesus never relinquished His authority to another. Of sound mind and in full control of His faculties, Jesus intentionally gave His life. It wasn't taken from Him as some supposed. Like Jesus, in marriage, our commitment must be to God, sustained by His grace. Each one's work, then, is to remain of sturdy mind and self-controlled. The degree each one is devoted to God determines his or her will and strength to overcome temptation.

The difference between our attempts to change our spouse and God changing our spouse is this. We settle for temporary changes in behavior. God settles for permanent changes in heart and soul. This is a far deeper work. It requires the Holy Spirit to go where human hands cannot. Only God's *Unveiled Love* can reach such depths in your spouse.

Marriage is not solely to produce offspring nor for the pleasure of man and woman. While both are germane, marriage was, is, and will always be about Christ and His Bride. It was always about preparing the Bride for His Son. Jesus's joy and ecstasy at the glance of His Bride was hidden momentarily in His suffering for her restoration. We *were* His joy upon giving His life for us. We *are* His joy while we live in His image and likeness. And we *will be* His joy for all eternity. Hebrews 12:2 (TPT) reads:

> We look away from the natural realm and we focus our attention and expectation onto Jesus who birthed faith within us and who leads us forward into faith's perfection. His example is this: Because his heart was focused on the joy of knowing that you would be his, he endured the agony of the cross and conquered its humiliation, and now sits exalted at the right hand of the throne of God!

Now Jesus waits for the full redemption of His Bride. The Apostle John shares his vision of the Bride in Revelation 19:7–8.

> Let us be glad, rejoice, and give him glory, because the marriage of the Lamb has come, and his bride has prepared herself. She was given fine linen to wear, bright and pure. For the fine linen represents the righteous acts of the saints.

Today, the Bride of Christ is preparing herself through right living, right behaviors, and right responses to people and circumstances. The sons of God are made up of men and women who believe and receive Jesus Christ as Savior.[78] Similarly, the Bride, is made up of men and women that believe and receive the Lordship of Jesus Christ. One of the main relationships God uses to train the Bride is marriage. One of the integral parts of marriage can best be expressed by a definition of the word "system." Here's how the word "system" appears, in part, in the *Merriam-Webster* dictionary: *a capability given by the practical application of knowledge.* Jesus built into marriage a system. Jesus used this same system, this same capability, which He created in mankind in the first place, to draw them to redemption.

The System God Uses to Change You and Your Spouse

In Secret #7, we spoke about living in Christ by adopting His mindset. The Father boasted in the Son. The Son boasted in the Father. Jesus became human in the likeness of a man. And then He offered Himself unreservedly to the Father. Let's take a closer look at how God used Jesus to facilitate men and women changing their minds about God.

Jesus revealed and repeatedly referred to different spiritual concepts by using allegories, actual examples and miracles involving bread. How it starts from wheat, how it is prepared, treated, cooked, served, eaten, and even how the leftovers were collected and miraculously filled baskets full of bread. By using the near universal system, like bread and the daily handling of it, we learn the process of change. God uses this process to change us, as well as our spouse. Think

---

[78] John 1:12

about this, most every other culture has a staple product like bread. In Northern China, it is called mantou. In Italy, it's called focaccia. And in India, it's called chapati. Germany calls it pumpernickel. The Navajo Indians of North America call it frybread. Ethiopians call it injera. Bread is the perfect system to teach the world about God's plan to redeem mankind. That's because all bread, regardless of culture has at least one thing in common. All bread is *breakable*. It can be torn in two. Breakability is at the heart of the change process. That Jesus would use a food item of universal appeal to drive home this truth is remarkable! Importantly, being broken, like bread, is a relational truth. A truth, a system that applies to marriage and any other relationship in which change is desired and/or warranted.

Brokenness the System of Change!

Brokenness is a theme in changing one thing into another. Jesus repeatedly broke bread and served it. When something is repeated, it means that it is important. Moreover, that we ought to give it our attention. Oftentimes, Jesus took bread, blessed it, broke it, and served it to his disciples and, on occasion, to thousands of others. Once, in the books of Matthew and Mark and twice in the book of Luke, the Bible (KJV) records these words:[79]

> As they were eating, Jesus took bread, blessed and broke it, gave it to the disciples, and said, "Take and eat it; this is my body." Then he took a cup, and after giving thanks, he gave it to them and said, "Drink from it, all of you. For this is my blood of the covenant, which is poured out for many for the forgiveness of sins."

There were other instances of bread and brokenness. When feeding the multitudes, Jesus repeated the habits of taking bread,

---

[79] Matthew 26:26; Mark 14:22; Luke 22:19 and 24:30 (KJV)

offering thanksgiving, breaking it, and serving it to others.[80] As mentioned before, there were leftovers! Nothing went unaccounted for in God's economy. Breaking bread was a habit. It was a lifestyle Jesus engaged with His disciples. After Jesus's death, the apostles carried on the practice of taking, blessing, breaking, and distributing the bread and drinking the cup of His blood. Observe the order in 1 Corinthians 11:23–25 (CSB).

> For I received from the Lord what I also passed on to you: On the night when he was betrayed, the Lord Jesus took bread, and when he had given thanks, broke it, and said, 'This is my body, which is for you. Do this in remembrance of me.' In the same way also he took the cup, after supper, and said, 'This cup is the new covenant in my blood. Do this, as often as you drink it, in remembrance of me.' For as often as you eat this bread and drink the cup, you proclaim the Lord's death until he comes.

Paul followed the order of Jesus by taking bread, blessing it by giving thanks, breaking it, and serving it. Paul then handled the cup in the same manner.

But what does all this have to do with God changing your spouse? Keep tracking with me. At one point, while establishing the order and habit taking, blessing, breaking, and serving bread, Jesus reveals something startling. Only John records the revelation. He does so, by quoting Jesus four times. Here's what Jesus says in John 6:35 (CSB).

> I am the bread of life. No one who comes to me will ever be hungry, and no one who believes in me will ever be thirsty again.

---

[80] Matthew 14:19; Mark 8:6; John 6:11 (CSB)

In verse 41 (CSB), Jesus says the following:

> I am the bread that came down from heaven.

Jesus repeats Himself in verse 48 (CSB):

> I am the bread of life.

Finally, in verse 51 (CSB), Jesus expounds on verse 35.

> I am the living bread that came down from heaven. If anyone eats of this bread he will live forever. The bread that I will give for the life of the world is my flesh.

John heard, received, and recorded a profound, life-changing revelation. It was so deep yet so subtle and easily overlooked that Matthew, Mark, and Luke failed to record Jesus's declaration. In these four verses, Jesus reveals the principle, process, and promise of changing others. It was true then and remains true for all that live the Christ life. This system is the most powerful influencer of change. There is no other tactical method that comes close to rivaling this principle, process, and promise. It is the way of Christ. And for every husband or wife that desires God to change his or her spouse, this must become the way too. It is interesting that two men were walking toward the village of Emmaus. They were talking about all that had transpired with Jesus when Jesus came up and began walking with them. The Bible says that the men were prevented from recognizing Him. Jesus interacted with them by asking questions and explaining the scriptures. Still, the men were clueless to Jesus's identity. Jesus accepted an invitation to visit further with them. At the table, Jesus took bread, blessed it, broke it, and gave it to them. Luke 24:31–32 (CSB) records their response.

> Then their eyes were opened and they recognized him, and he disappeared from their sight. They

> asked each other, "Were not our hearts burning within us while he talked with us on the road and opened the Scriptures to us?"

After installing the system of change, the recipients' eyes were opened, and they recognized Jesus. Their hearts burned as truth was imparted. But there is more. Luke 24:33–34 says that they got up immediately and returned to Jerusalem, gathered with the eleven disciples, and witnessed concerning the truth. They told the disciples how they recognized Jesus. Luke 24:35 (CSB) tells us plainly.

> Then the two told what had happened on the way, and how Jesus was recognized by them when he broke the bread.

Until Jesus did something familiar, He remained obscure to the men. They identified Jesus through the process of taking, blessing, breaking, and serving bread. That these two unidentified men were familiar with the process suggests that those other than the disciples saw Jesus engage it. They remembered! Perhaps in that moment they recalled Jesus declaring Himself to be the bread. The entire story of the two men is told in Luke 24:13–35.

Understanding the secret of God changing your spouse requires that we consider a sobering thought. In Matthew 21:42, Jesus was the stone that the builders rejected. He became the chief cornerstone. Jesus went on to say:

> Whoever falls on this stone will be broken, but on whomever it falls, it will grind him to powder.

The choice is ours. We can fall on the stone by choosing to engage God's system of change and thereby experience brokenness and ultimately wholeness. Or we risk the stone falling on us and grinding us to powder. I know these don't sound like typical triumphant faith-filled words. Still, they are Jesus's words. If for no other reason, we do well to consider them whole-heartedly. That's because

God is removing the grace to side-step this key component of transforming our souls and our spouse. It's all about you and it's not! Your spouse's greatest opportunity to manifest the changes you pray and fast about accompanies your brokenness. Hopefully, you now can see why marriage is not for the faint of heart nor for those whose egos must be carefully kept. And those who walk on eggshells around their spouse have a working reality of what this means!

Engaging the System

When you work with God's *Unveiled Love*, notwithstanding your spouse's willingness, God can change your husband or wife. When unwilling, God can influence his or her desire at best. Still, both require you to take part. Jesus shows us how. The system is fourfold. God's *Unveiled Love* takes, blesses, breaks, and gives your life to your spouse. Your spouse retains the choice whether to receive life or not. Throughout the gospels, Jesus's interactions with men and women make it clear that some will receive the life given to them by God. Others will not. Jesus did not try to control the outcome of His interactions with others. Instead, He maintained regard for the freedom of each person. Jesus did so by recognizing that each person had the God-given right to respond as he or she willed. Moreover, that each one must ultimately give account to His Father. Paul attests in Hebrews 4:13 (AMP).

> And not a creature exists that is concealed from His sight, but all things are open and exposed and revealed to the eyes of Him with whom we have to give account.

And in verse 12, Paul is explicit about the degree to which God knows each one. God distinguishes our soul and spirit, our actions from our reasons, and our thoughts from our motivations. This covers everything as it relates to each one's response. Jesus knew this. Honoring each one's freedom to respond gave His Father the greatest latitude in working with individuals' heart and soul. Jesus had neither a need nor a desire to coerce any to accept Him, the words He spoke, or the life He chose to live. Each person retained the right to refuse Him.

Working with God's *Unveiled Love* means adopting Jesus's mindset. It means loving God first and foremost in what we think and how we behave. It means refusing to engage in manipulation and control tactics to get our spouse to say and do what we desire. It means honoring their freedom and right to refuse our way of thinking and behaving. It means engaging the process and trusting God with the outcomes. God blessed Jesus, broke Him, and served Him to mankind. To this day, some receive. Some do not. Throughout all, Jesus trusted God to work everything in agreement with the purpose of His will for each of us. We must do the same in marriage. And we must do the same in every other relationship God gives us to be an agent of change.

Rejection

When your spouse rejects God's offer of life through you, your work is not in vain. God sees to it. Paul informs us in Galatians 6:9 (AMPC).

> And let us not lose heart and grow weary and faint in acting nobly and doing right, for in due time and at the appointed season we shall reap, if we do not loosen and relax our courage and faint.

Whether received or not, Jesus benefitted. Luke 2:52 (CSB) states the following:

> And Jesus increased in wisdom and stature, and in favor with God and with people.

Jesus matured. Jesus increased in favor both with God and people. When a husband or wife works with God's *Unveiled Love*, he or she benefits. This is true whether or not his or her spouse accepts

God's invitation to life. That's why I love working with God's *Unveiled Love*. It's a win-win! The giver is transformed. The receiver has an opportunity to be transformed. The entire process is coordinated by God. Marriage is brilliant in this way! It answers the transformational needs of both husband and wife. God can use one adverse situation, one conflict, one discontented spouse to bring about change in the marriage. It only requires one person working together with God's *Unveiled Love*. I have often heard it said of marriage, "It takes two to make it work." I agree. It does take two, and you and God make the two necessaries to create the conditions for your relationship to work. Still, your spouse always has the right to opt out.

What freedom this provides for you and your spouse! You can focus on what God is having you to do. Whether it is for you to stop doing something or start doing something is unique to you and your relationship. Let me explain.

Jane constantly felt the need to press Kevin to become the spiritual leader in their family. When they argued, she felt compelled to prove that she was right. Jane could run circles of scriptures around Kevin. Kevin experienced Jane as unkind. And although he would not say it, he appeared intimidated by her confidence. Kevin had enough and threatened divorce. That's what stopped Jane in her tracks. She prayed. A friend told her about Radical Love, a twelve-week marriage skill building course I wrote. In the course, Jane learned that she could spiritually lead her children in the disciplines of Christianity. And when she began doing so, she was satisfied and stopped harping on Kevin. Jane also learned that the ability to be quiet is as important as it is to speak up. She did not need to say everything that came to mind, nor did she have to be right. And that sometimes being right before Kevin made her wrong with God. Saying the right thing at the wrong time or with the wrong motive is wrong. Long story short, through Radical Love, Jane learned that what was acceptable growing up *was hurting her relationship with Kevin*. As she changed, her relationship with Kevin improved.

The flip side is this. Kevin responded to Jane's strong, unrelenting personality by avoiding emotionally difficult conversations. He internalized emotional pain, appearing agreeable even when he was not. Kevin had not learned to speak to emotionally powerful people beginning with his mother. He preferred maintaining relationship at the expense of his self-worth. In Radical Love, Kevin recognized that it was important for him to speak up. He understood that if the relationship was going to change, he must be willing to contribute what he thinks and feels. That others have the freedom to agree or disagree. And that Jane's disagreement did not make him less right. With coaching, Kevin learned to admit his thoughts and feelings and practice sharing them in a supportive relationship.

Both Jane and Kevin were committed to the process. Through Radical Love, God was able to take their lives, bless them in their unique aspects of His glory, reduce them to their real value, and offer new life to the other. A missing part of Jane's value was learning to be quiet. By doing so, she created space and the inspiration Kevin needed to show up and share his thoughts and feelings. As he did, Jane developed a newfound respect for Kevin.

A missing part of Kevin's value was learning to speak up. By doing so, he provided knowledge and leadership to their relationship. As Kevin found his voice, Jane no longer felt as though she had to figure out everything for them. Finally, she felt like she had a partner.

When Internal Change Looks Like Responding Differently

Dan can be charming and genuinely helpful. To most, he appears attentive and loving toward his wife. But Julie experiences otherwise. According to Julie, everything revolves around Dan. What she thought and felt mattered little. Dan can be physically aggressive by posturing and shoving. He has thrown things at Julie, only to suggest it was an accident. On several occasions, Dan has admitted being jealous of Julie and her relationships with others. His admission usually follows some sort of outburst that physically or emotionally threatens Julie. Dan is manipulative. Instead of taking responsibility for his wants and needs, he assigns them to Julie. He will say things like, "Aren't you hungry?" instead of saying, "I am hungry." Or "Don't you want to go get this or that" versus "I want to get this or that." Dan is contentious. When confronted about his behavior, Dan makes it about Julie's behavior. Dan is intelligent. He skillfully uses words to reframe events so that Julie doubts her memory, experience, and reality. Dan has an insatiable need for attention and believes he would be happy if Julie spent all her time with him. He feels the need to be right and listens to Julie only to improve his position. When attempts to blame Julie don't work or his behavior is indefensible, he dons the persona of a victim. Dan will lie, connive, and be mean on purpose without regard for the hurt or pain caused Julie.

Julie came to me several years ago. It did not take long to recognize Julie had been abused by powerful people in her life—some of it under the guise of Christianity. Julie believed that forgiveness was the proper response to Dan, because "that's just the way he is." Moreover, that serving others mattered most. Julie could also cite the scripture that says we should not return evil for evil. Julie reminded me of Luke 6:27–31 (MEV):

> But I say to you who hear, love your enemies, do good to those who hate you, bless those who curse you, and pray for those who spitefully use you. To him who strikes you on the one cheek, offer also the other. And from him who takes away your cloak, do not withhold your tunic as well. Give to everyone who asks of you. And of him who takes away your goods, do not ask for them back. Do unto others as you would have others do unto you.

And other verses like, Luke 6:35 (MEV) to heart.

> But love your enemies, and do good, and lend, hoping for nothing in return. Then your reward will be great, and you will be the sons of the Highest. For He is kind to the unthankful and the evil.

And 1 Peter 3:9–11 (TPT):

> Never retaliate when someone treats you wrongly, nor insult those who insult you, but instead, respond by speaking a blessing over them—because a blessing is what God promised to give you. For the Scriptures tell us: and find beauty in each day must stop speaking evil, hurtful words and never deceive in what they say. Always turn from what is wrong and cultivate what is good; eagerly pursue peace in every relationship, making it your prize.

Based on her understanding of love and forgiveness, Julie's response to Dan's repetitive, manipulative, controlling, and hurtful behavior was to accept his apologies, mature in forgiveness, and be a more loving wife. Given Dan's behavior, Julie's response may seem absurd. But I assure you, there are many Christian wives that learned the same.

Unlike Jane, Julie did not need to be quieter. Nor did she need to accept Dan's ungodly leadership. Unlike Jane, Julie did not have a problem saying "Yes." In a sense, she always said yes to or agreed with Dan by adapting to whatever situation arose. Julie accepted responsibility for Dan's feelings and behavior. She had a problem saying "No." Saying "No" went against the grain of Julie's Christianity. For Julie, vulnerability now means sitting up (not sitting down), standing up (not standing down), showing up, and saying, "No." There is scripture support for this response too. In Revelation 2, the Angel of the Lord commended the church at Ephesus for the following.

> I know all that you've done for me—you have worked hard and persevered. I know that you don't tolerate evil. You have tested those who claimed to be apostles and proved they are not, for they were imposters. I also know how you have bravely endured trials and persecutions

because of my name, yet you have not become discouraged.

In the epistle to the Ephesians, Paul instructed the believers likewise in Eph. 5:11-14 (TPT).

> And don't even associate with the servants of darkness because they have no fruit in them; instead, reveal truth to them. The very things they do in secret are too vile and filthy to even mention. Whatever the revelation-light exposes, it will also correct, and everything that reveals truth is light to the soul.

Paul is emphasizing the part of surrendering to God's *Unveiled Love* which is telling the truth with love. Love receives and connects. Truth divides and corrects. It becomes obvious then that love *and* truth work together to unite and direct husbands and wives into proper relationship with God and each other.

Julie was practicing love without truth. On the other hand, Jane practiced truth without love. Love without truth enables evil. Truth without love is repelling. Julie needed to mature in her ability to say "No" to Dan's behavior. Julie and Jane's situations both needed love and truth, not one without the other.

For Julie, this is as hard and scary, as it is for Kevin to open up and say what he thinks and feels in relationship with Jane. Sometimes, *Unveiled Love* is not about God changing your spouse, but rather about God changing your response to your spouse. By changing your response to your spouse, a new set of choices become available to your spouse.

Julie needed to change her response to Dan's behavior. She needed to add truth to their relationship. Julie needed to lay a boundary declaring abuse unacceptable and intolerable. Julie is yet early in establishing the strength of her "No"; therefore, Dan's response remains to be seen. Whether Dan responds favorably or not, whether the relationship survives or not, Julie benefits. The ability to say yes and no is integral to the Christian life. It's like muscles. They work in pairs. Both are required for movement. When one contracts the other relaxes. This is how they work together. The muscles complement each other by opposition. We require this (divine) tension to negotiate life and relationships. If our yes and no muscles are not working together properly, then we either become more contracted and inflexible or relaxed and permissive than is appropriate in relationships. Julie has a strong yes muscle and a weak no muscle. She frequently gave in and excused Dan's behavior to reduce the tension in their relationship. Julie confused her behavior with the gift of mercy. Julie was merciful, but almost always at the expense of being truthful with Dan. By developing her no muscle and denouncing Dan's abusive behavior, Julie exercises her freedom and authority to establish boundaries in her marriage. This also offers Dan an opportunity to reflect on his behavior and make different choices. This is how God's *Unveiled Love* works. Julie broke away from always saying "Yes" to preserve relationship with Dan. Although difficult, Julie is learning to use the word "No" and to object when not in agreement with Dan. Julie is finally showing up in marriage, telling her truth, and trusting God with the outcomes.

A Life Insurance Policy

Think about *Unveiled Love's* transformation system as a life insurance policy. One person pays the premium, another person gets the benefit. The benefit is available for receipt when the one paying the premium dies. More so than in any other gospel, John makes it clear that Jesus is going to the Father and the reason for this. Thirteen times in the Gospel of John, Jesus speaks concerning this. When Jesus speaks of going to the Father, He is talking about giving up His earthly life—*His soul and body*. John 13:3 (CSB) reads as follows:

> Jesus knew that the Father had given everything into his hands, that he had come from God, and that he was going back to God.

John 14:28 (CSB) adds this:

> You have heard me tell you, "I am going away and I am coming to you." If you loved me, you would rejoice that I am going to the Father, because the Father is greater than I.

A third time, Jesus speaks of giving up His earthly life in John 16:28 (CSB):

> I came from the Father and have come into the world. Again, I am leaving the world and going to the Father.

We know that Jesus became our sin and, by doing so, incurred the judgment of God. He did this so that we could be free and reconciled to God. Jesus told His disciples that it was also necessary that He go in order that the Father send the Holy Spirit—*the Helper and the Counselor that empowered Jesus*. John 14:25–26 (CSB) informs:

> I have spoken these things to you while I remain with you. But the Counselor, the Holy Spirit, whom the Father will send in my name, will teach you all things and remind you of everything I have told you.

When Jesus dies, resurrects, and ascends to the Father, the Father would send the Holy Spirit to us that believe. In John 15:26 (CSB), Jesus plainly says that the Holy Spirit will testify of Him.

> When the Counselor comes, the one I will send to you from the Father—the Spirit of truth who proceeds from the Father—he will testify about me.

What this means for us that believe is that the Holy Spirit will bear witness to the word of God, who is Christ, the life of God, the indwelling Christ, and the experiences of God, lived through Christ. This is what every believer can expect. Nothing more. Nothing less. What this means for husbands and wives is simply this. Jesus is God's life insurance policy for the souls of mankind. We are Jesus's beneficiaries. When Jesus gave His earthly life to God through death, the benefit of His life became available to us that believe. Upon Jesus's death, Jesus's life became available to us.

A contemporary example is the death of my father during the writing of this book. As one of his beneficiaries, a monetary benefit was made available to me. Now I have a life insurance policy and upon my death, my children and grandchildren will receive monetary benefit. That's how life insurance policies work. That's how God's *Unveiled Love* works. And God is the architect of this amazing system.

God established the system to reconcile, reform, and restore humanity to Himself. Marriage provides one of the best opportunities to see this system at work. That's because only God can change people for His glory and our good. He does so by working through men and women on each others' behalf. God can change you and your spouse if you are willing. All that is required is for you to engage God's *Unveiled Love*. Let us begin by thinking about saying, "I do," as having taken out a life insurance policy and naming your spouse the primary beneficiary. Then we can inquire of God as to what constitutes our life, that which He requires to facilitate the transformation of our spouse. God's mercy and truth attends His requests, along with grace to yield our lives. As this happens, not only are we transformed, but also our spouse is presented with unique opportunities to change as well. All need the assurance of mercy to face our sin, mistakes, and our unloveliness. All need truth to behave differently. And someone must go first. If not you, then who? The person in marriage experiencing the greatest dissatisfaction is the one who must go first. Although it may not be your fault, the dissatisfaction is your problem. God's *Unveiled Love* is the answer.

It's Who You Are Becoming that Matters

God's *Unveiled Love* is autocorrecting because at the heart of it is who you are becoming and how you are responding in relationship to your spouse. *Unveiled Love* is about you working together with an all-powerful, all-knowing, and always present God and Father. By doing so, you change. It's inevitable. As you do, you give your spouse the greatest opportunity to change too. Paul says as much in Colossians 3:23–24 (CSB).

> Whatever you do, do it from the heart, as something done for the Lord and not for people, knowing that you will receive the reward of an inheritance from the Lord. You serve the Lord Christ.

You are married. But you remain individuals, each one capable of thinking and deciding for him or herself. God deals with you as individuals. Recall Lot and his wife. Lot and his wife lived in the land of Canaan alongside Abraham's family. The land in which they dwelled together could no longer support both families. Abraham gave Lot first choice as to where he wanted to move. He chose Sodom. Sodom was steeped in sexual immorality. God planned to destroy Sodom and Gomorrah and the surrounding cities. He sent angels to warn Lot to take his family and run. The angels told them to run for the hills and to not stop or look back. Lot's wife stopped and looked back. She became a pillar of salt. The story is told in Genesis 19. Although they were married, God dealt with Lot and his wife as individuals.

Ananias and His Wife, Sapphira

The church Luke writes about in the book of Acts was radical. They were unified having all things as common.[81] They sold property

---
[81] Acts 2:44–45

and possessions and distributed them to according to those who had need. In Acts 5, Ananias and Sapphira sold property and presented part of the proceeds, as if it were the entirety of the money received from the sale. Peter confronted Ananias saying that he lied to God. Immediately, Ananias dropped dead. A few hours later, his wife came in, not knowing what just occurred. Peter gave Sapphira an opportunity to come clean by telling the truth. She did not. And this is what Peter said to Sapphira in Acts 5:9 (MEV):

> How is it that you have agreed together to test the Spirit of the Lord? Look! The feet of those who have buried your husband are at the door, and they will carry you out.

Though they were married, each one was held accountable. God did not deal with them as a couple, rather as individuals.

A Modern Example

A few years ago, I attended a conference with a well-known and well-respected minister. He had called out a pastor and his wife to prophesy to them. He provided details about their lives that only God *or Facebook* could have known. Every detail the minister revealed was readily available to any friend of the couple on Facebook. Many were amazed by his seeming accuracy. I was shocked by his brazenness. Then he called out my last name a couple of letters at a time, as if he were getting a slow download. Having just witnessed what I did, I was unmoved. He seemed to become tongue tied, before saying, "You want Moore of God, don't you?" This was true. But what he said next was equally suspicious. He assured the crowd that he could not read name tags, insisting he could not see that far away. I was sitting on the second row. I do not question his salvation. But what I experienced was not God. This minister was very vocal following the 2020 elections, carrying on into 2021. He gained media attention after making some questionable statements.

In the first part of 2022, I learned that he had left his wife. According to the wife, he was scheduled to minister in another state. She had reservations about him going and said as much. She encouraged him to stop and take some time to regroup. The wife admitted they were having marital problems. According to the elders in the church they founded together, he was engaging in ungodly behavior. They felt he needed help and accountability. Apparently, he refused, started a new church across town, and kept his scheduled ministry appointment. His wife had not heard from him since then. He did take a break from social media for a couple of months, he re-emerged announcing his break from social media was over. He continued by condemning the FBI raid on Trump's Mar-a-Lago residence. A few short hours after making this post, he had a heart attack and died. Again, I am not questioning his salvation. In fact, his wife says that she believes with all her heart that he is with Jesus. God knows. Surely, there is more to the story. And only God knows for certain the relationship between the details shared here and the outcome.

My point in relaying this story is this. He was a married man. However, God dealt with him as an individual. Whether married or not, each one will bear responsibility for his actions. Whether we are rewarded with blessings or consequences is entirely up to each one. Who you are and choose to become matters. For this is what informs your choices and behavior. That we are Christian does not exempt us. That you are married doesn't either. God will not always strive with a husband or wife that insists on doing things his or her own way. He is ever mindful of our impact upon others.

God's *Unveiled Love* makes it clear that He will deal with a troublesome spouse. Paul addresses this in verse 25 (CSB):

> For the wrongdoer will be paid back for whatever
> wrong he has done, and there is no favoritism.

God loves you. And God loves your spouse. He loves each of you more than either of you could ever love each other. And His love is holy. It is both merciful and truthful.

Speaking of eating and drinking, Paul tells the Corinthians that they are to do all things for God's glory!

> So, whether you eat or drink, or whatever you do, do everything for the glory of God. 1 Cor 10:31 (CSB)

What we eat and drink physically, mentally, and emotionally combined with our response determines who and what we become. But eating and drinking alone is not enough. We must digest what we eat and drink. We are disciplined by the truth (or lie) we eat and drink. We must be willing to respond to truth. Paul shares the fate of believers unwilling to adhere to the truth they received in 1 Corinthians 10:1–5 (MEV):

> I would not want you to be unaware that all our fathers were under the cloud, and all passed through the sea, and all were baptized into Moses in the cloud and in the sea; all ate the same spiritual food; and all drank the same spiritual drink, for they drank of that spiritual Rock that followed them, and that Rock was Christ. But with many of them God was not well pleased, and they were overthrown in the wilderness.

God equates proper nutrition with truth. Each one must decide to eat and drink. But also each one must choose to adhere to the truths taken in. In this manner, we become what we eat, drink, and exercise. Who you become in relationship with your spouse is what ultimately matters. That's because God uses changed lives to change a life. And this involves learning new responses in the face of adversity. When God's glory is our aim, that we must change is certain. We can love our spouse unconditionally, while relating to them conditionally. Julie and Kevin can love their spouses unconditionally, but they must also show up with boundaries that serve as conditions for relating. For Kevin, it meant stating his opinion and sharing his feelings with Jane more often. For Julie, it meant saying "No" to abuse. Julie and Kevin discovered that love does not give one the right to treat his or her spouse any way he or she chooses. The courage to show up and speak up or to show up and be silent is possible because everything comes from God and returns to Him. Paul expounds in Romans 11:36 (AMPC):

> For from Him and through Him and to Him are all things. [For all things originate with Him and come from Him; all things live through Him, and all things center in and tend to consummate and to end in Him.] To Him be glory forever! Amen (so be it).

In other words, whether consciously and intentionally, we are doing all things in response to God. Husband, wife, God considers that however you think of and treat your spouse is the same way you think of and treat Him. Jesus explains the principle in Matthew 25:31–46 (CSB). There are two possibilities. The first possibility is committing an act of commission, as said in verse 40 (CSB):

> Truly I tell you, whatever you did for one of the least of these brothers and sisters of mine, you did for me.

The second possibility is an act of omission as stated in verse 45.

> Truly I tell you, whatever you did not do for one of the least of these, you did not do for me.

Husband, wife, truthfully, I tell you that your Maker is with whom you must concern yourself. While it easy to believe you are doing things for or against your spouse, it is really God whom you are addressing. For most, this is not an ongoing working reality. Regardless, how we behave in relationships is to God's glory and our benefit or to God's dishonor and our guilt and shame. God sees all, hears all, and is concerned with all. This is what makes *Unveiled Love* so radical and shamelessly provoking. It only requires one willing husband or wife working together with God to facilitate change in his or her spouse. And if your spouse fails to accept this glorious invitation, it is not held against you, who offers his or her life as bread. God is just in this way. This is good news! It's incredible news! You are free! You oversee you! No more bribes, pay to play, or other temporary fixes to deep-seated emotional challenges. You can quit trying to fix your spouse—*you can't!*

I keep thinking of the Christian movie *Fireproof* (2008) in which Caleb Holt, the character played by Kirk Cameron, can't fix his spouse. Neither can his spouse, Catherine Holt, fix him. Caleb tries the "Love Dare" at the urging of his father. But it doesn't work, because he is still trying to change Catherine using Love Dare as a recipe. It isn't until Caleb has an encounter with the cross of Christ, that his entire motivation changes. He decides to follow God and trust Him with the outcomes whether favorable or not. This is how Unveiled Love works. He continues the forty-day challenge even after the forty days run out. In the end, it is God that changes Catherine by opening her eyes to the change and the new motivation to serve God in Caleb's life. God changed Caleb. And by doing so, Catherine became a receptive beneficiary.

Listen, if One Man (Jesus) could change the world by partnering with God, surely you can partner with God's *Unveiled Love*, enabling Him to change your spouse! Unaided by God's Holy Spirit, the human mind is incapable of comprehending this autocorrecting, life-transforming system. It just doesn't make sense. But then, in 1 Corinthians 1:18, Paul makes this abundantly clear:

> For the story and message of the cross is sheer absurdity and folly to those who are perishing and on their way to perdition, but to us who are being saved it is the [manifestation of] the power of God.

You Are the Bread

The life and material God uses to transform us is Jesus Christ. Jesus declared Himself bread—*living bread from heaven*. And as Jesus is in the earth, so are we. Husband, wife, you are the bread that God uses to transform your spouse. Your bread is represented by your manner and way. It's the how you think. It's how you do things and the way you respond to your spouse and others. It's how you sit, how you walk, how you stand. It's how you speak. It's how you interact with others. It's the habits you learned, the strengths you possess. It's the weaknesses you hide. It's your fears. It's your successes and failures. It's your hopes and dreams. Your bread is your time, your money, your possessions. It's everything about you—your past, present, and future all rolled up into one called you. Simply and profoundly, your bread is your whole life and everything concerning it. And the most frightening and most magnificent thing is this: God's *Unveiled Love* asks for it all. God desires an all access, *no-holds-barred* pass to your life and everything and everyone within it. Only you can make these things available to God. You can make it all available to God by offering it. And usually, this happens little by little over the course of your life.

This is the way God changes people. He uses one person (and people) to change another. In marriage, this person begins with you—that is, your life, for you are the bread. When you offer your life to God, He takes it seriously. Jesus always took the bread first.

Taking the Bread and Blessing It

In Matthew 14:19, Mark 6:41, and Luke 9:16 (MEV), Jesus took bread and looked to His Father, then He blessed it.

> Then He took the five loaves and the two fish, and looking up to heaven, He blessed them, and broke them, and gave them to the disciples to set before the crowd.

In these verses, the Greek word for "blessed" means to praise, set apart, and to cause to prosper. Jesus praised His Father. He set apart the bread and fish to God who would cause them to prosper to the fulfillment of all. When we can take our lives because Jesus set us free. We can give our lives to God because Jesus enabled us to reclaim our authority. When we give our lives to God, we acknowledge His worthiness and offer Him praise. By doing so, God sets us apart for His use and then causes us to prosper personally and relationally.

We see this in the lives of Noah, Abraham, David, Abigail, Esther, Ruth, and Job. Each took what they had and gave it to God, who in turn set each one apart for His use and their benefit.

In marriage, when we give our lives to God, acknowledge His right to all that we are and possess, and praise Him, we enable God to set us apart for His use in and ultimately our benefit.

The Breaking

When we give our lives to God, He sets us apart to be used as He desires. Oftentimes, this involves a breaking for which we are ill-prepared, initially reject, then resist before conceding. Much of Western Christianity minimizes or completely ignores this part of transformation. It is no wonder that husbands and wives expect the dating experience to continue well after they say, "I do." We date each other's strengths. We marry each other's weaknesses. And this is for a good reason. Only covenant relationships have the faith, durability, and permanence to handle the severity of the transformation process. God intends this of marriage. Marriage is strong enough to endure the rigors of this breaking. Yet many husbands and wives faint in the day of their adversity. And there are many reasons for this. Not all divorces are the same. While some may disagree, there are some divorces that best preserve the freedom, dignity, and well-being of one or both spouses.

Divorce—A Side Note

Nevertheless, the breaking that comes with divorce is severe. That's because truth penetrates pride, peels the well-plastered pretense, confronts behavior, invades thinking, and exposes the lies believed. For some, divorce is an admission that the cost of truth and the change that it demands is too much. For others, divorce is a remedy to abuse. Still for others, divorce is a license to commit adultery. Many Christians believe that Jesus's disapproval of divorce is with divorce itself. It is not. If you read the context of Jesus's statements on divorce, you will find that adultery is an integral part of every conversation. Upon exposing the Pharisees' dishonesty, greed, and taking advantage of the law, Jesus gives an example of what was likely a fairly common practice. That is, Pharisees' divorcing their wives to marry another to fulfill their sexual appetites. In Luke 16:18, Jesus tells the Pharisees that if they do this, it is the same as committing adultery.

> Everyone who divorces his wife and marries another woman commits adultery, and everyone who marries a woman divorced from her husband commits adultery.

You will find similar statements in Matthew 19:9 and Mark 10:11–12. I cannot find in scripture where Jesus talked about divorce apart from adultery. Jesus exposed the Pharisees' use of Moses's law on divorce as a license to commit sexual sin. Jesus called it adultery. In Luke 16:15 (CSB), Jesus said:

> You are the ones who justify yourselves in the sight of others, but God knows your hearts. For what is highly admired by people is revolting in God's sight.

I realize that this is not an exhaustive study on divorce and remarriage. However, my hope in these few lines is two-fold. First, that it will inspire you to review all scriptures on divorce, as I did.

Perhaps God will bring you to the same conclusion. Scripture denounces divorce as a license for sexual sin. Secondly, all divorce is not about sexual sin. Therefore, it behooves us to consider the circumstances that led up to one choosing divorce.

Like the Pharisees, some of us appear to be well-constructed, well-appointed houses. But God sees through to the bones, the actual framework, the plumbing, and the electricity. He knows what we think, how we think and why we think as we do. He perceived the Pharisees' reason and motivation. We may believe and even look godly to others, but God gets the heart of the matter. I jointly own an older home. Before purchasing it, I asked a couple of friends in residential construction to weigh in. Both said that the home has "good bones." In other words, the home possesses structural integrity and only minor renovations are needed. It's hard to see where we lack structure integrity. We need help. This is both the beauty and awfulness of marriage.

That all are born into sin means that our structural integrity has been ruined. We have developed ungodly ways of thinking and behaving to survive. By the time we reach adulthood, these thoughts, actions, and reactions harden like bones. They are natural to us. While we may limp to others, all is native to us. When a leg is broken and doesn't heal properly, it is called malunion. The treatment is to re-break the bone, align it properly, set it, and cast it so that it heals properly. This is our dilemma.

Sin broke the alignment between God's Spirit and our spirit. But it didn't stop there. Sin realigned our spirit with lies and deception. We learned to think, believe, and act on things that were not true about us and others.

Jesus did not come to improve us. Rather, He came to restore our structural integrity. First, God recreated our spirits. We have spiritual structural integrity because we have been reunited with God through Christ. Now we must take possession of our souls—our minds, will, and emotion and line them up with God's Spirit and Word. This is so we can think right, believe right, act, and respond properly. Jesus's life and work make it possible for us to function the way God created us. We now have opportunities to live how we are made, rather than how we were raised. Marriage, therefore, is uniquely suited for the breaking, realigning, reconnecting, and resetting our mind, will, and emotions. All this to restore our structural integrity.

It is only by this breaking do we become powerful people capable of doing the things Jesus did, and support God in changing our spouse. Jesus made it clear that he could do nothing of Himself.[82] Brokenness which led to dependence on His Father gave us the opportunity to know and experience God as Jesus did. The idea that we outgrow this complete and utter dependency upon God by somehow becoming little gods is outrageous. This kind of thinking is so far removed from anyone who has suffered by the will and hand of God.

David writes of this breaking in Psalm 51:8 (MEV):

> Make me to hear joy and gladness, that the bones
> that You have broken may rejoice.

From our brokenness comes a sweetness that satisfies us as well as others. A few sentences later in verses 16 and 17 (TPT), David explains further:

> For the source of your pleasure is not in my performance or the sacrifices I might offer to you. The fountain of your pleasure is found in the sacrifice of my shattered heart before you. You will not despise my tenderness as I bow down humbly at your feet.

Micah Stampley wrote a song called *"Take My Life."* In it, he writes:

> Brokenness
> Brokenness
> Is what I long for
> Brokenness

---

[82] John 5:30

Is what I need
(Gotta be broken)
Brokenness
Brokenness
That's what you want
For me
Take my heart
And mold it
(Take my mind)
Take my mind
Transform it
(Take my will)
Take my will
Conform it
(Conform my will)
To yours
To yours
Oh, Lord[83]

    There is just no substitute for a broken man or woman. They exude a humility that cannot be feigned. There is a sweetness in their words even when unpleasant to hear. There is a gentleness in the firmness that summons your soul. And despite dealing a sometimes fatal blow to your pride, you leave their presence hopeful and empowered.

    When grapes are crushed, we get wine. When the alabaster box is broken, a sweet-smelling perfume is released. Matthew 26:6, 7, and 12–13 tell the story of a woman who takes an alabaster box, filled with expensive oil, and pours it all over Jesus's head. Alabaster boxes were flasks with a narrow neck. They were made from stone. To get to the valuable contents, the neck of the flask had to be broken to pour out the oil. The alabaster box can be a prophetic gesture representing Jesus's life that is broken for us and the oil the Holy Spirit poured out upon us. But it can also represent our lives. The hard, stony exterior comprised of how we were raised, that is, how

---

[83] Micah Stampley, *The Songbook of Micah* (2005)

we learned to act and respond. Our hardness can be the things we learned to do to protect ourselves to avoid exposure and re-injury of our vital parts. It can be what we have come to rely on for self-worth, significance, and self-preservation. It's our sacred cow responses like "Don't go there," "Don't touch that," and all the other iterations of these phrases. These things God's *Unveiled Love* intends to crush, so that the most valuable parts of you emerge to others blessing and your benefit. It's not about destroying you, rather God desires to establish you in Christ and Him alone. To adopt Christ's way of thinking and acting, we must relinquish our own. And how can we have a choice unless our contrary ways are revealed. That's why Paul says that God's word is quick and more powerful than a double-edged sword.

> For we have the living Word of God, which is full of energy, like a two-mouthed sword. It will even penetrate to the very core of our being where soul and spirit, bone and marrow meet! It interprets and reveals the true thoughts and secret motives of our hearts. (Hebrews 4:12 TPT)

This is what occurs during the breaking. This needs to happen if we are to be useful to God and release life to our spouse and those God assigns us to influence. Transformation requires life for a life. That we become a living sacrifice for the healing of others. This is the currency of God's Kingdom and the autocorrecting nature of God's *Unveiled Love*.

Questions to Learn By

1. Why does the author say God's *Unveiled Love* is autocorrecting? How does this compare to "machine learning"?
2. God's *Unveiled Love* is a fool-proof, fail-safe system that ensures each of us has every opportunity to do what?
3. Read Ephesians 1:11–12. What does it say? What does it mean as it relates to *Unveiled Love*?

Questions to Grow By

1. While a husband or wife might make it easier for a spouse to commit adultery, who is ultimately responsible? What scriptures does the author give to support this?
2. "Marriage is not solely to produce offspring, nor the pleasure of man and woman. While both are germane, marriage was, is and will always be about Christ and His Bride." God is preparing the Bride to give to His Son. And He is using the same system He used to give us His Son. Scripture illustrates with bread. He took bread. Blessed it. Broke it. And gave it to us. What aspects of Jesus's life reflect each of these activities? Did any of these activities appear in your wedding ceremony? (i.e., Were you blessed by clergy, a justice of the peace? Did you take communion? Did you give each other rings?)
3. What is the system of brokenness? How does it apply to you in marriage?

Questions to Change By

1. The author suggests God's *Unveiled Love* is like a life insurance policy. That is, one person pays the premium and another gets the benefit. How does this apply to your marriage?
2. Your life is the bread that God uses to change your spouse. What does this mean? How does it apply to you? What in this offers hope?
3. How is this strategy different than other things you may have tried to improve your relationship?

Secret 9

Endure the Contradiction

> His (Jesus's) example is this: Because his heart was focused on the joy of knowing that you would be his, he endured the agony of the cross and conquered its humiliation, and now sits exalted at the right hand of the throne of God! (Hebrews 12:2 TPT)

Marriage is not a *wedding* event. It is a process. The relationship is designed to take a man and a woman from one place and state of being to another. We have already discussed the care with which this happens. In Secret #8, we talked about the technology God uses to transform the souls of men and women. God's *Unveiled Love* is precise, tamper-proof, and reliable. The person who engages this Love inevitably experiences more freedom, more authority, and personal power. One client who I have been helping apply the secrets of God's *Unveiled Love* to his marriage had this to say: "My wife has not changed as much as I desire, but I feel more respected. I no longer walk on eggshells. I speak my mind." Another client had this to say, "I stopped assuming responsibility for my husband's feelings and behavior. It's like a burden has been lifted." Still, another tells me that she sees everything differently. "It's not just my marriage that has been impacted, but all of my relationships!" If God's *Unveiled Love* only changes you, it's worth it! It's a change that lasts a lifetime and beyond.

Sadly, many couples spend an inordinate amount of time and money on planning their wedding and honeymoon. Courtney's parents spent over twenty-five thousand dollars on her wedding in the late '70s. To put this in perspective, today Courtney's parents would have spent approximately one hundred and ninety thousand dollars on the wedding. Six months later, Courtney and Tommy were divorced. My parents offered the option of a larger wedding or a sizable down payment on a house. I chose the wedding because I considered the day, rather than the life we would live after the day. I do not condemn any that choose a grand wedding day, how can I? I simply offer that couples consider planning a life that includes a wedding day. Jesus kept a long-range view that enabled Him to endure the contradiction between His joy and His trials. There is always an inconsistency between what we desire and what we are currently experiencing. There may be many reasons for this. I wholeheartedly believe that one reason for this is that we have opportunities to conform to Christ's will, manner, and way. This is so that our souls are transformed and mirror our recreated spirits which are in the image and likeness of God.

And since we cannot change ourselves or each other for that matter, we need an effective strategy that we can successfully engage. Moreover, we need a vision and a hope compelling enough to remain engaged. God's strategy was brokenness, culminating in the cross. We were Jesus's hope. We were His joy. We were the reason He endured the contradiction between what He saw and hoped for and what He experienced.

In both Old and New Testaments, God's people endured contradictions between what they believed and hoped for and their present experience. Faith demands this. Noah, Abraham, Joseph, David, Hannah, Naomi, Esther, Peter, Paul, Timothy, and we could go on, all endured inconsistencies, like Jesus, until what they experienced conformed to their hope. What once were ceilings became the floors of testimony—all to God's glory, their benefit, and blessings to many others! Each one discovered the life, the freedom, and authority God reserves for those committed to enduring the contradiction between what they desire and their current experience. Since we can't change ourselves nor do we pay for or own change, another must become involved with us and be willing to pay the price. You cannot change your spouse. You can choose to be involved, intentionally working with God's *Unveiled Love* and pay the price. The price can include any number of things and is unique to marriage. At least one common cost is the willingness to endure contradictions between what you see and what God desires you to see.

I have and always will condemn abuse of all kinds—*spiritual, mental, emotional, physical, sexual, financial, et.al.* This is true for the married and unmarried, children and adults, men and women. Moreover, this book does not advocate maintaining any behavior that perpetuates abuse by enabling the abuser. Disabling an abuser can look different, depending on the circumstances. Sometimes it can look like saying or doing something new and different. At other times, curtailing abuse may involve law enforcement and/or the court system. Still at other times, it may involve temporarily (or permanently) terminating the relationship with the abuser. In all cases, pastoral or professional counseling and other community resources can aid.

When addressing paying the price to facilitate the changes you want to see in your spouse, here is a general rule of thumb. Safety first. Support second. Strategy third. Do you feel safe to exercise your free will without harmful, immobilizing retaliation? You must be able to maintain your freedom to think and act independent of your spouse. Engaging *Unveiled Love* requires this. Therefore, ensuring your safety and that of your spouse and your children is of the utmost importance.

Secondly, who will support you? God's *Unveiled Love* is about you growing and changing. It depends on you changing the way you think and act in relationship to your spouse. And since you cannot change yourself, support and accountability are vital to sustainable success. The result is a powerful and persuasive opportunity for your spouse to also grow and change. That's because when you change, everyone in relationship with you must change—*whether favorably or not.* In his book, *Leadership Pain: The Classroom of Growth,* author

Samuel Chand writes, "Growth equals change; change equals loss; loss equals pain; so inevitably, growth equals pain."[84]

The process of growing and changing is a vulnerable enterprise. Not only do we need safety but also outside assistance. For many, working through the change process alone with God, in our prayer closet, is undeniably appealing to the ego. But prayer and communion with God alone is not how He converts the souls of men and women. Pride aside, if we desire true and lasting change whether for ourselves or our spouse, then we must accept aid from others. As you will soon see, it's non-negotiable. Lack of support prevents change. It's a deal breaker. Support makes the enterprise of growing and changing less threatening, more doable, and most successful. Support may be from a trusted family member or friend, a pastor, professional, a small group, or some combination of any of these mentioned.

Lastly, the third rule of thumb is strategy. Whatever your plan to facilitate God changing your spouse, safety and support are crucial. Still, without effective strategy, faith will remain the substance of the hope that your spouse will change. God's *Unveiled Love* provides strategy that has been tried, tested, perfected in, and proven by His Son, Jesus Christ. By becoming who God intends as a man or woman, husband or wife, your spouse has the greatest opportunity to measure up to his or her divine design. But it will cost you something, *if not everything*.

The Cost

Jesus advises us to count the cost of our endeavors. Transformation always costs somebody something. That we desire our spouse to change will cost us something. Paul talks about the price Jesus paid so that God could redeem us and reconcile us to Himself. Let's just say we weren't cheap. Recall, Paul's explanation of the price in Hebrews 5:7–8 (CSB).

---

[84] Samuel Chand, "Leadership Pain: The Classroom for Growth," Thomas Nelson Publishers, Nashville TN (2015)

> During his earthly life, he offered prayers and appeals with loud cries and tears to the one who was able to save him from death, and he was heard because of his reverence. Although he was the Son, he learned obedience from what he suffered.

God delivered Jesus, but not before he suffered emotionally and physically. Letting go of life hurts. It is part of the transformation process. It is part of Jesus's devotion to God. It is always important to say that God does not suffer humanity. We suffer because we do not love. We suffer when motivated by God's *Unveiled Love* to make decisions that result in loss to ourselves or others. It may be the loss of relationship, opportunity, money, or possessions. Whatever we value, therein is life. When we give up something of value for something of greater value, we feel the loss. And it can hurt—*indescribably so at times.*

Even though it may feel like it, our decisions will seldom bring us to the degree of suffering Jesus experienced. And when in pain, God issues grace, that is the ability to endure and respond to Him. Marriage is a life for a life. It's letting go of our life, that is, the value we attach to our way of doing things and our mental and emotional survival skills. This hurts. But this exchange is God's method for transforming you and your spouse—a life for a life!

Earlier you read about Julie's misunderstanding of Christianity. On one occasion, Julie admitted being fearful of Dan. Julie described being unable to breathe, move, or speak freely in her own home. She did not feel safe. Julie used to believe that she needed to forgive Dan and submit to him. Submit to what—*abuse?* Julie seemed unable to confront Dan's abusiveness. She may not have recogized it for what it was, evil. She was reluctant to tell him that his behavior was—unacceptable. She may even have feared taking even more drastic measures to ensure her safety and well-being. This is not the kind of suffering the Bible endorses nor Jesus displayed. It gives Jesus no joy and God no glory to see His children abused and oppressed.

Jesus was neither bound nor paralyzed spiritually, mentally, or emotionally. He confronted evil. He told the truth. He did not just forgive the Pharisees and conform to their reality. Julie's misinformed beliefs about submission in marriage contributed to her tolerating abuse. This led to unnecessary mental and emotional pain. This may seem obvious to some, but I have found that those in abusive relationships misunderstand or fail to recognize in others, the same breaking and suffering they themselves are experiencing. Jesus retained His freedom and authority to think and respond to His Father among the wicked, the religious, and the perverse. He did not conform to evil. Jesus came for this reason to overcome evil. First John 3:8 (AMPC) sums it up nicely.

> [But] he who commits sin [who practices evil-doing] is of the devil [takes his character from the evil one], for the devil has sinned (violated the divine law) from the beginning. The reason the Son of God was made manifest (visible) was to undo (destroy, loosen, and dissolve) the works the devil [has done].

As I have already said multiple times, God does not support or condone abuse cloaked in Christianity. God's *Unveiled Love* doesn't either. God does not hurt us nor cause us to suffer. But when we do suffer whether self-inflicted or at the hands of another, God is present. We can take courage in Paul's words in 1 Corinthians 10:13 (TPT).

> We all experience times of testing, which is normal for every human being. But God will be faithful to you. He will screen and filter the severity, nature, and timing of every test or trial you face so that you can bear it. And each test is an opportunity to trust him more, for along with every trial God has provided for you a way of escape that will bring you out of it victoriously.

That our character will be tested in marriage is normal to the Christian life. That we will be abused in marriage is not. Still, many will say that God hates divorce. To these, I say God hates abuse more!

Who Pays?

Consider this. Jesus did not go to those he wanted to change and ask them to pay for it. He assumed the cost—*the inconvenience, the discomfort, and the loss of something of value for something of greater value.* He gave up His life because He decided our life was more valuable. Your life is valuable, as is your spouse. You must see your life is valuable. God's *Unveiled Love* doesn't work if you don't know and appreciate your worth to God. It only works when you perceive your own value.

Have you ever received a gift from someone who no longer valued the item he or she was giving you? I know of a friend whose mother valued her expensive collection of jewelry. She also had quite a bit of costume pieces. Occasionally, she would give a piece of jewelry to her daughter. It wasn't the expensive stuff, rather costume jewelry that was often dated. The mother held on to the real, expensive jewelry. My friend confided that because her mother didn't value the jewelry she received, neither did she. The jewelry ended up in the bottom of a drawer or the trash. When we try and give our spouse something that contains little to no value to us, we shouldn't expect that it will have value to him or her. Only life can produce life. Jesus was, and is still alive. He gave up His life to God for us that we might receive life. When a husband or wife gives up his or her life to God for a spouse, that life becomes available to the spouse to receive. Both the life given up has value and the one receiving life has value. In God's economy, esteeming your spouse as more valuable assumes you know your own true value. Recently, I considered what some call the Aaronic blessing. It is God's prayer for the people He delivered from Egypt. It's found in Numbers 6:22–27 (CSB).

> "The Lord spoke to Moses: "Tell Aaron and his sons, This is how you are to bless the Israelites.

> You should say to them, 'May the Lord bless you and protect you; may the Lord make his face shine on you and be gracious to you; may the Lord look with favor on you and give you peace. In this way they will pronounce my name over the Israelites, and I will bless them.'"

The entire prayer is beautiful. It is full of love, affection, and protection for His people. What I find most fascinating is the use of the word "bless." It is used three times. "Bless" is the Hebrew verb "barak." It means to kneel. Jeff Benner, founder of the Ancient Hebrew Research Center, adds, "A related Hebrew word is 'barakah', meaning a gift or present. From this we can see the concrete meaning behind the verb barak. It is to bring a gift to another while kneeling out of respect. The extended meaning of this word is to do or give something of value to another."[85]

Now consider the magnitude of these words. The God of the whole universe and the entirety of creation kneels to offer the gift of His protection, His presence, His perpetuity, and His peace. He kneels out of respect to those He desired to receive Him. Do you see this? The One with greater authority kneels before the one with lesser authority. The One, who is the gift, kneels before the one without. The One with strength kneels before the one without strength. Who else did this? Jesus.

When Jesus knew His time of departure had come, He bowed to wash His disciples' feet. Wait; Jesus is God in the flesh. This Jesus was about to go through the most unimaginable, horrific experience of His life. Shouldn't the disciples kneel and wash His feet? Shouldn't the disciples serve Him? They call Him Teacher and Lord, positioning themselves as students and adherents. Shouldn't this scenario have played out the other way around? Like His Father, Jesus, the One with greater authority kneels before those with lesser authority. The One who is the gift bows before those in need of the gift. The One with the strength bows before those without strength.

---

[85] https://www.ancient-hebrew.org/definition/bless.htm

And who else does this? Those that engage God's *Unveiled Love*. These are intentional in relationship. They understand how God transforms the souls of men and women, married and not. They are not waiting on reciprocity to get what God promises them. They are not relying on their spouse to meet their needs. They see their spouse as an opportunity to learn, grow, and become the person God desires. And because they are becoming more and more secure with who they are in Christ, they are free—*not needing to prove themselves, fend for themselves, or live for themselves.* These perceive their value. Their worth is a settled matter. Therefore, they are free to esteem their spouse's value ahead of their own. For those immersed in God's *Unveiled Love*, Philippians 2:3 is a living reality.

> Do nothing out of selfish ambition or conceit, but in humility consider others as more important than yourselves.

You Are More than Enough

You have an abundance of what your spouse has in short supply. And you know you do. It's the thing you want him or her to say or do. It's the thing you already do so well. We have mentioned this before. It's the serious, task-oriented wife who wants her husband to be more serious and task-oriented. It's the kind and gentle husband who wants his wife to be kinder and gentler. You see, you have what your spouse needs. But if you are holding on to it, it is unavailable for them to receive. Will you withhold the fix because you can't give it directly to your spouse? God's *Unveiled Love* requires all things to go through Him to be of lasting value to others. Scripture offers this support.

Abraham's Example

God promised Abram a son and that he would be the father of many nations. Upon this promise, God changed his name to

Abraham.[86] In Genesis 22, God instructs Abraham to place his son, Isaac, on the altar. Many offer reasons why God would instruct Abraham to do this. I suggest this. Isaac was the promised son, through whom Abraham would become the father of many nations. But Isaac was born in sin. God sets apart, cleanses, and makes exchanges with those He chooses to do the greater works. The altar of God is holy. The altar Abraham built and placed Isaac upon separated Isaac (from himself), cleansed Isaac, and exchanged his sinfulness for righteousness. Abraham's willingness to offer Isaac on the altar of God was counted as a sacrifice. Abraham's willingness to offer Isaac to God became legal tender. God accepted Abraham's offering as a valid and sufficient exchange to become a great nation and a great name. Perhaps all will not agree with this explanation. However, God is holy, and He requires holiness, that is our sanctification. Isaac was given to God that day. Abraham had to go through God before becoming the Father of many nations. And Isaac had to go through God before he was given to the nations. God's *Unveiled Love* follows the pattern of Abraham and Jesus. Whatever changes you desire to see in your spouse, you must offer yourself to God as an acceptable and pleasing exchange. Many husbands and wives want their spouse to change so they can remain the same. These have no interest or intention to behave differently. They think if their spouse changes, everything will be fine. In this, they err. When a spouse changes, it gifts the other with opportunities to behave differently. Some will. Some won't. But those that commit to God's *Unveiled Love* operate on a whole other level.

Like Abraham was in receipt of Isaac, God's answer for the nations, you are in receipt of God's answer for your spouse. But the answer must go through God before delivery to your spouse. Commonly, we see what our spouse needs and try to answer it. We may even be right. But we go as far as to force-feed the answer we think is right and best. No wonder so many have difficulty receiving from their spouse. Who wants to be force fed?

---

[86] Genesis 17:1–6

It doesn't work! When we keep trying, we become frustrated and our spouse becomes resentful. Even though what you are saying or doing may be right, unless cleansed, the underlying motives are smeared with pride, self-preservation, and selfishness. Our motives are not pure because we say so or even believe so. Pure motives, like silver, must be tried by fire until all the dross is removed. The silversmith, not the silver, determines this. When he can see his reflection in the silver, all the dross has been removed.

Your knowledge, skills, talents, and abilities are the answers your spouse needs. But they must be cleansed of any ulterior selfish motive. And the only way to do that is to get the answer out of our hands. The answer along with our bright ideas, and cleverness must be placed on the altar—separated to God, cleansed of impurities, before being given to your spouse. Sound familiar? As Jesus would later do with the bread, Abraham did with his Isaac. Abraham *took* Isaac up the mountain, *blessed* him, *broke* him on the altar, and gave him to God. Then God gives Isaac back to Abraham. Solomon tells us the following in Ecclesiastes 11:1 (AMPC).

> Cast your bread upon the waters, for you will find it after many days.

If we receive life in marriage, it is because we let go of life. And if our spouse is to get life, we must let go of life. That's the way it works. We cannot hold on to what our spouse needs and at the same time think our spouse is able to receive it. Even if our spouse was interested in taking what we offer, it would look like tug of war. Each time our spouse tried to take us up on the offer, he or she feels our tug of resistance. After a while, one or both give up, increasing the temptation to step outside the marriage.

The Way of the Cross

God's *Unveiled Love* is unique. It's not new-age, psychology, or simply behavior modification. It's the way of the cross. It is how God conducts change. Most are familiar with hair, makeup, and wardrobe makeovers. Makeovers are quite common. Generally, makeovers are conducted by another with knowledge, experience, and expertise in the area we want made over. The cross is God's makeover for humanity. He alone has the knowledge, experience, and expertise required. The prophet observed this very thing in Jeremiah 18:1–10 (MSG).

> God told Jeremiah, "Up on your feet! Go to the potter's house. When you get there, I'll tell you what I have to say." So, I went to the potter's house, and sure enough, the potter was there, working away at his wheel. Whenever the pot the potter was working on turned out badly, as sometimes happens when you are working with clay, the potter would simply start over and use the same clay to make another pot. Then God's Message came to me: "Can't I do just as this potter does, people of Israel? God's Decree! Watch this potter. In the same way that this potter works his clay, I work on you, people of Israel."

The good news is that God is still performing makeovers! God used Jesus's faith, life and surrender to give humanity another chance to know Him. Jesus, working together with God's *Unveiled Love*, is responsible for the opportunities we possess to believe, experience, and know God as we do. Let me say this again. It was and is Jesus, not us, that is responsible for our transformation. One man working with God's *Unveiled Love* brought about amazing opportunities for us to know God and each other intimately. Are you tracking? Husband, wife, when either one of you give your faith, life, and surrender to God and work together with God's *Unveiled Love*, your spouse has new and fresh opportunities to believe, experience, and know God. You are God's gift to your spouse, whether he or she recognizes this or not.

Here's the Big Idea

Jesus did not ask us, the recipients of God's gift and grace, to also pay for it. Nor will God ask your spouse to pay for the changes He wants to make and you desire for your spouse. Paul says it this way in Romans 5:8 (TPT).

> But Christ proved God's passionate love for us by dying in our place while we were still lost and ungodly!

Jesus took the hit and suffered the loss for us. In marriage, all have been hurt by the words and actions of a spouse. All of us have indulged the appetites of the flesh. Human vice is endless. Our learned emotional responses are tied to our survival. Even our strengths are learned ways of thinking and behaving to avoid that which we fear. Our spouse pays for it when we over-indulge the flesh, succumb to vice, use anger to neutralize perceived threats, and employ our strengths to stay alive at his or her expense. In marriage, husbands and wives hurt each other. None are immune from causing emotional injury. These are some of the expenses spouses incur. How each one responds determine what use God makes of it. For instance, a husband or wife lashing out in response to his or her spouse's disregard for punctuality is unlikely to produce a sustainable regard for time. If punctuality is a recurring challenge, then in those situations when punctuality is critical (i.e., catching a plane, paying bills, or meeting tax deadlines) make different arrangements. Perhaps one can drive separate cars to the airport, take responsibility for paying the bills or separate bills and bank accounts, or file separate taxes. I recognize that the alternatives may be more costly to the wallet, but trading agitation and anxiety for peace might very well be worth it. Still, this may not be feasible for some. In these cases, I maintain God does have an answer that will allow you to maintain a posture compatible with *Unveiled Love*. That God's Love is *Unveiled Love* means that your marriage relationship may not look like everyone else's. That's because what God may have you do is not what He may have others do. Therefore, prayer, accompanied by wise counsel, is good. When you incur costs for things we neither asked for nor desired, our response is a key component in God making over your spouse. Add to the costs, our hurt and pain. When all is kneaded together, it becomes the bread we offer to God. When we offer our bread to God and respond as He desires, we are paying for the changes we want to see in our spouse.

At the beginning of secret 8, I shared my experience concerning my mother and pastor's daughter visiting us one weekend. I explained that God allowed me to know an unusual peace despite reason for distress. What was my bread? I had to let go of the need to appear perfect before important people. I had to let go of the need for everything to be in perfect order. I had to let go of the need to do things my way. I had to let go of the need to be responsible for others' feelings, whether they belonged to my mother, pastor, or then husband. I had to let go of the need and idea that I could fix it. And I had to let go of the anger I felt as this had been a chronic problem. Letting go is how I offered these things to God. The things I let go were not on a checklist, readily available for me to see. But as each thought and feeling came to my awareness, I admitted it and offered it to God, trusting He would accept it. By faith, I know He did. I thanked Him. He separated me from each one and gave me His love and contentment in exchange. I was able to recall scripture and say them out loud. Scriptures like, God is working all things together for my good because I love Him, and He called me for His pleasure and purposes. I remembered that God is a present help in my need. I thanked God for setting me free of having to fix it and assume responsibility for others' feelings. Oh yeah, this one was huge! As one who loves hot, long showers to both relax and cleanse, the cold water was a rude awakening. To my surprise, I was able to thank God that the cold shower of my awakening to no hot water still made me clean. And I had peace. I had peace because what the enemy used to try and derail me, God used to establish a new level of faith and love.

This was the bread God used to prompt, inspire, or provoke my then husband to go up and down the stairs, countless times to ensure three ladies had hot baths. This was not clever psychology on my part. Unknownst to me at the time was God's *Unveiled Love* working with me, and me with Him. It would be years later, even now as I write this book that I understand what truly transpired. And though my marriage did not last, I am forever changed. I have no regrets. Marriage showed me some of the best of times and some of the worst of times. I am older, wiser, and at rest in Him. And I am more willing, though not always eager to offer God what he desires. I know Him as a promise keeper—*for my labor has not been in vain.*

A Word About the Use of Ultimatums

According to *Merriam-Webster's Dictionary*, an ultimatum is a final condition or demand issued to another. An ultimatum can be used to manage the behavior of an offending party or to manage one's own behavior. Ultimatums issued to control a spouse's behavior may work, but in many cases, the benefit is temporary. That's because ultimatums serve to regulate behavior and may have little to no impact on the heart and soul that produces the behavior. When issuing an ultimatum to an offending spouse, keep in mind it will likely be less effective than using an ultimatum to govern your own behavior. It's the difference between what you would have your spouse to differently versus what you will do differently.

Let's apply this to Julie and Dan. Dan is abusive. Julie now recognizes that much of Dan's behavior serves to provoke a reaction from her, which inevitably results in her catering to him. It's manipulative and controlling. Julie can issue one of two ultimatums to Dan. Which one do you think would be most effective?

Ultimatum 1: "Dan, if you don't stop abusing me, then you will have to leave."

Ultimatum 2: "Dan, I no longer tolerate your abusive behavior. If you continue, I will leave."

The first ultimatum is passive, placing the burden on Dan to change his behavior or leave. The problem is this. Julie can't change Dan's behavior nor make him change. While she may be able to enlist the help of law enforcement to force Dan to leave, this will not occur without verifiable proof of abuse. Typically, this looks like physical injury. Given these things, in most cases, issuing an ultimatum that places the responsibility on your spouse to change is pointless.

Conversely, the second ultimatum is assertive. Julie retains the freedom, responsibility, and authority to act in her best interest. She tells Dan that his abusive behavior is unacceptable. Moreover, she will no longer tolerate it. That if he chooses to continue to act abusively, she will exit the relationship. Exiting the relationship could look like separation, taking out a restraining order preventing contact, temporarily moving in with family or friends, seeking counsel to identify an acceptable way forward, and/or divorce. Each abusive relationship is different. Each one ought to be considered on its own distinctions.

Ultimatums are most helpful in the governance of self. That's because this kind of ultimatum relies on your freedom, authority, and ability to direct your own behavior.

Promises, Processes, and Principles

The promise that God can change you and your spouse is plain. This is the reason Jesus came. He came to reconcile us to God. He did this by incurring God's judgment on our behalf, thereby setting us free to take part in the reformation process. First, we must be reformed and restored to God in our thinking and behavior. Then, we gain favor and influence with God and man. We best support God's efforts to change our spouse when we engage this transformational process for ourselves. A progressively changing husband or wife is an irrefutable testimony of God's grace and power. And as one spouse continuously engages the transformation process, his or her life becomes available for God to give to the other. I am reminded of the words the Lord spoke in Zechariah 4:6 (CSB).

> "Not by strength or by might, but by my Spirit,"
> says the Lord of Armies.

Not human will power, nor human ability, nor human effort alone, will change you or your spouse. It requires one person's faith engaging the technology of transformation for God to bring about what we desire to see. This technology, also called God's *Unveiled Love*, is fool-proof, fail-safe, spouse-safe, and spouse-proof! This means that human incompetence, error, or misuse cannot derail God's *Unveiled Love*. God has His own way of automatically compensating for these things to prevent failure. God's *Unveiled Love* works plain and simple. It is the only thing that delivers long-term results. It can take the hostile minds, intentions, and actions of a husband or wife and inspire him or her for His glory and your benefit. It's a process. And God invites each of us to take part. That's because marriage is a life for a life.

The process requires the whole life of one for the whole life of the other. Jesus demonstrates. Jesus gave His whole life—*body, soul, and spirit* in covenant relationship with God. God, in turn, gave us the life of Christ. God's *Unveiled Love* takes one life, blesses it, breaks it, and gives it to another. The instrument that makes this continuously possible is the cross. By engaging the technology of transformation, Jesus single-handedly relieved us of having to live in sin, guilt, and shame. He made us free. He made it possible for us to reclaim our authority. Jesus made it possible for us to do the same for our spouse. Paul explains in Galatians 2:20 (CSB):

> I have been crucified with Christ, and I no longer live, but Christ lives in me. The life I now live in the body, I live by faith in the Son of God, who loved me and gave himself for me.

Verse 19 (MSG) informs us what this looks like.

> What actually took place is this: I tried keeping rules and working my head off to please God, and it didn't work. So I quit being a "law man" so that I could be God's man. Christ's life showed me how, and enabled me to do it. I identified myself completely with him. Indeed, I have been crucified with Christ. My ego is no longer central. It is no longer important that I appear righteous before

you or have your good opinion, and I am no longer driven to impress God. Christ lives in me.

Paul engaged the technology of transformation. He received God's *Unveiled Love* for himself first and then tells us he is poured out as a drink offering for others. It reminds me of the instructions flight attendants give in the event of an emergency. We are reminded to put the oxygen mask on ourselves first and then assist those around us. Husbands and wives ought to receive and engage God's *Unveiled Love* for themselves first.

As Paul encourages Timothy to exercise self-control in everything, to endure difficulties and fulfill his assignment, he also tells him the following:

> For I am already being poured out as a drink offering, and the time for my departure is close. I have fought the good fight, I have finished the race, I have kept the faith (2 Tim. 4:6-7):

This same Paul wrote half of the New Testament. The transformation technology called God's *Unveiled Love* worked for Jesus. It worked for Paul. And it will work for you! Jesus is so sure of this technology that He instructs the disciples in this manner. Paul passes the technology on to fellow believers in 1 Corinthians 11:23–26 (CSB).

> For I received from the Lord what I also passed on to you: On the night when he was betrayed, the Lord Jesus took bread, and when he had given thanks, broke it, and said, "This is my body, which is for you. Do this in remembrance of me." In the same way also he took the cup, after supper, and said, "This cup is the new covenant in my blood. Do this, as often as you drink it, in remembrance of me.' For as often as you eat this bread and drink the cup, you proclaim the Lord's death until he comes."

For Paul, communion was more than a remembrance. It became his lifestyle. Jesus engaged God's *Unveiled Love* for God's glory, Paul's benefit, and our blessing. One man working with God's *Unveiled Love* transformed Paul's hostile mind, willful intent, and evil actions into one of God's greatest friends!

The process worked then, and it works now. It demands a life for a life. Whatever you desire to see in your spouse, he or she will need an opportunity to become it. Your faith and participation in God's *Unveiled Love* is your spouse's best chance for this to happen. God promises to do this and even more than we can imagine according to Ephesians 3:20 (TPT).

> Never doubt God's mighty power to work in you and accomplish all this. He will achieve infinitely more than your greatest request, your most unbelievable dream, and exceed your wildest imagination! He will outdo them all, for his miraculous power constantly energizes you.

He also shows us how by spelling out God's Unveiled Love—the technology of transformation—and by giving us living proof through the lives of and fail-safe. It works exactly as it should every single time and in every single relationship where it is employed. It always presents the intended recipient with an opportunity to think, feel, and behave differently. And if they do, the transformation lasts for always.

The Principle

God's promises and processes are held together by principles or laws that reflect truth. This is what makes them so overwhelmingly successful. There are many laws undergirding God's *Unveiled Love*. One principle is the law of sowing and reaping. What we do earns favor and blessings or consequences. Seedtime and harvest support transformation technology. Genesis 8:22 declares the law.

> As long as the earth endures, seedtime and harvest, cold and heat, summer and winter, and day and night will not cease.

Paul clarifies the principle in Galatians 6:7–10.

> God will never be mocked! For what you plant will always be the very thing you harvest. The harvest you reap reveals the seed that you planted. If you plant the corrupt seeds of self-life into this natural realm, you can expect a harvest of corruption. If you plant the good seeds of Spirit-life you will reap beautiful fruits that grow from the everlasting life of the Spirit. And don't allow yourselves to be weary in planting good seeds, for the season of reaping the wonderful harvest you've planted is coming! Take advantage of every opportunity to be a blessing to others, especially to our brothers and sisters in the family of faith!

The principle of sowing and reaping aids and benefits the one who engages God's *Unveiled Love*. That's because when we engage this transformation technology, we plant good seed. We sow to the Spirit of Life that is in Christ Jesus. We both win and offer our spouse opportunity to choose differently.

Fred's Story

The principle also works in reverse. To the spouse who insists on being irresponsible, selfish, hurtful, and unrepentant, the law issues consequences. Here's a true story. Fred is a wildly successful businessman. He enjoys all the external props of success—homes, cars, a boat, a four-wheeler, and just about anything else he fancies. He knows just about everyone in his sphere of influence. And they know him. He is likeable and helpful. Fred always has a story that will make you laugh or bring you to tears. He can be very enjoyable and generous. He has a wife and three young children whom he loves dearly and for whom he would do most anything.

Yet Fred is an alcoholic and habitual drug user, which repeatedly affects his behavior. He exhibits unrestrained profanity, sarcasm, and obscene language. During some part of most days, Fred is usually high. He has even blacked out, which means his wife and children are persistently exposed to this abuse. Despite his awareness of the adverse impact upon his family, Fred is unable to stop himself. He has gained considerable weight and has recently learned he has high blood pressure. Without intervention, it is easy to imagine the effect of these seeds will have on his physical health. But what about the long-term impact on his wife and children? What emotional toll is it taking upon them? Who might they become? Will anger reside in their bosom? How might they treat their bodies, spouses, and children? Fred is sowing seeds of irresponsibility, selfishness, and harm. The law of seedtime and harvest demands retribution.

Hopefully, Fred and his family will receive the help needed to avert complete destruction. Fred's story is not over. I am believing the best. I am doubtful that his wife is presently engaging God's *Unveiled Love*. If this were so, I imagine opportunities for a better outcome. Still, the outcome belongs to God. He retains final authority in everything. Speaking of the church at Corinth, Paul had this to say concerning he and Apollos.

> I have planted, Apollos watered, but God gave the increase. So then neither is he who plants nor he who waters anything, but God who gives the increase. Now he who plants and he who waters are one, and each one will receive his own reward according to his own labor.[87]

The principle of sowing and reaping is true. God is responsible for the outcomes. Each one will bear the burden of his or her

---

[87] 1 Corinthians 3:6–8 (MEV)

actions. Our families and friends are either blessed or become collateral damage.

God's *Unveiled Love* works because it adheres to unchangeable laws like sowing and reaping. Some are favorably provoked and inspired by the physical, mental, and emotional pain they experience. They learn, grow, and change to their own benefit and that of others.

Jeff and Carol's Story

Jeff loved the idea of being his own boss. So he chose commission sales. It was the closest thing to owning his own business. It makes sense. Jeff can sell. But over the years, he has proven inconsistent. He does well, flounders, and then bottoms out. He has gone from one company to another, all with the same outcome. About a year into a new job, Jeff has trouble selling, resulting in missed quotas. After several years of feast or famine and Carol's job keeping their heads just above water financially, she had enough. Carol and Jeff had been married for six years when they began having children. For those six years, Carol was supportive as they could easily bounce back. However, when they began having children, it became harder and harder to recover financially. One evening, Carol told Jeff she could no longer support the manner he chose to make a living. It was too stressful. She suggested he find a salaried job and, if he was still interested in sales, to do it as a hobby. Jeff took to heart what Carol said. He found a job in retail sales, a salaried sales job. It was a great solution. Jeff started working for a tire company. He no longer had to generate his own sales. Rather, people came into the store because they needed tires. For Jeff, it became a matter of which tires met each customer's expectation and budget. Jeff liked it, and Carol was happy. Their financial security and outlook improved! With help from Carol, Jeff experienced James 1:1–4 (TPT).

> My fellow believers, when it seems as though you are facing nothing but difficulties, see it as an invaluable opportunity to experience the greatest joy that you can! For you know that when

your faith is tested it stirs up in you the power of endurance. And then as your endurance grows even stronger, it will release perfection into every part of your being until there is nothing missing and nothing lacking.

The promises, processes, and principles of God, work together to transform the souls and lives of men and women. God's *Unveiled Love* is so effective because it offers the promise and hope that your relationship can be different. It provides the process by which God makes it happen, and it is supported by unchangeable laws.

Here's the thing. Neither you nor your spouse can change yourself. God and at least one other human being are required to produce desirable, true, and lasting change. Your God-given destiny includes all the desires, challenges, pleasures, and opportunities to develop godly character. The same is the case for your spouse. For all this, we require each other.

For David, destiny was the throne. Jonathan comforted, challenged him, and carried him to the throne. Jonathan gave his life—*his bread*. David ate. For Ruth, destiny was becoming part of the lineage of Jesus Christ. Naomi escorted, encouraged, and instructed Ruth concerning Boaz. Naomi gave her life—*her bread*. Ruth ate. For Esther, destiny was to deliver God's people. Mordecai prepared and advised Esther. Mordecai gave his life—*his bread*. Esther ate. And how about Peter? His destiny was to belong and be loved. Jesus accepted Peter. He affirmed Peter, always restoring him to relationship. Jesus gave His life—*his bread*. Peter ate. Then Peter devoted himself to Jesus by pouring out his life—*his bread* to the Gentiles.

All these were transformed and catapulted to destiny by another. Jonathan, Naomi, Mordecai, and Jesus were blessed in offering their lives. Jonathan received provision and protection for his family for the remainder of their lives. Naomi received a son (Obed) to nurse and mother. Mordecai received honor as well as the king's ring of authority. He had also appointed him over the house of Haman. Jesus received the Jews and Gentiles.

It is God who makes us and not we ourselves. And He always uses other people on our behalf. Every promise has a process. And people are always part of the process of bringing promises to reality. Your desire to see your spouse change requires your participation. But it's not how you think. Nor does it occur the way you want. It's more like re-gifting. You receive a gift. Then you give the gift to another. We are God's gift to our spouse, and they are a gift to us. Everything we possess, we first received. No one, absolutely no human being, is self-made. We require each other to become who God desires. Remember Paul's words in 1 Corinthians 4:7 (CSB):

> For who makes you so superior? What do you have that you didn't receive? If, in fact, you did receive it, why do you boast as if you hadn't received it?

But also we require and must maintain our freedom and authority to voluntarily offer our lives to God. This is our bread. And as God gives us daily bread, so we ought to give Him our daily bread. When we do, He re-gifts it to our spouse. God's *Unveiled Love* is effective because each couple has what is needed for each one to become who God desires and accomplish God's respective and collective will for their lives. Paul affirms this when sharing the example of our role model who is Jesus in 2 Corinthians 8:9 (CSB).

> For you know the grace of our Lord Jesus Christ: Though he was rich, for your sake he became poor, so that by his poverty you might become rich.

Every husband is rich. Every wife is rich. Each one possesses an aspect of God's glory. Also, each one has strengths, skills, abilities, and godly character traits the other does not. Paul summarizes in 2 Corinthians 8:13–15 (MEV).

> I do not mean that other men have relief, and you be burdened, but for equality, that your abun-

> dance now at this time may supply their need, and their abundance may supply your need—that there may be equality. As it is written, "He who gathered much had no excess. And he who gathered little had no lack."

Equality in marriage is not having the exact same thing or being able to do the same things. Rather, equality is the emptying of what one does have to supply the need of the other. This is what is meant by unequal gifts, albeit equal sacrifice. Therein, is unity. In all, there must be a willingness.

> For if there is a willing mind first, the gift is accepted according to what a man possesses and not according to what he does not possess.

True and lasting transformation for you and others only happens through relationship. This is the way God designed it. You are the living bread God desires to use to transform our spouse—*not by imposing your strength upon your spouse, not by correcting your spouse, not by manipulating and controlling your spouse's access to people, places and things, not by trying to make him or her behave to your satisfaction, not by raining down fire and brimstone, not by taking revenge, not by embarrassing or humiliating, not by meeting his or her needs, not by being dutiful, nor by any other human scheme—good or bad,* but by God's profound *Unveiled Love*! This includes enduring the contradiction presented by the cross. The condition of many marriages today, perhaps even some of our own, provides ample proof that human will and effort alone is futile. Marriage is a life for a life and settles for nothing less.

God shares your desire to see your spouse change in a particular area, manner, or way. He gave you faith to see your spouse's potential and to partner with Him that this potential can be realized. That's because without faith, it is impossible to please God. Moreover, we must believe that He rewards the faith of the person that seeks Him.[88] God keeps His promises. That's why Paul advises us in Hebrews 10:23 (CSB).

> Let us hold on to the confession of our hope without wavering, since he who promised is faithful.

God's *Unveiled Love* working in you, for you, and on behalf of your spouse, adds to your faith the desire to do what pleases Him. It's our faith that wins God's approval—*not the outcome.* Whether your spouse accepts God's invitation and opportunity to grow and change matters not, God will bless you anyway. What matters is that we endure the contradiction between what we have and what we desire.

Every promise you are holding on to for your husband or wife involves contradiction. There is immediate contradiction between the way your spouse is and the way you (and God) desire him or her to be. And since transformation is a process, you must endure the contradiction until that which you desire manifests. In the meantime, you are taking part in a process that allows God to re-gift your life to your spouse. Every process hangs on a principle or truth that transcends each couple's unique circumstance. You can endure the contradictions because you win! You win because in the process, God is making you over. He is training you how to speak and behave in a manner that reflects His eternal nature. And whether your spouse accepts the resulting invitations to be transformed, you cannot lose who you become, nor that which God has planned for you personally!

So again, I encourage you to endure the contradiction by holding dear to Paul's words in 2 Corinthians 4:16–18 (MSG):

> So we're not giving up. How could we! Even though on the outside it often looks like things are falling apart on us, on the inside, where God is making new life, not a day goes by without his unfolding grace. These hard times are small potatoes compared to the coming good times, the lav-

---

[88] Hebrews 11:6

ish celebration prepared for us. There's far more here than meets the eye. The things we see now are here today, gone tomorrow. But the things we can't see now will last forever.

And in Ephesians 3:20 (TPT).

Never doubt God's mighty power to work in you and accomplish all this. He will achieve infinitely more than your greatest request, your most unbelievable dream, and exceed your wildest imagination!

Questions to Learn By

1. "Marriage is not a *wedding* event, rather a process." What does the author say marriage is designed to do?
2. Why do we need an effective strategy to bring about change in marriage?
3. What does it mean to endure contradiction? Give a biblical example of someone who endured a contradiction until he or she got what they desired.

Questions to Grow By

1. What is the technology or four-step process God uses to transform the souls of men and women?
2. Partnering with God to facilitate change in your spouse is a process that mirrors what Jesus did with bread. Each time he took it, blessed it, broke it, and gave it to others. Can you identify any of these experiences in your own relationship? If so, describe.
3. What is the easiest part of God's transformation technology to apply to your relationship? What is most difficult? Give examples.

Questions to Change By

1. As stated in secret 8, you are the bread God uses to transform your spouse. Your bread is your life and is made of many things. Make a list of strengths, skills, possessions, hurts, pains, beliefs about yourself and others that make up your life. In making the list, consider gathering feedback from others (i.e., family, friends, children, coworkers) to identify strengths and weaknesses.
2. What has made you unwilling to offer your strength or weakness to God? For instance, fear of being out of control might make a person with strong administrative skills reluctant to offer these skills to God. Or a fear of being hurt again might make a person reluctant to give up angry outbursts.
3. Take some time and imagine a scenario in which you did give this very thing to God. And instead of fear of loss or pain, you experienced gain and joy. Describe what this would look like for you. How might this favorably impact your spouse?

Secret 10

Celebrate Victory!

Love never fails. (1 Corinthians 13:8 AMPC)

We can celebrate victory because God's *Unveiled Love* always prevails, even when it doesn't seem like it. Paul reassures us in Ephesians 1:11–12 (MSG).

> It's in Christ that we find out who we are and what we are living for. Long before we first heard of Christ and got our hopes up, he had his eye on us, had designs on us for glorious living, part of the overall purpose he is working out in everything and everyone.

The Amplified Classic Translation reads slightly different and is worth mentioning:

> In Him we also were made [God's] heritage (portion) and we obtained an inheritance; for we had been foreordained (chosen and appointed beforehand) in accordance with His purpose, Who works out everything in agreement with the counsel and design of His [own] will, So that we who first hoped in Christ [who first put

our confidence in Him have been destined and appointed to] live for the praise of His glory!

If God is going to carry out His will, then it begs the question, where does our free will come in? If God is going to have His way, if His will trumps all, then why does it matter that we have free will? Why should we even bother to engage *Unveiled Love*? Here is how I reconcile God's sovereignty and our free will. God is sovereign. He retains final authority over all creation. He has established laws to govern the universe and all creation. These laws have predetermined ends. Adam was told that he could eat freely from any tree in the Garden of Eden, except from the tree of the knowledge of good and evil. And if he ate of this tree, he would surely die. Romans 8:2 refers to this as the law of sin and death. In this same verse, Paul speaks of another law. It is called the law of the Spirit of life in Christ Jesus. One law ends in death, the other law ends in life. In similar fashion, other laws like the law of love in Matthew 22:37–40, and the law of sowing and reaping in Galatians 6:7 all end in either blessings or consequences. We can choose to obey God's laws or violate them. This is our free will at work. The blessings or consequences that follow are God's Sovereignty at work. He alone has decided the rewards and punishments for every law that governs the universe and mankind. God does not override our will. He doesn't have to. God's laws serve His purposes. His laws reflect His nature, His goodness, as well as His Holiness and justice. Paul explains God's laws this way in Romans 11:22 (AMPC).

> Then note and appreciate the gracious kindness and the severity of God: severity toward those who have fallen, but God's gracious kindness to you—provided you continue in His grace and abide in His kindness; otherwise, you too will be cut off (pruned away).

God's laws are good, but also severe. Those that obey God's laws experience blessings, which give rise to even more blessings. Those that violate God's laws experience penalties. If we continue to violate God's laws, the after-effects become more severe. In His sovereignty, God makes the rules about life and relationships. We get to choose how we respond. In this way, God's sovereignty does not interfere with our free will and our free will does not interfere with His sovereignty. Sovereignty and free will are perfectly compatible, as they are each managed by laws. The remarkable strength and humility of God is that he subjects Himself to His own word. God's word is law. In Psalm 138:1–2 (AMPC), David declares this alone is worthy of worship.

> I will confess and praise You [O God] with my whole heart; before the gods will I sing praises to You. I will worship toward Your holy temple and praise Your name for Your loving-kindness and for Your truth and faithfulness; for You have exalted above all else Your name and Your word and You have magnified Your word above all Your name!

We can celebrate victory in marriage because it, too, is governed by laws. So even when all seems dire, you are never on your own. God's laws are present to guide, support, and reward you. When you take part in God's *Unveiled Love*, you come to terms with His will and His way. And I can tell you this, married or not, the reward is peace. It is peace that we need. Neither money nor possessions can buy this peace. That's because peace is a person. His name is Jesus Christ.[89] In Job 22:21–22 (AMPC), we find the Bible's position on the matter.

> Acquaint now yourself with Him [agree with God and show yourself to be conformed to His will] and be at peace; by that [you shall prosper and great] good shall come to you. Receive, I pray

---

[89] Ephesians 2:14

> you, the law and instruction from His mouth
> and lay up His words in your heart.

The secrets shared in *Unveiled Love* are based on God's laws and principles and applicable to every man, woman, husband, and wife. These laws and principles are true. They are unchangeable, irreplaceable, and unbreakable. They last for always. Psalm 119:60 (CJB) says so.

> The main thing about your word is that it's true;
> and all your just rulings last forever.

It is a mistaken thought that someone can break the law. When we disobey the law, we, not the law, suffer the consequences. Unlike the breaking discussed in the secret 8, the breaking spoken of here is specific to actions that violate God's laws.

Several years ago, I worked with a couple who had been married for over ten years. Both were Christian and very involved in their local church. They did well financially and enjoyed the benefits of an upper middle-class lifestyle. Both were active in employing some of the secrets in God's *Unveiled Love*. They made good progress. It was several years later that I learned the husband was found guilty of embezzling lots of money from his company. He went to jail. He lost his job, his home, his marriage, and many other relationships. I would later see him on social media—*a broken man*. The law found him out and imposed penalty. That's what laws, truths, and principles do. Laws honor and bless compliance, and they dishonor and punish non-compliance. We can celebrate victory because God's everlasting and unchangeable laws, truths, and principles govern *Unveiled Love*. This means they are not subject to the fickle, doubleminded, often self-serving opinions of men and women. This includes your husband or wife. When you engage *Unveiled Love*, you are working with God, not a man or woman. Therefore, you can celebrate because you can choose to work with these laws as an independent act of your free will. When you do, God assures that you will be honored, blessed, and your spouse and others will be given the benefit of opportunity to grow and change.

God Is True to His Word

The idea that God is causing you to suffer in marriage, or that He just isn't answering your prayers, is the result of misunderstanding the relationship between law and choice. God doesn't have to hurt you to inspire you to follow Christ. Violating His laws will hurt you as well as those around you. This is the strategy of God's will. This is what Paul means when he said God works everything out according to the design of His will. The design of God's will is comprised of laws and their corresponding systems. It's the framework in which we operate our free will. There is no conflict between God's sovereignty and our free will. This is settled, undisputable truth. Our free will engages the laws that uphold God's sovereignty. It's unavoidable. It's by divine design. Therefore, when we use free will to cooperate with God's *Unveiled Love*, we can celebrate victory. Once again, Job 22:21–22 (AMPC) informs us.

> Acquaint now yourself with Him [agree with God and show yourself to be conformed to His will] and be at peace; by that [you shall prosper and great] good shall come to you. Receive, I pray you, the law and instruction from His mouth and lay up His words in your heart.

And if for no other reason, celebrate victory because God is true to His word. Numbers 23:19 (CSB) agrees.

> God is not a man, that he might lie, or a son of man, that he might change his mind. Does he speak and not act, or promise and not fulfill?

God keeps His word.

Love Doesn't Hurt

Still, each one must resolve the internal conflict between God's sovereignty and their free will. If not, then we are likely to reject and retreat from God's *Unveiled Love*. That's because we will conclude that His love hurts. We fear hurt and pain. The thought of reliving it is unpleasant and, therefore, undesirable. So we will refuse love. This can even look like attacking or hiding from God and our spouse.

However, God's *Unveiled Love* is always good. It never hurts. Using the words "always" and "never" imply absolute, irreversible, and unchangeable conditions. That's why I suggest when describing your spouse's behavior, these words be used little or not at all. Your spouse's behavior is reversible and can change. To say, "You always _____" or "You never _____" removes the possibility of your spouse behaving differently and you thinking differently about your spouse. Kathy routinely tied Brad's irresponsibility to his father. She would say things like, "You act just like your father. You never think of anyone but yourself." Yet as she was saying this, Kathy was earnestly praying and perhaps even fasting that God will change her husband to be more considerate of her and their children. It seems and is counterproductive. In Kathy's mind and apparent in her words, Brad will never change. He will always act like his father in her eyes. This is misplaced hope for change, works against God's *Unveiled Love*, and renders her prayers and fasting ineffective. When working with God's *Unveiled Love*, Kathy might say something like this: "Brad, I experience you to be selfish. You seem to show no consideration for me or the kids. It reminds me of how your father treated you and your mother." Kathy makes the same point as in her previous statement, but there is one key difference. In this statement, there is real hope and opportunity that Brad can change the way his family experiences him. But also Kathy's words lend faith and support to God's *Unveiled Love*. Her words work together with her prayer and fasting.

That God's *Unveiled Love* doesn't hurt is an idea that few stop to unpack. And because it is a reason to celebrate the victory, it is worth unpacking here. God's *Unveiled Love* never has, never does, and never will hurt us. This is settled law. And like with God's sovereignty and our free will, each one must settle this in his or her soul. When we violate God's *Unveiled Love*, we suffer. We also suffer for what we may do in response to this love. Giving up something we value hurts. Like Julie, in secret 8, imagine saying "Yes" to others and "No" to yourself your entire life. Then God's *Unveiled Love* requires you to begin saying "No" to others and "Yes" to yourself. Or how about those of you whose default switch to anything asked of you is "No" or "How much does it cost?" Then God's *Unveiled Love* urges you to say "Yes." Or instead of asking how much something costs, ask "Is this something God would have me or us do?" For some, the thought of making such a change is spiked with fear and felt with anxiety. It is not God's *Unveiled Love* causing fear and anxiety. Rather, it is leaving that which is familiar and comfortable to us—even though it hasn't gotten us that which we desire. When we experience fear and anxiety, we sense an emotional or physical threat to our survival, and it doesn't matter, at the time, that our survival is based on a lie. It's how we manage to stay alive and attached to the people, places, and things that matter. When our survival is threatened, we hurt. God's *Unveiled Love* does not threaten our survival, rather it creates pathways to survival that are based on mercy and truth.

Other things that hurt include the loss of financial stability, the absence of emotional and sexual intimacy, betrayals, rejection, and setbacks. But God's *Unveiled Love* causes none of these things! To say otherwise is a lie that is intended to provoke distrust in God. God's *Unveiled Love* and the secrets shared in this book are the answer to all these things. God's *Unveiled Love* gives life. It does not take life away. Jesus makes this crystal clear in John 10:10 (AMPC).

> The thief comes only in order to steal and kill and destroy. I came that they may have and enjoy life, and have it in abundance (to the full, till it overflows).

There is nothing in Jesus's words that so much as hint that He (who is God in a human body) is out to get you or hurt you. Any thought or feeling to the contrary does not come from God. God's

Unveiled Love is always good. It never hurts. We can celebrate victory because while what we sometimes do for love in marriage can and does hurt, God's *Unveiled Love* always gives us joy. This is a gift and blessing!

Celebrate His Blessings

Like many of you, I have often been reminded to count my blessings. Generally, it means that we should stop and reflect on the good things that have happened to us and for us. But it wasn't until very recently I came to understand an even deeper meaning to counting our blessings. In fact, it is more than just a good idea. Recounting the good and amazing things God has already done for us is the foundation of confidently celebrating victory when working with God's *Unveiled Love*. It's the difference between the wilderness and your promised land. It's the difference between a barren land and a land flowing with milk and honey. It's the difference between eating manna or milk and honey. It's how we endure the contradiction between what we are experiencing and what we want to experience."

Israel's Example

Israel witnessed God perform miracles, signs, and wonders in Egypt. He spared their firstborn, loaded them down with gold and silver and possessions, ushered them out of Egypt, split the Red Sea, gave them dry ground to cross over, and watched the same sea devour their enemies. Then they made their way into the wilderness. It was a new place. It was an empty place. It was unfamiliar. It wasn't the promised land flowing with milk and honey. But also it wasn't the slop they ate in Egypt. They were free and no longer slaves.

In Numbers 11, we learn that the Israelites grumbled and complained about hardship. They hated the space between Egypt and Canaan. It represented a contradiction between what they had been promised and what they experienced. They neither had a mind to endure nor a foundation with which to do so. God became angry and said as much by burning the outskirts of their camp. The Israelites cried to Moses for relief and Moses appealed to God who relented.

Shortly thereafter, the Israelites, comprised of a mixed multitude, craved food other than the manna God provided. They asked for whomever would provide them meat. They complained. They imagined the slop they were fed in Egypt was more desirable than manna and said as much. Numbers 11:5–6 (AMPC) reveals the Israelites' thoughts.

> We remember the fish we ate freely in Egypt and without cost, the cucumbers, melons, leeks, onions, and garlic. But now our soul (our strength) is dried up; there is nothing at all [in the way of food] to be seen but this manna.

Manna was a pastry cooked with the finest oil. It tasted like cake. It was good, filling, and nourishing. Manna was gathered, prepared, and consumed daily. It required effort. It was monotonous. Whether it was the lack of variety to their diet or wanting the certainty of Egypt instead of the uncertainties they faced in the wilderness matters not. What does matter is that they had not built a foundation to stand confidently in uncertainty. After such mighty displays of God's authority and power on their behalf, the Israelites should have had more faith in God. But they did not. They did not count their blessings. Therefore, they neither had faith nor room to receive the new blessings God had stored up for them. Instead, the Israelites grumbled.

Chaim Bentorah Biblical Hebrew Studies adds the following: "The word in the Hebrew for grumble is 'yalan.' This means to worry, fret, complain etc. The word explains itself with its own built-in commentary. It is spelled Yod, Lamed and Nun. The Yod represents no foundation, irrational actions, the Lamed shows narrow thinking, self-importance, and the Nun shows lack of faith."[90] What we can learn is that the Israelites did not lay a proper foundation by

---

[90] https://www.chaimbentorah.com/2015/11/word-study-they-grumbled-ילן/

continually recalling and celebrating the wonderful and miraculous things God had already done for them. The foundation and ability to endure the contradictions, difficulties, and discomfort is celebrating victory and counting our blessings. Israel did not. They became irrational in their thinking, believing that the leftover, half-eaten slop they were fed as slaves in Egypt was better than being free and eating from the hand of God. They were convinced and said so. When we do not celebrate the victory of things God has already accomplished on our behalf, then we are likely to deceptively re-characterize them as unfavorable and yearn for what we had before. Numbers 11:6 (AMPC) tells us how Israel felt about the matter.

> But now our soul (our strength) is dried up; there is nothing at all [in the way of food] to be seen but this manna.

When we do not celebrate the tangible things God has done, we forfeit laying the foundation necessary to endure the contradictions. We also lose the strength and ability to properly respond to God. Eventually, this leads to giving up, quitting, and walking away. Proverbs 24:10 (AMPC) offers this.

> If you faint in the day of adversity, your strength is small.

The Message Translation says it matter-of-factly in this way.

> If you fall to pieces in a crisis, there wasn't much to you in the first place.

The Israelites did nothing to advance. They did not celebrate the victories God had already won for them nor the provision and protection they experienced. They collapsed because they had no foundation of praise for the good things God had already done for them. They had no footing enabling them to see and believe for anything greater. The Israelites became self-reliant and faithless. As a result, many of them did not enter the promised land. Numbers 14:29 (ESV) records this.

> Your dead bodies shall fall in this wilderness, and of all your number, listed in the census from twenty years old and upward, who have grumbled against me.

If we do not lay a proper foundation of celebrating the victories God has obtained for us and the things He has provided for us, then we will become self-reliant and lack the faith necessary to continue working with God's *Unveiled Love*. Whatever God's dream for you, your marriage, your family, and all that concerns you, one thing is true. It has no possibility of coming to pass unless we cooperate by celebrating victories. Counting our blessings is how we move through the difficult, uncertain terrain that leads to God's promises for us. I can't underscore this enough. Celebrating victory is essential to your ability to stay engaged with God's *Unveiled Love*.

Guarantees Worth Celebrating

God is trustworthy. His promises and guarantees are reliable and worth continually celebrating. God promises to love us whether we make our eternal bed in heaven or hell. As we have said, God decided to love us as a sovereign act of His will. We can receive it or refuse it. When we refuse love, we incur the consequences. That's the law. That we suffer doesn't remove God's love, albeit it does affect our relationship with Him. Psalm 139:7–8 (CSB) assures us of God's love, regardless of our nearness to Him.

> Where could I go from Your Spirit? Or where could I flee from Your presence? If I ascend up into heaven, You are there; if I make my bed in Sheol (the place of the dead), behold, You are there.

Whether or not a husband or wife adopts and displays God's *Unveiled Love*, the same principle applies. His *Unveiled Love* may be accepted or it may be refused. When it is refused and a spouse's behavior is injurious, then the injured one might become tempted to choose separation or divorce. Though not often included in marriage sermons, this may be the most loving thing one can do and for all concerned. I am not advocating divorce, rather suggesting that the highest act of love sometimes is releasing a continuously defiant spouse from his or her commitment to marriage. We should not assume that a husband or wife who makes such a prayerful and grueling decision does not love their spouse.

For those taking exception to this position, please keep in mind that God values and, therefore, honors freedom. His laws provide restraint for those with impure motives and the irresponsible. Remember all things are naked and open to Him whom we must give account. God sees clear through to our motives and is skillful at separating them from our actions. This God guarantees. Mark 4:22 (TPT) makes it clear that no motive will go unchecked.

> For there is nothing that is hidden that won't be disclosed, and there is no secret that won't be brought out into the light!

For readers considering divorce, I encourage you to ask and allow God to reveal your true motives and respond to Him accordingly. The very next verse, that is, Mark 4:23 (NIV) advises.

> If anyone has ears, let them hear.

We can celebrate because we can always count on God to be who He says He is and do what He says He will do. God's faithfulness must become more than an occasional thought or a belief we confess. His faithfulness must become deeply imbedded in our souls. This is what God's *Unveiled Love* requires if we are to walk confidently in relationship with Him and others. This is especially so, when you are working with God's *Unveiled Love* and your spouse isn't. You must not only think and believe God is faithful to perform His will and word, but you must also know it!

Outcomes Belong to God

That said, neither this book nor I guarantee that by engaging "The Secrets of God's *Unveiled Love*," you and your spouse will live happily ever after. The fact is, some will and some won't. Some husbands and wives will mature spiritually, mentally, and emotionally and their relationship will improve immensely. Delightfully, they will remain married. These couples enjoy greater freedom, share deeper love, and intimacy.

Some husbands or wives will mature, but their spouses will not. The fact of the matter is that some of these marriages will end in divorce. My desire is for healthy, emotionally maturing men and women in marriage. As a minister, counselor, and coach, it is neither my right nor responsibility to advise divorce. Rather, it is for me to help individuals mature in hearing and following God's word.

We can celebrate the victory because God knows the end of a matter from the very beginning. Through a system comprised of laws, all things will work to the benefit of the one who loves God and cooperates with His *Unveiled Love*. It may not be the outcome we desire and for which we prayed and hoped. But in the end, it will be best for all. To the faithful, God's best will be good in this life and the life to come. But for the unfaithful God's best may not always end desirably. This is the beauty and strength of God's *Unveiled Love*. The goodness and severity of God's laws is that they bless one and punish another all in the same stroke!

Karlee's Story

Karlee and Andy both were Christians. Karlee was introduced to Christ in college and insatiably took to reading God's word and learning about God through an on-campus ministry. By the time she graduated, her heart was set on serving God in full-time ministry. Andy discovered God sometime later but was equally engrossed in learning about Him. Both worked and volunteered in various ministries. They did so for many years. They took classes, Radical Love being one of them. Karlee was more aggressive in applying the principles to her life. The principles helped but did not eliminate their conflict. But by applying the principles and with the help of a coach, Karlee was able to distinguish her contribution to their recurring arguments and adjust when appropriate. Karlee stopped receiving information from Andy that did not resonate with what she knew and understood of herself.

Karlee told Andy that she was willing to own her behavior but was no longer willing to accept responsibility for his behavior. And she got better at communicating the adverse impact of his behavior upon her. Karlee began showing up. She was no longer willing to accept the error, the lie, that both she and Andy believed and unknowingly the church reinforced. For over twenty years, Karlee believed, albeit struggled with the lie. The lie exploited Karlee's desire to please God. The lie resulted in Karlee feeling and being made to feel rebellious. The lie was the misapplication of Ephesians 5:23–24. That as head or source of the wife, Andy had the authority to dictate who Karlee would be and what she was able to do.

It culminated when Andy and Karlee were sitting in their car. Karlee told Andy that her desire was to support him by accepting direction from him. However, she made it clear that Andy did not have the right to dictate or direct who she is. Furthermore, any permission she had given him based on the lie that they both believed was revoked. Karlee told Andy that from that moment on, she would be making these decisions for herself with help from God and His word. God gave her this right and responsibility and it could not be delegated nor usurped ever again. This was a game changer for Karlee. It was empowering. Karlee had the tools to re-evaluate her participation in marriage and other relationships and make healthy changes.

It was hard work because it was heart work. Karlee had allowed this lie to dominate her interactions with Andy for far too long. It was difficult for Andy too. He had as hard of a time accepting the changes as Karlee had initiating them. Andy was unable or unwilling to see it any way other than what they had been taught and how they had behaved through most of their marriage. It reminds me of the command Jesus received from His Father in John 10:18–19. God commands Jesus to retain authority to own and govern His life. This included who He would be and what he would do. Verse 19 (MSG) records the Jews' response.

> This kind of talk caused another split in the Jewish ranks. A lot of them were saying, "He's crazy, a maniac—out of his head completely. Why bother listening to him?" But others weren't so sure: "These aren't the words of a crazy man. Can a 'maniac' open blind eyes?"

Perhaps Andy thought Karlee was crazy. Or perhaps, Karlee's decision to take control of her life, beginning with establishing boundaries around her personhood, meant less control for him. Andy did not stay. Instead, he opted out of marriage. Andy told Karlee of his plans to end the marriage, and eventually, they divorced.

Karlee was left with no home, no car, divided children, few friends, and a meager income. It was devastating. At times, Karlee doubted her decision to take control of her life. However, she continued to believe that her decision to set healthy scriptural boundaries would result in healthier relationships between herself and others. Taking part in God's *Unveiled Love* did not result in a happily ever after for Andy and Karlee. After the divorce, things seemed to get worse for Karlee. But God went about making lemonade out lemons. It reminds me of Paul's words in Romans 8:28 (TPT).

> So we are convinced that every detail of our lives is continually woven together for good, for we are lovers who have been called and designed for a purpose.

That was several years ago. Since then, God has given Karlee new friends, homes, cars, and vacations. It is important to underscore the word "given" used here. Karlee told me that she paid for none of these things. Today, Karlee is well and advancing. Through *Unveiled Love*, she was able to raise questions about marriage being governed by hierarchy, that undermined the will and capacity for each to think, feel, and take part as each one decides. Karlee wanted a relationship based on truth. She wanted for her and Andy to create a relationship that could withstand worldly and religious pressure to conform to the traditions of mankind. Even though this did not happen, Karlee no longer doubted her decision to reclaim her freedom to navigate her life and trust God with her needs.

Author Stephen Covey sums it up best, "Independent will is our capacity to act. It gives us the power to transcend our paradigms, to swim upstream, to rewrite our scripts, to act based on principle rather than reacting based on emotion or circumstance."[91]

Andy and Karlee could have swum upstream together and that would have been amazing! Another couple did just that.

Lynn's Story

Lynn loves Bernie. It's obvious in the way she speaks about him and holds space for him whether present or not. They have been married for quite some time. Like many, they struggled with how to do marriage. Trapped in a hierarchical model they were frustrated often. Lynn found out about *Unveiled Love* and inquired about coaching to learn how to apply the principles to her marriage. Lynn was especially excited upon learning that God's *Unveiled Love* did not require Bernie's participation. After our coaching relationship ended with her firm grasp on the principles, Lynn continued practicing them faithfully. In her own words, here is what she has to say today: "The biggest part of my testimony was letting go of the expectation of how 'our' marriage should look and embracing how our marriage looks and what it is. We are both emotional. It helped me to be able to identify what was mine vs. what was his. I have taken complete responsibility for myself and have let my husband off the hook completely. We are experiencing a greater degree of freedom

---

[91] https://nichequotes.com/stephen-covey-paradigm-quotes

and understanding than at any other time in our marriage. A most recent example is with leading worship. I was prepared to pack my equipment, set it up, lead, break it down, and do everything myself. Although my husband is able to assist me and sometimes he does, this time he did not. Sometimes, he is working, and at other times, he just doesn't want to help. Before, I would be upset if we agreed to do something together and then he reneged. But this doesn't bother anymore because I am responsible to manage my music. And whenever he can help, it truly is a gift that I can receive. We are better because I took the initiative and learned the Secrets of *Unveiled Love*. They work!"

Bernie and Lynn's marriage looks different and feels different than many marriages. But what is apparent is love. Each one is free and empowered to create the marriage that glorifies God and works for them. Their marriage looks very different than Ric and Darlene's, but nonetheless persuasive of the power of God's *Unveiled Love*.

Ric and Darlene's Story

I have known Ric and Darlene for many years. They are both Christians and have been from the time that they met in the winter of 1996. They dated for three years and married the first time in 2001 and divorced in 2002. Darlene divorced Ric for financial reasons, having never seen his paystub and rarely saw his money. Darlene explains that Ric was living like he was a single man, staying out sometimes until three or four in the morning, promising to help with the expenses. She adds that she was raising her young son from her previous marriage and didn't want him to be expose to this behavior. Ric agrees with Darlene's perspective on how things went during that time and adds that he came into the relationship having not yet healed from the hurt he experienced in his previous marriage. He said that he was living as a hurt single man. Darlene admitted that although she loved Ric, she hated the pain caused by Ric's irresponsibility.

Once the divorce was final, Darlene had second thoughts, wondering whether she had done the right thing in God's eyes. After the divorce, Ric moved away and began seeing an old female friend. During this time, for two nights in a row, Ric vividly heard God say, "Go home and get your wife." But Ric did not have a wife and the one he had divorced him. Unable to shake the words God spoke to him, he ended the relationship with his female friend and arranged to move in with his aunt to be closer to Darlene. Shortly thereafter, Ric and Darlene met a few times in the parking lot of a library not far from her job. Ric used to watch her drive in to work just to ensure she was okay. These meetings rekindled their love for one another.

They started going to church together and learned about a marriage course called Radical Love—a twelve-week marriage skill building course. They enrolled in the course. As the author of Radical Love, I trained facilitators to implement the course in their local church. The pastors of the church Darlene and Ric attended were two such Radical Love Facilitators. I later met Ric and Darlene in one of the Radical Love weekly classes.

Darlene remembers feeling shame because the class, pastor instructors, and other class members alike knew she divorced Ric. While Darlene was committed, she was reserved in class. Ric was more outspoken in that he was willing to share everything for the sake of their marriage. But he was also sensitive to Darlene's fear and shame, not wanting to expose her. Through Radical Love, Ric and Darlene were exposed to some of the introductory principles contained in God's *Unveiled Love*. Each one embraced the principles. In 2003, at the end of the last class, Ric and Darlene were remarried in front of forty witnesses.

Ric and Darlene became RL Facilitators. And for the past fifteen years, Ric and Darlene have overseen the marriage ministry in their local church. They have ministered to hundreds of couples separately and in small and large groups. When speaking with Ric and Darlene about sharing their story, I found it noteworthy that while Ric assumed responsibility for poor participation the first time they were married, he did not become a victim. When asked about this, Ric offered the following explanation: "I was responsible for many of the things that happened in our relationship. I grew up not respecting money. My wife was different. She is her own person. I had to mature. While not always (showing it), I love my wife—who she is and how she is. It has been and is to my benefit."

Darlene admits that her mouth was part of the problem the first time they were married. She said, "I would talk until three in the morning or until I heard what I wanted to hear. I was trying to tell Ric what to think and say." She, too, had to mature and welcomed the challenge. Absent from a recent conversation with them was blame. Neither one blamed the other, rather both seemed more content to learn and own their own contribution to their relationship. They did not blame nor did they deny the reality of the other. During our conversation, they made room for each other's opinion without trying to justify themselves. There was an ease about them that was refreshingly pleasant.

Ric and Darlene are not starry-eyed. They still experience conflict. But both agree that it doesn't last long as before. When they take the time to really hear each other, oftentimes, they discover they are saying the same thing. God's *Unveiled Love* takes up where Radical Love leaves off, showing husbands and wives how to practically work with God when their spouse isn't.

The Bride of Christ

In all, we must remember that it is ultimately about the Bride of Christ. We can celebrate victory in Ric and Darlene's story and in Lynn and Bernie's stories. But also we can celebrate victory in Karlee's story. That's because God is doing one thing with anyone that takes part in His *Unveiled Love*, that is making a Bride suitable for His Son. It is the same God who leads each of us according to His will, which He upholds by His laws. Marriage is not for the faint of heart. It is designed to make a bride out of each of us for Jesus Christ. I remind you of Solomon's words.

> There are sixty queens and eighty concubines and young women without number. But my dove, my virtuous one, is unique; she is the favorite of her mother, perfect to the one who gave her birth.

> Women see her and declare her fortunate; queens and concubines also, and they sing her praises: Who is this who shines like the dawn, as beautiful as the moon, bright as the sun, awe-inspiring as an army with banners?

Verse 9 in the Message Translation begins with these words.

> There's no one like her on earth, never has been, never will be. She's a woman beyond compare.

As there are many sons, albeit One Son, there are many daughters, albeit there is One Woman and Bride of Christ. Obviously, husbands and wives look different physically. How they may think and express the attributes of God also varies. But it must be the same Spirit of God motivating all. The Bride is beautiful. And what makes her beautiful is the preparation of the soul made agreeable to God and Christ by the help of the Holy Spirit. How is she preparing? The Bride is re-establishing the supremacy of God and Christ in her life, family, and community. She is renouncing idols. That is, anything and everything used to sustain her life and significance in this world. It could be a job, a position, a credential, fame, fortune, possessions, or a person—*including a husband or wife*. Virtually anything and anyone can become an idol and compete for our worship. The Bride is renouncing all such things. Jesus writes to the disciples about His Bride in Luke 14:26–27 (TPT).

> When you follow me as my disciple, you must put aside your father, your mother, your wife, your sisters, your brothers; it will even seem as though you hate your own life. This is the price you'll pay to be considered one of my followers. Anyone who comes to me must be willing to share my cross and experience it as his own, or he cannot be considered to be my disciple.

Not only is the Bride preparing herself by reestablishing the supremacy of God and Christ in every area of her life and relationships and renouncing idols, but she is also regarding the holiness of God and finding her rest in God alone. Although relevant and influential in speaking and helping others, the Bride doesn't use profanity, showmanship, gimmicks, or clever speech to satisfy itching ears. She regards the purity of God, Christ, and Holy Spirit and desires to be as they are—*pure in motive, word, and action*. Finally, the Bride finds her rest in God, not in men or women. These are the aims of the Bride of Christ. That is, to love God and fellow man and woman in like manner. The Bride is men and women who make it their sole aim to love God and their spouse as Jesus did when on earth. God's *Unveiled Love* is an invitation to partake of the life of Christ. Jesus invites us in Revelation 22:16–17 (TPT).

> I, Jesus, sent my angel to you to give you this testimony to share with the congregations. I am the bright Morning Star, both David's spiritual root and his descendant." "Come," says the Holy Spirit and the Bride in divine duet. Let everyone who hears this duet join them in saying, "Come." Let everyone gripped with spiritual thirst say, "Come." And let everyone who craves the gift of living water come and drink it freely. "Come."

God's *Unveiled Love* is a rare and extraordinary opportunity to become united with Christ and in Christ with those who accept it. God's *Unveiled Love* is calling you to deliver you, cleanse you, direct you and instruct you in the ways of Christ and His Bride. All this to your beautification, edification, and benefaction of your spouse and others. When we hear God's call and accept Jesus's invitation, we become partakers of *Unveiled Love*. We show off and celebrate God's glory in the earth—to our spouse, families, to our church and communities, as well as, to all God gives us to impact. Together, with God's *Unveiled Love*, we become the embodiment of Christ in the earth!

Finally, like Paul in Ephesians 3:14–21 (CSB), I pray.

> I kneel before the Father from whom every family in heaven and on earth is named. I pray that he may grant you, according to the riches of his glory, to be strengthened with power in your inner being through his Spirit, and that Christ may dwell in your hearts through faith. I pray that you, being rooted and firmly established in love, may be able to comprehend with all the saints what is the length and width, height and depth of God's love, and to know Christ's love that surpasses knowledge, so that you may be filled with all the fullness of God. Now to him who is able to do above and beyond all that we ask or think according to the power that works in us—to him be glory in the church and in Christ Jesus to all generations, forever and ever. Amen.

I celebrate your victory!

Questions to Learn By

1. What is one reason the author gives for celebrating victory?
2. When we violate God's laws, who suffers?
3. Why doesn't God have to hurt you to inspire you to follow Him?

Questions to Grow By

1. Can you think of a time you held God responsible for misfortune? Explain. Given what you have read or heard, how might you view that misfortune now?
2. What reason does the author give in saying "love never hurts"? What do you think about this?

3. Can you think of a decision you made to love someone that hurt or cost you something personally? What was it like? (What did you do? How did it feel? Did you regret it? Would you do it again? Why or why not?)

Questions to Change By

1. Counting your blessings is the space between your wilderness and your promised land. Like the Israelites, without this foundation, we are likely to succumb to grumbling, complaining, and ultimately forfeiting God's promises. If you have been grumbling, complaining, blaming, demanding, insisting your spouse change, then now is a great time to ask God to forgive you. Here are a few scriptures that can help.

> But if we walk in the light as He is in the light, we have fellowship one with another, and the blood of Jesus Christ His Son cleanses us from all sin. If we say that we have no sin, we deceive ourselves, and the truth is not in us. If we confess our sins, He is faithful and just to forgive us our sins and cleanse us from all unrighteousness. (1 John 1:7–9 MEV)

> Confess your faults to one another and pray for one another, that you may be healed. The effective, fervent prayer of a righteous man accomplishes much. (James 5:16 MEV)

A simple heart-and-soul-motivated prayer is better than many words. Here is an example.

> *Father, according to your Word, I have sinned. I have complained, blamed, and demanded my spouse act a certain way. Please show me all the ways I have*

dishonored You and my spouse's freedom to think and act for him or herself. (Pause and acknowledge all that Father shows you. Continue.) Father, thank You for accepting my confession and forgiving me of these sins. Wash me through Jesus's blood, and I will be clean. Now help me confess my faults to my spouse that I might receive prayer and be healed. In Jesus's name.

2. Be intentional about setting a time to discuss these things with your spouse.
3. List and daily recount your blessings to strengthen the foundation and your endurance to ensure your receipt of God's promises. Consider updating your list regularly.

About the Author

Since 1986, Kim has helped hundreds of individuals and couples overcome hurts, habits, and hangups, impacting their relationships. Widely considered a relationship expert, Kim has written and published courses and books and conducted train-the-trainer workshops and seminars. She speaks at churches, retreats, and national conferences. Kim has coached ministry leaders, business owners, professional athletes, and those struggling with life-dominating issues. As a speaker, Kim is relevant, captivating, and compelling.

Imagine, then, the embarrassment and humiliation when, in 2013, Kim's husband announced to both her and others that he no longer wanted to be married. By mid-2016, Kim officially became a "divorcee." She was devastated. Everything she believed and knew was shaken, challenging her faith at its very core.

A New Journey of Discovery and Revelation

During the healing process, Kim realized that, for much of her life, she feared rejection if she let her voice be heard publicly or even privately. Despite her convictions, she retreated behind a wall of silence. Kim's breakthrough came when she admitted and confronted her fear of rejection. She learned how to face it by receiving God's love and acceptance for herself. Out of this journey of discovery and revelation came her 2016 book, *Face It with Love: The Guide to Conquering Fear*, and her new book, *Unveiled Love: 10 Secrets to Working with God When Your Spouse Isn't!*

Her ongoing journey continues to this day. Kim now shows up, speaks up, and, when appropriate, "shuts" up. She is passionate about helping others experience God's unveiled love and acceptance and the freedom that accompanies truth.

When not writing, speaking, or coaching, Kim stays busy enjoying life with her family and friends. She has two daughters, two sons-in-law, six grandchildren, friends, and Cash—a four-legged, 7.5-pound miniature pinscher. A former decorated competitive swimmer, Kim continues to be a water enthusiast, whether it is boating, jet-skiing, or just lounging by the ocean, lake, or stream!

Printed in the USA
CPSIA information can be obtained
at www.ICGtesting.com
CBHW020244081124
16958CB00048B/395